ALL THE $#!T I WISH I KNEW IN HIGH SCHOOL

All the $#!T I Wish I Knew in High School

TOM BORAK

Team T&A

Contents

Dedication   vii

1	This is what it's all about	1
2	What it means to be a man	9
3	Let's be honest: it's time to stop lying to yourself	27
4	Lie #1: Real men don't cry	47
5	Lie #2: Who I am right now is who I'm destined to be	67
6	Lie #3: I should have it all figured out by now	95
7	Lie #4: Failure is final	125
8	Lie #5: Money is the key to happiness	147
9	Lie #6: The more friends I have, the better	167
10	Lie #7: I am special	183
11	The truth of the matter	209
12	The truth about sex and pornography	213

13	The truth about love	243
14	The truth about bullying	279
15	The truth about drugs and alcohol	305
16	The truth about strength and fitness	331
17	The truth about nutrition	353
18	The truth about school	375
19	The last word	393

FOR IVAN

Chapter 1

This is what it's all about

If you are like most young men, your high school years are full of questions that you desperately want the answers to, but are too afraid, ashamed, and embarrassed to ask:

- I have no idea what I want to do with my life. My friends seem to have everything mapped out already! Am I going to be left behind? Am I a failure?
- It feels like everyone is hooking up but me – am I missing out? I really want to have sex, but what if I'm bad at it? Should I be in love first? How do I know if I'm in love?
- Everyone keeps telling me I need to "man up." What does it even mean to be a real man? Am I allowed to show emotion? Do real men *ever* cry?

- Do I need to go to college if I want to be successful in life? What if I don't get straight A's, or can't afford it? What if I don't *want* to go to college?
- I jerked off *four* times yesterday! Is something wrong with me? Am I some kind of pervert?
- I'm a complete loser. I don't have a girlfriend and I get picked on all the time! Is this what my life is destined to be? Will things ever change, or should I just call it quits?

Do any of these thoughts resonate with you? If not, there are undoubtedly other questions on your mind that you're frantically seeking answers to. Everyone who has gone through high school has questioned themselves, their choices, and sometimes their very lives, among many other things. These questions are sensitive and personal. They leave you feeling vulnerable, and open to potential judgment and ridicule by your friends, family, and others. As a result, you keep them to yourself, suffering alone. In the following pages, I will do my best to answer these questions and many more.

This book is a conversation starter. It is not a self-help book with step-by-step instructions designed to ensure your success, or even point you in a specific direction. In fact, it is quite the opposite. This book is an open window, offering you the opportunity to eavesdrop on private conversations that have relevance in your life without anyone knowing you're there. It is a door, left slightly ajar, offering a chance to explore some difficult topics with others who, like you, are looking for guidance, reassurance, and encouragement in this tumultuous chapter of your life.

The contents of these pages are intended to be shared and discussed amongst friends. Each section contains personal stories from my life – true stories that chronicle my own experience wrestling with these very same questions. Many of the topics I cover are likely the same ones that you are already talking about with your friends – as well as several that may still feel too uncomfortable to discuss, even with those closest to you.

I hope that talking with your friends about *my* experiences will help break the ice and give you the confidence to begin sharing your own ideas and experiences. This book is a tool that will add depth and nuance to your conversations, adding an invaluable layer of information that you will never be able to find on your own until much later in life because it only reveals itself through experience, context, hindsight, and perspective.

This book is a resource for all the young men out there who do not have a father who is playing an active role in their life. It's also for all the young men who are too afraid, intimidated, ashamed, or embarrassed to talk with their fathers about these topics – like I was.

I struggled mightily with these thoughts and questions in high school, but I was too proud – and too naive in some cases – to acknowledge that I didn't know the answers. In other cases, it turned out that I wasn't even asking myself the right questions! Other topics were too embarrassing and shameful to discuss. I know now that I was not alone in feeling this way, and neither are you.

When I started this project, it was intended to be a private endeavor. I set out to write a series of letters to my younger self – myself in high school, specifically – to give him the answers to some of his most pressing questions. I wanted to assure him that no matter how difficult or impossible things seemed at the time, everything would turn out alright. I wanted him to relax, knowing that the consequences of actions and decisions that he felt would define his life forever – for better or for worse – would ultimately turn out to be mere footnotes that have all but faded into obscurity over time as the rest of his story unfolded.

I ultimately realized that keeping this knowledge for myself was pointless. I cannot go back in time to share this information with my past self any more than you can jump forward in time to learn from your future self! I decided to shift gears and address these letters instead to my nephew, Ivan, who reminds me very much of myself at his age. I hope that he will use this information to his advantage. I hope that in reading my correspondence to him, you will also find answers to some of your own questions. If you find something of value in these pages, I encourage you to take it for yourself. If not, leave it and move on.

I am not a therapist, psychologist, or any other kind of expert. I'm not rich, famous, or powerful either. I'm not special. I'm just an average guy, like you, trying to make my way in the world. I just have a 20-year head start, which affords me the opportunity to share some insight with you.

With that said, I recognize that my vantage point as a straight, white man – and thus the narrative of my stories – will differ from many in my audience. However, while I cannot write from any perspective outside of what I have actually lived and experienced, I truly believe that the core of what I share in these letters transcends race, socio-economics, sexual identity, and any type of disability you may have. What I have discovered to be true applies at the *human* level, and we all stand equally in that category.

As you read, remember that your path is unique. Your life – your feelings, emotions, challenges, goals, and victories – cannot be contained, defined, or dictated by any book. Each of us has to walk our own path and discover who we are, decide who we ultimately want to become, and plot the best course to get there based on the circumstances that are laid out before us.

Your starting point is inevitably influenced by circumstances you cannot control: your race, sexual orientation, community and cultural values, and your family's socio-economic status, among others. These identity markers are only a starting point. They will not define your future unless you let them. Regardless of where you find yourself right now, I encourage you to look beyond the hand you've been dealt to see the bigger picture of what your life can become.

My hope is that this will be a book you keep and refer back to for many years to come. There may be references and situations I discuss in this book that you may not fully understand at this point in your life. Don't worry about it! Some of them may become relevant in two or three years, and some may not make sense until much later in life, depending on how your personal story unfolds. In other instances, you may find yourself relating one of my stories to a particular event, person, or thing in your life right now, but when you revisit these pages in the future you will find an entirely different meaning in the words – equally as valuable, but in a different frame of reference.

Skip around if you want. Pick and choose the topics that are most important to you. There is a flow and structure to the order of these letters, but for the most part, each one can stand alone. Use these pages as a reference, or guidebook. Make notes in the margins about what you're thinking and feeling as you read and include the date you make each note. Bookmark the pages you want to come back to. When you look back on these pages in the future, you'll truly be able to measure how far you've come!

A note to parents

I'm writing this book for the young men in the high schools of America, and those who are about to join them. However, I sincerely hope this book will also help build new bridges between mothers, fathers, and their sons.

Most of the content in this book is comprised of my opinion. With that being the case, I fully expect and welcome those with a different point of view to share their own thoughts. To any parent who reads this book and disagrees with something I say, consider it an invitation to start your own conversation with your son! Share your experience and perspective. Give him your personal point of view and explain why you disagree with mine. Encourage him to think critically about both sides of the argument and formulate his own opinion. By talking about these differences openly and honestly, we will collectively expand the minds of our young men, creating a stronger and much healthier society.

To the parents who read this book and generally agree with what I have to say, you're not off the hook! Consider this your invitation to connect with your son, discuss these topics, and share *your* story. Be prepared for him to disagree with me and you. For myself, and every man I've met, young and old alike, finding commonalities and building a connection with our fathers is one of the deepest desires of our hearts. Don't let this opportunity pass you by. Even if you disagree on some things, an open and honest dialogue between father and son is one of the most valuable gifts we can give one another.

I hope you enjoy these letters, and perhaps find some insight for your own benefit. I believe much of what is written can be applied at any age in life – I just wish I'd known it sooner.

Chapter 2

What it means to be a man

Dear Ivan,

When I was younger, I wrestled relentlessly with this question: What does it mean to be a man?

When I was 10, I thought it meant swearing and flicking people off. When my brothers and I would go off to play in the woods with our friends or paddle our canoe around the small lakes in our neighborhood, we delighted in using as many curse words as we could. We made a pact that we would never tell on one another. It made us feel tough, like outlaws throwing caution to the wind. It made us feel more grown up.

When I got to high school, I thought it meant being able to grow facial hair. I envied the guys a couple years older than me who had a few whisps of hair sprouting from their chins and the baby-soft beginnings of a mustache forming on their upper lips.

At every new milestone in my life, the definition of manhood changed. It was a moving target, and nobody could tell me exactly when, how, or *if* I would ever become a man.

I know this is a question you also wrestle with. You have probably received conflicting information from different men in your life: your father, grandfather, teachers, coaches, and now me. Who is right? How do you make sense of it all, and how can you know for sure that you are – or will be – a man?

This is perhaps the greatest question any of us have as we are going through our adolescent years. Does the fact that you have a penis automatically qualify you? Having a penis makes you a *male*, at least at birth, but it doesn't mean you're a man. What additional characteristics and traits does a man have that "separates the men from the boys?" How do you *become* a man? Does having sex make you a man? Going to war? Drinking alcohol? Being a good athlete? On the other hand, what makes you *less* of a man? Do men cry? Are you less of a man if you show emotional vulnerability or any hint of weakness? These are all relevant questions that each of us has to explore in discovering our own true definition of what it means to be a man.

I believe there is a distinction between being a male, being masculine, and being a man. The lines are blurry, but they're there, nonetheless. It's kind of like the colors in the rainbow – you can see the individual colors, but they all blend together from one to the next and there is no clear line where one begins and the other ends.

Everyone has his own opinion of what it takes to be a man. For some, it's the physical maturation of the body – reaching a certain age, growing hair under your arms and on your face, chest, and groin. For others, it's the conquest of definitive hurdles like having sex for the first time or taking your first shot of whiskey (hence the expression, "That'll put hair on your chest!") For others still, it requires proof that you are able to *survive* on your own – moving out or your parents' house, getting your first job, and supporting yourself financially.

Many of these notions of manhood are based on the experiences of a person's familial or cultural history, in other words, how you were raised. How was your father brought up? What have you learned from him about what it takes to be a man? If your father isn't present in your life, how does the community around you expect you to act as a man?

These are the foundations of learning what being a man is all about and why everyone has a slightly different answer to this question. Ultimately, it is up to you to determine how you will define manliness and how you will eventually influence others around you to achieve that status.

Before we get too far, let's establish a baseline for masculinity. I'm going to give you two lists. I want you to determine which of these two columns you would consider more manly.

Male A	Male B
Plays with stuffed animals and keeps a baby doll in his room.	Shoots action figures with his pellet gun, pretending to be a sniper behind a 50-cal rifle.
Looks away when a girl's bikini top falls off at a high school pool party.	Sits in the front row at a strip club with his buddies.
Gets cut from the school baseball team and a girl makes the team over him.	Breaks an opponent's wrist with a 90-mph fastball.
Cries when he watches Disney movies.	Watches war movies and gets jacked up to fight.
Goes to the gym with some buddies and winds up puking outside after some light curls and bench press.	Deadlifts more than 500 pounds, squats more than 450 pounds, and is a two-time state champion in Weightlifting.
Sips wine coolers and other fruity drinks at parties.	Enjoys good whiskey, neat – no ice or mixers.

Cries when he gets his nose bloodied and retaliates by calling his aggressor a name and punching him in the stomach.	Breaks an elbow and an ankle snowboarding and never sheds a tear.
Sings in the choir, plays in the marching band, and gets leading roles in the school musical.	Starts for the varsity baseball team.
Is terrified to speak to girls he's romantically interested in.	Makes out with random girls in bars.
Gets bullied at school and often calls his mom to come pick him up because he has a "stomachache."	Is one of the most popular kids in his class.
Lives at home with his parents, even though he's graduated from college.	Lives in a house with several roommates in a different city than his family.

What do you think? It seems pretty clear cut to me. Male A sounds like a complete wuss! Am I right? Male B is clearly the man's man.

You may be thinking that I set this up, cherry-picking traits on the extreme ends of the spectrum, to ensure that you agree with my assessment of manliness. I can forgive you for thinking that, I mean, the differences are pretty extreme. On the other hand, I wonder if part of you feels some compassion or even some similarities and a sense of camaraderie with Male A? Do you feel like Male B is a little bit of a caveman? A "bro" or a "meathead," who is probably pretty dumb and won't amount to much in the real world?

Regardless of which side you gravitate toward, the question remains: which of these is the more *manly* person? There is only one right answer. Which do you choose?

Your response is probably based on a combination of your own personal experience and situation combined with cultural ideals of manliness that have been forced upon you – what you see portrayed on TV, in advertising, and the movies. Maybe this comparison has made you pause as you really think about what you think it means to be a man. Maybe you quickly identified with one side or the other.

Here's the kicker: whichever side you ultimately decided on – you're right. There is only one right answer because there is only one person in that chart. It's me. Every single one of those statements is a description of me at some point in my life. Some of them are a few years apart and some occurred simultaneously. Go ahead and read that list again. Tough to believe, isn't it? All of these statements are true of me in my life at one point or another.

I used to be ashamed of the characteristics in the left column. I tried to hide them from everyone, including my family and my friends. I tried hard to change them. I was successful with some of them, like transforming from a weak kid who couldn't handle a light workout without puking to being able to lift respectable amounts of weight. I do everything I can to avoid a fight, but if someone directly threatens me or my family, you'd better believe that I'm ready to unleash hell!

On the other hand, there are things that fall into the right-hand column, plenty of which are not listed, that I look back on with regret. I have definitely done things because they seemed like the "manly" thing to do at the time, but ultimately went against my morals and values. This is all part of the journey of growing up and discovering who you are and deciding who you *want* to be.

Despite my desire to change certain things, there are characteristics on the left side of that list that I've had to accept as a part of who I am. I'll readily admit that I *like* Disney movies, but I still cry at *The Lion King* every time Simba talks to the spirit of Mufasa in the stars. Every. Fucking. Time. There's actually a line from that movie that will be crucial to you as you grow and learn more about yourself and your personal definition of manliness. No, not "hakuna matata" (Swahili for no worries). It's actually in that scene that makes me cry. Right before he disappears, Mufasa says to Simba, "Remember who you are."

Before you can remember who you are, you need to *learn* who you are. You will be influenced by your immediate surroundings. Again, these include your family, religious, social, and cultural expectations. The expectations placed on you by these external sources should be viewed as options or guidelines in your search, not necessarily the law that you must obey.

You can absolutely find examples of men who completely embraced all of the expectations and norms assigned to them by their surroundings. Many of them lead wonderful lives, stitched neatly back into the social fabric from which they were cut.

On the other hand, there are countless examples of men who come from broken homes, socially marginalized segments of society, or strict religious upbringings, who have rejected these pressures and carved their own definition of what it means to be a man.

Tyler Perry is an American actor, writer, producer, and director. He is wildly successful and is worth a *billion* dollars at the time I'm writing this. He also has a generous spirit, giving his money and time to help others in need, whether it's donating millions of dollars to support relief efforts for natural disasters or practicing random acts of kindness in his community. If you look solely at the man he has become, you would not guess how his story started.

Tyler Perry was one of four children growing up in New Orleans. His father was violent and abusive, once beating him so badly that he blacked out for three days. In addition to the physical violence he endured at home, Perry suffered sexual abuse at the hands of four different adults over the course of his childhood. He was only about six-years old the first time he was molested. It got so dark that Perry eventually attempted suicide – the only option he believed he had left at the time.

The turning point for Tyler Perry occurred while he was watching an episode of Oprah. He heard a comment on the show about how writing about difficult experiences could lead to personal breakthroughs. He began writing, inspired by his personal experiences, and that ultimately changed the trajectory of his life.

The familial and cultural framework of Perry's childhood could have easily shaped his definition of what it means to be a man. If he had mirrored what he saw around him as the ideal of manliness, he could have become a violent, abusive person – possibly a sexual predator himself. Instead, Perry undertook the incredibly difficult challenge of building his own definition of what it means to be a man, one step at a time, ultimately becoming the person he is today.

It is also possible for a person to reach adulthood believing and defending the definition of manhood that was imposed upon them until an event occurs in their life that directly affects them, forcing them to reevaluate their definition of manliness, change their course of action and dramatically alter their life's path in pursuit of a new definition.

Dax Shepard is an American actor, writer, director, and podcast host. Like Tyler Perry, Shepard did not have an easy childhood. His parents divorced when he was three-years old, and he was subjected to a revolving door of his mother's boyfriends passing through his life. Growing up on the outskirts of Detroit, Shepard subscribed to the definition of manhood he saw around him: fast cars, strength and toughness, the ability to drink and fight, and the constant pursuit of sexual conquest.

This lifestyle led him into substance abuse and addiction. Even after achieving some success in Hollywood, the definition of manhood he had adopted in his youth was still etched in his psyche and he had to live up to it. At his lowest point, Shepard found himself sitting in an airport bar on a return trip from a Hawaiian vacation, so hung over and sick from the drinking and drug use on the trip that he had to drink even more just so he could get on the last leg of his flight home.

When you are addicted to drugs and alcohol, your body can become dependent on having those chemicals in your system, even though it's toxic. Depriving the body of these substances for too long can actually cause it to go into shock. Ironically, your body needs *more* of the poison to function normally. In that moment, Shepard realized he *hated* who he had become and decided he needed to get sober and *stay* sober.

Dax Shepard will be the first to tell you that he's not perfect. He has had some relapses during his journey of sobriety, but his life is unquestionably better overall. He goes to therapy to work through his issues and learn to discover and accept his true self. He still loves going fast and racing cars and motorcycles, but that in itself does not define manliness for him anymore – it's just a part of who he is. At the time I'm writing this, he is in his mid-40s and has realized that the definition of manliness that he was introduced to in his adolescence is not the *only* definition. He is moving forward with an open mind about what it means to be a man.

I used celebrities for these two examples because their lives are public, and they have spoken openly about their pasts. The stories of others are my only frame of reference because I most closely associate with the first group I talked about – fitting neatly, for the most part, into the cultural fabric from which I was originally cut. Fame has nothing to do with manliness. The point is you have the opportunity to make intentional choices to affect your life and create the path you want to walk, regardless of the circumstances you are born into. It will be harder for some than others, but the potential and possibility is real for all of us.

I want you to take a moment and think about how you currently define manhood. Make a list – you can do it right here in the margin if you want. What characteristics do you currently associate with being a man? How does this list make you feel? How do you measure up?

Are there things on your list that make you uncomfortable? Do you have thoughts or feelings that you believe go *against* your current definition of manhood?

As you go through life, you will face all kinds of challenges and events that will test your definition. Each of these episodes will give you a new opportunity to build and modify your definition of what manhood means to you. Some of these episodes will reaffirm your beliefs. Others will give you reason to doubt what you have long held as true. All will build, in some way, your definition of who you are.

I don't think anyone can ever fully realize who they are. It's a constantly changing and evolving process, but as you grow, more and more of it will solidify, allowing you to continue to build over time. Who you are today is much different than who you will be when you look back on this point in your life from 10 or 15 years in the future. I'm speaking from experience here!

Some of the foundation of who you are may be predetermined for you. Your race, sexual orientation and socio-economic status are things that you cannot change as a child. They will make up the base of who you are – the foundation on which you can begin to build your own identity as a man. Regardless of your eventual achievements, these foundations will remain. They do not, however, get to dictate who you become. The coming years of your life represent an opportunity to determine who you are in *spite* of where you come from – not because of it. As you face each new idea, challenge, and test, you will be able to look at the foundation you have built and use that to decide if the new information before you fits in with who you are or, perhaps more appropriately, who you want to be.

You may not recognize these crossroads every time they emerge. In many cases, you will be swept up in the prevailing popular sentiment and carried off without even realizing you had a choice. As you grow, you will look back on these times and ask yourself, "what if I had done that differently?"

One example for me, which I discuss at length in a later letter, occurred in the 4th grade, when some of my classmates were singled out and picked on for being different. Today, with my current moral compass and values, I would have done my best to make them feel welcomed and invite them to join me in our community. At the time, however, I was happy to go along with the actions of the majority of my classmates because I was constantly seeking the approval of others and didn't want to do anything to put myself at risk. I didn't feel like I really had a choice. When I look back at regrets in my life, this example stands out as one that makes me wonder, "what if I had done that differently?"

You will also experience points in your life when you will clearly have a choice before you. It is in these moments that knowing who you are and what you stand for plays a critical role in how you respond. Some will remain easy choices. You may very well agree with the majority and knowingly allow yourself to join that momentum. Some will be incredibly difficult. You will risk being alienated by people you love and letting down those who have shared common interests and beliefs with you in the past.

A couple years after I got married, I was playing in a very competitive baseball league in Denver. Our team traveled to Las Vegas to play in a tournament against teams from across the country. I liked these guys – I'd been playing with them for two years at that point and the camaraderie was strong. I saw it as a great opportunity to get away for a bit, hang out with the boys in a new place, and play some good baseball. After we got knocked out of the tournament in the semi-final round, a bunch of us decided to spend our last night in Vegas out on the strip.

The night started out great. We had a couple drinks at a German-themed beer hall, talking about different scenarios we'd faced in the tournament and laughing about the antics of some of our teammates. As the night wore on, things began to turn. We eventually found ourselves at a casino bar, where we were approached by a group of women. We chatted amiably for a bit, but then some of my friends, including some who were married, took some of the women out on the dance floor. Eventually, the entire group was pulled away from the bar to mix it up with the music.

As I was dancing alone, I watched one of my married teammates leave the group with one of the girls, saying they were heading back to his room. Another, who had just gotten married a few months earlier, started making out with the girl he was dancing with. I could see where this night was heading, and realized I had a very clear choice to make. I could stay, be "one of the boys," and cheat on my wife, or I could leave and risk being outcast by my teammates for witnessing their infidelity and not being a part of it.

I left. I walked out of the casino, texted my wife to tell her that I loved her and I was excited to be coming home to her the next day, and I walked back to the cheap motel I was staying at a mile off the strip. I still felt guilty – not for leaving, but because I had stayed so long. I knew I loved my wife and I didn't want to do anything to compromise our relationship, yet I had waited until I was standing right at the intersection of right and wrong to make that call. I vowed never to put myself in that situation again, and I've stuck to it.

This is where manhood is forged. The courage to listen to who you are and stand for your beliefs at the risk of personal injury, whether physical or emotional, is the truest test of a man's character. As John Wooden, the great American basketball coach, once said, "Be more concerned with your character than your reputation. Your character is who you really are, while your reputation is merely what others *think* you are."

Your character will be tested throughout your life. You will face internal challenges – battling your conscience – as well as external challenges from people and situations. The choices you make in those situations will ultimately define the man you become. I found this beautiful parable during some aimless internet wandering and I believe it speaks directly to this battle:

> A wise old man was talking to a boy and said, "There are two wolves always fighting inside me. One is filled with anger, hate, jealousy, shame and lies. The other wolf is filled with love, joy, truth, and peace. This battle rages inside of you and all men."
>
> The boy thought for a moment and asked, "Which wolf will win?"
>
> The old man answered, "The one you feed."

As important as it is to believe in yourself and have conviction in what you believe, it is equally important for you to *understand* the issues on which you take a side. This is especially important in the world we live in today, where attention spans are short and inflammatory soundbites are meant to heighten your emotions and launch you into a rage-filled crusade. I'm not necessarily saying that your outrage is unjustified – I'm saying that you must show the restraint to look into an issue from multiple perspectives and fully understand, to the best of your ability, what is truly happening. You must learn to fight the mob-mentality that is fracturing our country today. I challenge you to understand the causes for which you stand and be able to defend them beyond pointing to a news headline you read online or regurgitating an opinion you heard without taking the time to form your own thoughts on the matter.

These are the characteristics of a real man. Keeping a level head and understanding what he is supporting and why he is doing it, even if what he is supporting is unpopular with others.

You should not feel ashamed of where you come from. It is what it is, and just like I shared with you who I am – for better and for worse – in that list, you must learn to embrace who you are at your core and accept it. The sooner you are able to do this, the sooner you will be able to affect real change in the areas of your life that you desire: making choices based on who you are and who you *want* to be, not who others think you should be.

There is nothing inherently wrong with you. After years of trying to hide truths about myself, I have learned that there is nothing inherently wrong with me. My definition of what it means to be a man has changed over time. Yours will too. I have learned that the projection of a "man" imposed on us by society is an empty shell. You can worship the muscular appearance, lavish lifestyles, and hyper-sexualized exploits that are presented to you by Hollywood, but that doesn't define a man. A man is defined by what is within him. How does he treat others? Does he have a healthy love for himself and his community? Does he respect women and those weaker and less fortunate than himself? Does he have a strong moral compass and conviction in his beliefs?

Do you?

Your path to discovering your character and personal definition of manhood will be long and winding. You will face internal and external challenges along the way. Embrace the journey and the experiences, both good and bad. Learn from your mistakes. I'll be here for you when you have questions.

Love,
Tom

Chapter 3

Let's be honest: it's time to stop lying to yourself

Dear Ivan,

When I was a sophomore in high school, I had a summer job as a cashier at a sporting goods store making $6.50 an hour. Some of my friends had jobs making $8-10 an hour, which made me feel like I was being ripped off. After a month of growing frustration, I decided I would even things up on my own.

Every day, right before my lunch break, I would straighten up and re-stock the snack section next to all the cash registers. When I was sure nobody was looking, I'd slide a candy bar into my pocket. Then I'd take my lunch break and happily enjoy my "bonus." One time, after observing my pattern for a few weeks, one of the managers confronted me in the break room and asked me about it. I lied and said my mom bought packs of full-size bars for me to bring to work. He was satisfied with that explanation.

The close call only made me bolder. I started upping the ante. On the days I worked a closing shift, I'd take my company shirt off and carry it under my arm as I went through the closing procedures. Right before I walked out, I'd grab a bag of beef jerky or some other snack, cover it with my shirt, and head for the exit. I did this for the rest of the summer.

Sometimes, sitting in my truck in the parking lot, I'd start to feel guilty about my actions, but I always rationalized it by telling myself that I was making up for the low wage I was being paid. It couldn't be stealing if it was *owed* to me, right?

In the next several letters, I'm going to talk a lot about the lies you tell and how they impact your life. I'm not talking about the lie you told your mom about where you were on Saturday night or the lie you told your teacher about why you missed third period. I'm not even talking about the lie you told your friends about what *really* happened between you and your girlfriend after the movie last weekend. I'm talking about the lies you tell *yourself* – the carefully-woven tapestry of thoughts, ideas, excuses, and rationalizations that you have created to protect yourself from the fear, insecurity, and weakness that you live with every day but don't want others to know or see.

I lied to my manager about the source of those candy bars I ate with my lunch every day. That was bad, but the worse lie was the one I told myself: that I was *justified* in my actions because I was owed something. The fact of the matter is that I wasn't owed any more than what I agreed to be paid when I took the job. If I'd wanted more money, I could have looked for another job, but I was too lazy to do that. Instead, I told myself a lie that went against my morals and values. I compromised on who I was because I was too lazy and ashamed to face the truth. These are the lies that will get you into trouble.

These lies are like a protective barrier: a suit of armor you wear to ensure that you will fit in, that others see you the way you want to be seen, and ultimately, to give you a place to hide when you're feeling vulnerable. This armor creates an *audience-friendly* version of yourself, an outward-facing caricature that you believe the people around you will like, even if it's not necessarily a true representation of who you really are, how you really feel, or what you're really thinking.

Armor is not impenetrable. It always has weak points. There will be times when your armor is more of a liability than an asset, which can get you into trouble. You may find yourself in a situation where you feel obligated to do something out of peer pressure that you really don't want to do. The *audience* – everyone around you – is expecting you to act a certain way based on the character you have created, the version of yourself that you have introduced them to. You will have to choose between living up to the audience's expectations and going through with something that you are uncomfortable with, or showing a different side of yourself, opening yourself up to potential ridicule, embarrassment, and shame – like puking your guts out in front of your friends the first time you try dipping tobacco.

I got to observe this firsthand during my senior year of high school. It was the beginning of baseball season and the team was in a good mood. We were excited for a new season in which we were expected to do well. We changed into our practice clothes in the locker room, some of us in sweatpants and three-quarter sleeve shirts, others in old baseball pants pulled up high, with holes in the knees and the seats from sliding into bases. We walked down a winding gravel road through the woods that led to the athletic fields, carrying our equipment. We walked as one large, shapeless mass, broken into smaller groups of two or three guys. We were close enough to hear the conversations of others around us if we wanted to, but the gravel crunching beneath our metal cleats and the sounds of other student athletes on the nearby tennis courts and softball field gave a sense of privacy. We reached a slight bend in the road, where the path led away from the tennis courts and softball field and turned toward our baseball diamond.

As I rounded the bend, I saw some of my teammates forming a semi-circle around our first baseman, Jordan, who was standing next to our assistant coach, Nolan. Jordan had just turned 18, which was old enough to buy tobacco, and had been talking a big game recently about how he was going to start dipping like a *real* ballplayer. Nobody on our team had dipped tobacco before, but Coach Nolan did, and we all looked up to him as someone to model ourselves after. Coach Nolan was in his mid-20s. He had already done a tour of duty with the military, where he was stationed overseas in a combat zone. He had played college baseball, which nearly all of us aspired to do, and he was jacked. He must have worked out every day. He was a walking representation of what we thought a man should be.

By now, the entire team had gathered around. We all watched as Coach Nolan took the green can of wintergreen Skoal from his back pocket, held it between his thumb and middle finger, and flicked his wrist several times. With each flick of the wrist, his limp index finger slapped into the side of the can with a satisfying smack, packing the loose tobacco in the can into a more compressed mound at the bottom. He pulled off the top of the can, grabbed a pinch of the finely-cut tobacco between his thumb and index finger, and placed it in his mouth between his lower lip and his gums, creating a visible lump. We silently took mental notes, watching him pack it with his tongue. The mound inside his lip moved around as if he had a small mouse living in there. After he was satisfied with the positioning, he turned and spit a perfect arc of dark brown tobacco juice into the grass beside him. He turned back to us and smiled, then turned and offered the can to Jordan.

Jordan had a choice to make. He could continue to play the role of "tough guy" and try tobacco as he'd been bragging about, or he could change his mind and decide that he wasn't up for it – not right that moment anyway. The lie Jordan told himself was that he *had* to try tobacco because he'd been talking a big game about it and we were all here watching him.

Coach Nolan warned Jordan that the tobacco might make him feel sick, but Jordan felt like he couldn't back out of it now. He took a small pinch – less than the amount Coach Nolan had used – and put it in his mouth. We all crowded around and watched. Less than a minute later, Jordan's knees began to wobble. We could see the blood leaving his face as he grew pale and began looking around slowly, like an animal that knows it's trapped and is hoping to find a way out before anyone else sees it. There was nowhere for him to hide. Jordan spit out the tobacco, braced himself against a nearby tree and started heaving violently. We all laughed at Jordan and made fun of him for being such a wuss ... but nobody else wanted to try it after that.

I was happy and content to make fun of Jordan for something that I would not have had the guts to do myself. *My* armor was still intact. I hid my own fear and insecurity behind the jokes and insults I hurled at Jordan, along with the rest of the team.

Jordan's armor let him down because his body physically rejected the substance he put in his mouth. If he had refused to go through with it, we probably would have made fun of him in that moment, and maybe for the rest of practice that day, but it would have been forgotten. Instead, Jordan wound up puking his guts out and the team didn't let him forget it for the rest of the season and the memory is still with me today.

The lies you tell yourself and the armor you build up to defend those lies can reach beyond physical actions like dipping tobacco. You can create lies around personal philosophies and belief systems like religion, for example.

Regardless of what religion you have been raised to accept – if any – you probably believe that *your* religion is the right one. In some cases, this can create rifts between people who would otherwise share very similar values and potentially be great friends.

Think about all the personal conflicts and international wars going on today that are rooted in opposing religious beliefs. It's so fractured that these groups even fight amongst themselves! Catholic and Protestant Christians have literally fought wars over who's version of Christianity was right, while citing the same *Bible*. Sunni and Shiite Muslims still clash over religious hierarchy, even though both groups read the same *Qur'an*. Throughout the course of history, millions have fought and died over these beliefs.

If you're having trouble processing this concept, let's try a little thought exercise. Imagine a family, much like yours, living in a small house in a neighborhood. The family is made up of three kids and two parents. The youngest kid is in middle school and the two older ones are in high school. Think about these kids. What do they look like? Would you be friends? The parents want their kids to grow up with a good education so they can get a steady job in a strong economy, get married and have families of their own. They work every day in pursuit of being good stewards to the community around them and living a virtuous life in peace.

Can you see them in your mind?

What religion are they? What race or nationality are they? Are they gay or straight? How much money do they have?

The family you imagined probably looks very similar to your own and shares your beliefs, because those are the values that you hold dear and most comfortably identify with. Guess what? Someone with a completely different religious belief, racial background, and sexual orientation than you can read that same description and see *their* values and beliefs supporting those very same fundamental principles. The passage doesn't mention anything about religion, so it can actually fit people with no religious affiliation or belief at all!

Go ahead and try it again. Think of a family that's different from yours, a family that is different from the vision that immediately popped into your head the first time. Now re-read that passage. Does it still fit?

The thing is, when you step back and look deeper than the surface-level beliefs and arguments, most people have a lot more in common than they think. Over time, as a result of this shallow thinking, your armor can become less of a protective mechanism and more of a dungeon that you have effectively trapped yourself inside.

Here is my challenge to you: when you are confronted by a person whom you disagree with, refrain from immediately feeling attacked by their beliefs and ideas. Instead, take a step back and look below the surface. Try to see things from their perspective. This will allow you to think deeper about the issues around you and help you understand – not necessarily agree with – but *understand* other points of view. By taking a look at the bigger picture, you can begin to decipher which of your beliefs are true and which are lies constructed around a blind spot you have acquired somewhere along your path.

Let me make one thing clear – there is a difference between *holding a belief* and *believing and defending a lie*. Beliefs are good. They give structure to your life and help guide you on life's path. It is only when you hold your beliefs to be true *to the exclusion of all others* that you run into trouble. At that point, when you believe that nobody else can be right unless they share your exact same belief, you will create conflict.

Let's look at religion one more time to illustrate this. I'm going to use Christianity and Islam for this example, but it can be true of any denomination in any religion. Suppose a Christian and a Muslim family live next door to one another. If these families are both *holding a belief* that their faith is the one true religion, they can still coexist peacefully and get along just fine. They can look across their yard, wave, and see their neighbors as upstanding citizens. They can send their kids to the same school and let them play together. This works as long as their personal beliefs do not impose on their neighbor's belief system. Within their own homes and minds, they can pray, eat, and perform rituals that are integral to their faith without demanding that their neighbors do the same.

On the other hand, if they are *believing and defending a lie* that all people must think like they do or else they are a threat, they will look across their yard and see an enemy: someone who is defying the one true religion. This may cause them to send their kids to private or religious schools, not talk to one another, and live in a state of constant tension as the hate builds up within them for no other reason than a difference of opinion over religious beliefs.

Surrounding yourself only with people who echo your thoughts and ideas is a great way to minimize your life. At best, it will lead to a life devoid of experiencing the cultures and insights of people who are different from you, even if hate doesn't build up. The opportunity to experience the breadth of humanity is a gift and can lead to a much richer and more fulfilling life. Think about it this way: if the only ice cream flavor you ever tried was plain vanilla, you could still say you really like ice cream, but you'd be missing out on hundreds of flavors – some of which you might discover you like *more* than vanilla! My advice is to expand your palate and try as many as you can.

You can find examples like this all across the world. Religion is a major contributor to many of the social problems experienced in hundreds of countries, yet if we collectively take a step back and look at the underlying values of the imaginary family in our thought exercise, much of this tension and fear could be let go and we would have a lot less conflict amongst ourselves.

I don't mean to pick on religion. It is just one example. This same scenario can play out across a wide variety of social beliefs and causes: vegans vs. omnivores, Democrats vs. Republicans, gun control advocates vs. the National Rifle Association, even Yankees vs. Red Sox. The beliefs will change from person to person, but the underlying truth is there – we have more in common than we think.

The lies you tell yourself can be especially harmful when you construct them on a foundation of external circumstances you cannot control. Someone who is abused as a child, whether emotionally or physically, may construct the lie that they are unclean, unworthy of being loved, and that their life is a mistake. This person may then have trouble creating and maintaining close relationships, whether in business, romance, or any other area in their life.

This lie, built on a bad childhood experience, may cause them to create a suit of armor to hide this "truth" – that they're unlovable – and act in ways that will hide and deflect the shame they feel. This can present itself in several ways, including becoming a bully and perpetuating the abuse. A bully may believe that by being mean and hurtful to people, effectively pushing others away, they can hide their own personal shame and the belief that they are unlovable, while proving to themselves that they are better or more powerful than someone else.

The lie that you are unlovable can manifest in other ways too. Some people simply clam up and stay to themselves, refusing to be social or open up to others. In doing so, they eliminate any possibility that others might validate that lie. They may believe that refusing to be vulnerable with other people is the best way to avoid another rejection. If nobody can get close enough to realize that they're unlovable, they cannot be disappointed when the "truth" eventually comes out!

Regardless of the way it shows up, whether through bullying, social isolation, or any number of alternative manifestations, the lie that you are unlovable, or not *deserving* of love, care, and compassion creates a dangerous suit of armor that can lead to a miserable, lonely life.

Does this resonate with you? If so, how can you change your own mind?

I challenge you to start by accepting the *possibility* that some of the thoughts and ideas you have about yourself and the world around you may be lies, or perhaps *partial* truths. Give yourself permission to investigate alternative narratives, zoom out, and explore a larger field of view. By accepting the *possibility* that another person's point of view may be more correct than your currently-held belief, you allow yourself an opportunity to investigate the roots of your own beliefs and objectively weigh the evidence presented by both sides. In other words, you give yourself room to grow as a person.

Without straight-up acknowledging that your current belief is a lie, while remaining open to the possibility that it *might* be, you give yourself a neutral space to really think about your feelings. Take a step back from the idea or situation you are facing. Ask yourself *why* you believe what you currently believe. *Is it true*? Or is it just a convenient story you tell yourself to soften the blow of reality?

The story I told at the beginning of this letter is an example of a lie I told myself. Internal conflicts can be easier to apply this practice to because you don't have to admit that you were wrong to anyone but yourself. Applying this same exercise to an external conflict can be more difficult.

I grew up a die-hard Yankees fan. Both of my parents are from New York, and even though my dad's job with the Air Force had us moving somewhere else in the world every three years, the one constant was our summer trip back home to see our grandparents. My uncle watched the Yankees every night, and I'd be right there on the couch beside him. I loved listening to my grandma talk about the dynastic Yankees teams of the 50s and 60s, with Mickey Mantle, Whitey Ford, Yogi Berra, and the rest. I was steeped in Yankees lore and my blood ran as blue as their iconic pinstripes.

When I started college in the fall of 2000, the Yankees were in the midst of another dynastic run. They were the reigning world champions, having beaten the Atlanta Braves in the 1999 World Series to secure their third championship in four years. I was as arrogant as ever – everything everyone hates about Yankees fans – I believed they were perfect. I hated the Braves, but as fate would have it, my roommate and suitemate were both Braves fans.

We were all watching the playoffs together, and when the Braves lost in the first round, I started gloating again. It started gently, but slowly escalated to a low simmering tension. One night, as the playoffs continued without the Braves, the Yankees' right fielder, Paul O'Neill, got called out on strikes and threw a temper tantrum in the dugout, smashing a water cooler and a bucket of baseballs with his bat. My suitemate made a comment about how the Braves might be out of the playoffs, but at least they didn't have any crybabies on their team. I immediately sat up and turned on him.

"What do you mean, crybabies?" I asked. "Who's a crybaby?"

"Paul O'Neill is acting like a little bitch!" he replied, pointing at the screen, where O'Neill's antics were on full display.

My suitemate was not a small dude. He played baseball for our college team, he was in good shape, and he outweighed me by at least 25 pounds. In that moment, however, the simmering rage inside of me exploded and I flew out of my chair, grabbed him by the throat, and threw him up against the wall before my roommate could react.

"He's not a little bitch," I screamed. "He just plays with a lot of passion, which is more than can be said for those losers sitting at home!"

Before things escalated any further, my roommate got between us and settled us down. Once the rage had subsided, he rationalized with me and asked me to think about what we'd all just seen transpire on TV. He asked me to imagine what I'd think if I had seen a player from a team I hated react in the same way that Paul O'Neill had. I'd never considered that before. The truth is, if I'd seen someone from the Braves or Red Sox go berserk on a water cooler after striking out, I'd have said something very similar, if not worse!

As I cooled down and thought about it rationally, I *understood* why he said what he said. I still didn't agree with him in this particular case, but I understood where he was coming from. He wasn't attacking *me* personally, but that's how I had taken it. My roommate helped me step back and disengage my personal feelings, allowing me to effectively look at the situation from my suitemate's perspective. I had to acknowledge that he wasn't wrong.

Everything was cool after that. He'd still trash the Yankees every chance he got, and even though I obviously disagreed, and we still had heated arguments, we both understood where the other was coming from and it didn't affect our friendship. At the end of the day, we both loved baseball.

What's the takeaway here? Take the time to weigh your belief against the conflicting evidence or idea that you're up against. You may choose to maintain your current belief; you may choose to adopt a completely new position; or you may choose to *amend* your original position to accommodate some new information, blending the two, and creating an entirely new perspective, like I did. In any case – you are growing! You are opening your mind to new possibilities, taking in what makes sense to you, rejecting what does not and building your *new* truth on the sum of the evidence.

This is a process that should continue for the rest of your life! Never stop questioning your beliefs, no matter how fundamental and unshakable they may seem at the time. If the answers to those questions support your belief, you will only strengthen your position. If they expose your old beliefs as no longer true, give yourself the flexibility to pivot, reclassify that old belief as a lie, and take your next step forward.

You may be wondering if you really need to go through all that work. It's so much easier to just believe what you *want* to believe. It's convenient. Isn't everyone entitled to their own opinion?

It's easy to see these lies we tell ourselves as harmless. After all, if nobody knows your truth but you, how can it hurt anyone? The problem is that they can hurt YOU. Lies, like all thoughts, are a conception of the brain – an ethereal phantom – you cannot actually touch them. As you undoubtedly know from experience, some thoughts and ideas can change over time whether you consciously think about them or not.

As a child, I believed that girls were gross. There were certain girls on the playground that should not be touched, under any circumstances, because they were infected with cooties. When I really wanted to anger one of my male friends, I would take a glove or jacket from one of these girls – holding it by the exterior lining to avoid personal contamination of course – and wipe it all over my friend's chair, or worse, sneak up behind him and put it over his head and declare that he was now infected. This construct worked because all the boys I hung out with shared the same belief.

Thankfully, I reviewed that belief a few years later after a boatload of irrefutable evidence emerged. This new evidence, which I saw with my very own eyes, suggested that girls are beautiful, not gross. They now had boobies, not cooties. I discovered that being in close proximity to a girl was 100 percent more likely to result in sweaty palms and unwanted, unprovoked, and inconvenient erections than anything else.

One day, as I covertly tucked yet another sneak-attack boner behind the waistband of my underwear to avoid detection, it occurred to me that I had reclassified my belief that girls were gross and had cooties as a lie. I quickly and joyously acknowledged my new truth: that girls were the best thing ever created.

This is just one example of how your beliefs can evolve over time and why it's healthy for them to do so. What if I had been completely closed-minded and never bothered to re-evaluate my beliefs, where would that have left me? I would be an unmarried man in my late 30s, probably having never even gone on a date, much less actually *kissed* another human being. How stupid does that sound? What kind of idiot would be so inflexible and set in his ways to do that?

In this example, my thoughts were a product of biology – the systems and hormonal responses in our bodies that emerge over time to ensure that we're on the path toward sexual maturity and reproduction, but I think the example still works.

I encourage you to take the same steps with your other thoughts – the lies you tell yourself that do not have that biological safety net. These are the lies that have the greatest potential to cause trouble for you.

In the letters that follow, I'm going to tell you about some of the lies and traps that will influence your life. Some of these lies, if you begin to think about them now, will help you navigate high school on a level that I wish I'd been able to. In the long run, they will help you build and maintain healthy relationships with others around you, become a productive and successful member of society, and may even save your life.

Examining your beliefs to separate the lies from the truths can be downright painful. You will uncover wounds so deep that they cut right to the very heart of your being. It's important to realize that pain is not always a bad thing. It's immediately obvious when you touch a hot stove that you don't want to leave your hand there and contemplate whether or not the pain is worth enduring for the betterment of your life in the long run, but emotional pain *needs* to be felt and acknowledged before you can truly begin to unravel the truth from the lies.

As you read on, I'm going to ask you to take off your armor and open your mind to what I have to say. You may not agree with all of it. You may not even understand all of it right now, and that's fine! These letters are the stuff I wish I had known when I was your age. They are the lessons I have learned the hard way and they are the truths that I live by now. They have also been true for many of my most successful friends, acquaintances, and work colleagues over the years.

I encourage you to view these letters not as a roadmap, but more as guideposts to help answer some of the questions that you undoubtedly have now and point you in the right direction at different crossroads in your life's journey.

Let's get to it!

Love,
Tom

Chapter 4

Lie #1: Real men don't cry

Dear Ivan,

Do you ever feel like crying? Are there times where things happen in your life that are beyond your control and your emotions create a feeling of turmoil inside of you? I'm sure you know the feeling I'm talking about – perhaps you are even replaying a particular incident in your head right now. What do you do when you feel like crying? How do you cope with the overwhelming emotion?

In my last letter, I alluded to your suit of armor – the metaphorical defense you wear around others to protect yourself emotionally. While we traditionally think of armor as a way to keep things *out,* I also explained how it can be used to keep things in.

One of the greatest lies you will ever be told is that real men don't cry and don't outwardly show emotion. You don't have to have someone say this directly to your face to get the memo. As a young man growing up in our present culture and society, this message is instilled in us and we're reminded of it on a daily basis. This lie is incredibly important to identify early on because it underpins so much of what I will be sharing with you in the next several letters.

I'm going to come right out and say it: I'm a crier. If crying had a fan club, I'd be in it. If crying was a product, I'd sell it door-to-door. If crying was a candidate for office, I'd be its campaign manager. I am an advocate. I recommend crying to everyone! I'm dead serious about this. Crying is a natural outlet for sadness, grief, anger, and even joy – it's healthy and cathartic, even if it's sometimes uncomfortable and hard to do.

Even so, at your age and with everything you have on the line from a social status perspective, I understand that crying in public doesn't feel like an option. I had a hard time going to certain movies when I was in high school. I knew the happy endings in romantic comedies almost always made me tear up, so any time I took a girl on a date, especially if we were going with a group of friends, I was in for a battle to keep those tears in check. When the movie reached the tear-jerking conclusion, I used to bite my tongue so hard that the pain I was feeling was the primary thing my body focused on and I could minimize any tears. My eyes still got blurry from time to time, but I found that I could dry them out fairly quickly by holding them open really wide. When they were mostly dry, I would fake a yawn, which gave me an excuse to rub my eyes and erase the remaining evidence.

It's ok if you don't want to cry in public, whether it's at the movies or elsewhere. I get it, and that's totally fine – but it doesn't mean you have to keep those tears bottled up when you're finally alone or around people you love and trust. If you *do* cry in public, that's fine too. It means you're becoming more comfortable accepting who you are, even if some of the others around you are too self-conscious or emotionally disconnected to acknowledge their own feelings.

I'm easily moved to tears of joy at the happy conclusion of a cheesy rom-com or watching videos of people reunited with their dogs after a long separation. However, I have had many experiences where a traumatic event or a series of events triggers something inside of me and I feel the weight of worry, anger, sorrow, and grief building in my chest, but I cannot cry. It's not that I'm purposely holding it back. It's more like my body reacts subconsciously, putting up an emotional wall to separate me and keep me safe from those feelings, boxing them up and storing them somewhere else in my body. Sometimes I feel like my body is physically present, but I'm mentally distant – like my body is physically standing in the police interrogation room with the suspect, but my feelings and my mind are watching from another room behind a pane of one-way glass. The tears just won't come, even if I'm alone.

I vividly remember getting the call from one of my high school baseball teammates telling me our friend Jeff had just been killed in a drunk driving accident. He attended a rival high school, but we had played Senior League Baseball (the step above Little League) and been on the All-Star team together. I remember that he was the one hitter I hated to face because he seemed to always know what I was going to throw. In one Senior League game, I had him behind in the count, but he'd fouled off several good pitches, including my best curve ball. I decided to throw him a change-up – a pitch I hadn't used yet in the entire game – and catch him by surprise. Jeff sat back and crushed that ball a mile to center field for a home run. He was a good kid. He was respectful and nice to everyone, even when we faced off on opposite sides in high school. I was in a state of shock when I got off the phone, but I did not cry – I was just numb.

There were three high schools in my immediate area, so while our high school teams were all rivals on the field, we all knew one another socially from playing in the mixed Senior League divisions together. All three of our high school teams came to his wake to say goodbye to our friend. I remember feeling very uncomfortable standing in line waiting to walk by his open casket. It was my first personal experience with death, and I didn't like it. I remember looking at his face. He looked mostly the same as I remembered him in life. His face seemed a little gaunt, but perhaps that was just because I was used to him smiling. Seeing him lying there with his eyes closed and his mouth in a solemn, neutral expression was unsettling – as if I was looking at a version of myself in some strange out-of-body experience. I did not cry.

At the end of the viewing line, I saw his parents. I had seen them numerous times before in the stands at baseball games, always smiling and full of pride. Now they were standing in front of me, absolutely wrecked with grief. I looked into his mother's tear-filled eyes and I saw the question: why did this happen to *my* son? I can't imagine how hard it was for her to stand among this crowd of young men who were her son's age – his friends and teammates – and know that hers was the only one who was no longer alive. I took her hands in mine and simply said, "I'm sorry for your loss." That was all I could come up with in that moment. My heart was heavy. The grief felt like a boulder lodged in my chest and the weight of carrying it made me physically exhausted, but I did not cry. It was an extremely uncomfortable situation, and I left as soon as I felt I'd stayed the appropriate amount of time to pay my respects.

I often reflect on this episode in my life and wonder why – of all things – the untimely death of a friend and peer did not bring me to tears. At different points in my life I have felt like crying at the overwhelming prospect of a school paper or project that I felt sure I would fail, the death of a loved one, hearing from a close friend that they lost a child, a mass shooting, or terrorist attack, among others.

Many men – of all ages – have been conditioned by our culture to keep these feelings inside. Keep a straight face. Remain calm. Never let them see you cry. I suspect that in those moments – when the event is occurring in real time, or I've just been made aware of it – I am unable to fully process its true impact on me. Sometimes I can feel the pressure building and the lump in my throat feels like the cork of a champagne bottle that's just been shaken and is ready to burst. How do you let it out? How do you relieve that pressure?

These days, when I feel that internal pressure, I will often carve out some time to be alone and purposefully pick out the saddest movie I can find, or re-read the part in the novel, "Where the Red Fern Grows," where (spoiler alert!) Billy's dogs die and he buries them side by side on a hill on his family's farm. I use these tools as a catalyst to get the tears flowing and then I can go back to the thing I *really* want to cry about and just let it all out. It works every time – no shit, I just teared up while *writing* about it – and I feel incredibly relieved afterward. The pressure in my chest is gone and I can recalibrate and move on. It's very similar to when you are sick and you know you're going to throw up. The worst part is the agony of sitting there with waves of nausea washing over you, waiting for it to happen. Once you finally puke, you feel so much better! For me, watching that movie or reading that book is the equivalent of sticking a finger down my throat to just get it over with.

Crying is also a sign of empathy. I am a very empathic person, which means I am often able to feel and relate to the emotions of people around me. It also means that certain things make me cry very easily. To use the vomit reference again, you know how when you watch someone else throw up it can make you feel like you have to throw up too? Especially if they're close to you, right? The smell, the sound, watching their body convulse ... it's almost enough to make you gag a little right now, isn't it? Well, crying is kind of like that for me – it's contagious.

I'm not triggered by *all* crying. If I see a kid crying because he's scared to sit on Santa's lap, I don't cry. If I see some nutjob raving and crying because the barista got their coffee order wrong, I don't cry. I don't cry when I witness physical pain either, even if it's my own. One time I hit a tree while snowboarding and broke both bones in my left ankle. My foot was literally hanging from my leg, attached only by ligaments and skin. It was the worst pain I've ever felt in my life, and I almost puked, but I never cried. However, seeing someone in emotional distress is a different story.

My wife, Annah, is *not* a crier. It takes a lot for her to burst into tears. She is actually amused by how easily and often I cry. When we are watching a movie or some other show together and something emotional happens, her immediate reaction is to look over at me to check and see if I'm getting choked up, which I almost always am. We mostly watch uplifting content, and as I've told you, sharing someone else's happiness and joy are triggers for my "happy tears."

Recently, however, we went on a long road trip and listened to an audiobook to pass the time. It was a historical fiction novel that was set during World War II. In one scene, a group of young girls are being kept in a rural farmhouse as "entertainment" for the officers of the occupying enemy force. One of the girls escapes, but she is recaptured. As punishment, and to deter the others from trying a similar plan, the girl is pinned down by two men, fighting, and screaming, while a third cuts off her feet with a saw. The rest of the girls being held captive in the house are made to watch as their friend bleeds out and dies.

As I listened to the story unfold, I grew more and more angry. The atrocities committed in war – particularly those inflicted upon civilians – make my blood boil. I was raging mad, but I wasn't even close to crying. When the chapter ended, I exhaled loudly and muttered, "damn," under my breath. Then I turned to look at my wife. Annah had tears streaming down her face and her eyes were red – she had clearly been crying for a while. That passage had evoked a much different emotional response in her than it had in me. She turned to look at me and I could see the hurt in her heart and feel the profound sadness that she felt for that girl and all the others in that house. Seeing *her* crying immediately set me off in response to her emotion, and the two of us had a good sob fest for the next few minutes.

Boys and young men in the United States, as well as many cultures around the world, are taught from a young age that we cannot be vulnerable. It's considered weak to share how you *feel* unless that feeling is exhibiting the socially accepted norms of masculinity: anger, aggression, sexual conquest and general badassery. Sharing feelings of vulnerability, like loneliness, heartache, sadness, shame, and fear is discouraged and mocked. We are asked to push all those feelings down and lock them away inside ourselves. Showing any outward expression of these vulnerable emotions is like blood in the water for social sharks, and you risk being torn to pieces by the cruel words and actions of your peers and sometimes even your own family.

The idea that men don't cry and should not express vulnerable emotions is a complete lie and an absurd standard! Without an outlet for these "unmanly" emotions, they can fester and create a toxic sludge in your soul, weighing you down and dragging you toward depression and self-loathing. They can manifest as "emotional baggage," which you may feel the need to hide, in order to fit in socially.

Just the other day, I came home from the store and my arms were full of groceries and I was carrying a bag of dog food up the stairs from the garage. I was trying to carry everything all at once (because that's the manly thing to do, duh) and it was getting heavy fast! My dog greeted me at the top of the stairs, wagging her tail and excited to see me. She wanted to smell everything that I was carrying, and she wouldn't get out of my way! Because my arms were getting tired, my patience was very thin, and I snapped at her to get out of the way and kicked at her a little bit when she still didn't move.

Think about that – she was happy and excited to see me. She was interested in everything I was carrying because she wanted to know where I'd been all that time we'd been apart (and also if I'd brought her any treats) and I reacted by yelling and kicking at her. What kind of message does that send to her? It's not her fault that she didn't know I was under a lot of stress at that moment. She's only a dog! I felt so bad in the aftermath of that situation. I spent the next ten minutes loving her, petting her, and making sure she knew she was a good dog. Thankfully, dogs are very forgiving creatures.

Let's trade places in this scenario. Imagine that the heavy load you're carrying is your emotions: that loneliness, heartache, sadness, shame, and fear. You're not just carrying it up the stairs – you're carrying it *everywhere*. Instead of a dog greeting you when you get home, it's a person – a friend, sibling, or parent. Just like my dog didn't see or understand that I was carrying a heavy load, this person isn't going to see that burden you're carrying, so they become the dog in this version of the story. Imagine that they are excited to see you and want to give you a hug and talk about your day. If you are stressed and exhausted from carrying around your emotions all day, you are likely to lash out at them for no apparent reason they can perceive. It may not be physical – you don't have to push or kick them to lash out. Verbal attacks can be just as damaging, and unlike dogs, people can be much less forgiving – especially if it becomes a pattern.

If you want to see this in real life, just think about the biggest bully you know. Bullies can seem intimidating, but in most cases, their actions toward others are actually a reflection of *how they feel about themselves*. You may think of bullies as being full of anger and hate – those "manly" emotions – but anger and hate are often produced when loneliness, sadness, shame, and fear are mixed together and brought to a boil.

When a person is so filled with shame that he or she literally hates themselves – when that stew of emotion boils over – the result is often an outward attack on someone else close by. Bullies choose targets they perceive to be weaker than themselves because it gives them an outlet to let go of some of that toxic mix of loneliness, sadness, shame, and fear. It's a pressure release valve that is safe for them because they don't expect any resistance from their target. If bullies tried to unload on a stronger target, it would not work because they'd get their ass kicked, which would have the opposite effect: it would reinforce and *add* to their shame and fear. That's why the commonly prescribed antidote to facing a bully is to punch them right in the nose. You may still get your ass kicked that day, but they'll probably leave you alone in the future because you're no longer an *easy* target.

I'll break this down further and share a lot more about bullying in another letter, but for now I just want to give you a little insight into how toxic it can be to keep all your emotions bottled up.

Sometimes the person you lash out at is *yourself*. This can be particularly dangerous. Because you are hiding your feelings from everyone else, the people in your life who care about you may not be aware of the emotional load you're carrying. You can attack yourself both mentally and physically without anyone else knowing for quite a while.

When I was in middle school, I was bullied by a couple of boys in my grade. Again, I share this story in its entirety in the letter about bullying, so you can read all the details there. What I don't share in that letter is the depth of the fear, depression, and internal shame I felt and how I wrestled with it.

I did not understand what I had done to make these boys hate me. I spent hours staring in the mirror, trying to find the flaws that made me so unlikeable – so *unlovable*. I spent many nights crying silently in my room with dark thoughts passing through my mind like the shadows of vultures circling over a dying animal – as soon as one would pass, another would take its place in an unending cycle. The longer I ruminated on my situation with no clear answer, the more I drifted into a state of depression and despair. If there is no one reason for why I'm being treated this way, then *all of me* must be the reason. I started to hate the person in the mirror looking back at me. I hated the zit-faced *loser* with the gap in his teeth that braces hadn't yet closed. I hated the plastic-looking hair that was locked in place by way too much styling mousse. I hated the *weakness* in my heart, and I was ashamed that I was too afraid to stand up for myself.

On more than one occasion, I thought that it would be easier to kill myself than live one more day in the misery of shame and depression that overwhelmed me. I did not think through *how* I would do it or what would happen to my family afterward. All I could think about in those moments was how relieved I would be if I could just disappear.

I hid all of these feelings deep down inside. I didn't share them with anyone, including my parents or brothers. I didn't want my mom or dad finding out I was being bullied and dragging me into the principal's office for a meeting with my bullies and their parents! The *whole school* would find out how much of a little bitch I was, and I would get bullied even more! I tried to put on a mask of confidence and happiness, afraid to show any sign that something was wrong.

Thankfully, I had the presence of mind to recognize that killing myself was a terrible idea. I loved my family and I wanted to be around them. I loved playing video games and baseball with my brothers, and I was not ready to give that up. As the oldest, I also felt a strong sense of responsibility to be a good role model for my brothers and I could not do that if I was dead. I do not remember when, where, or how I found my path out of that dark place, but I did. I endured those emotions and that trauma for almost a year, but eventually it passed. Even so, the scars are still with me today, which is how I'm able to relay this story to you.

When you don't value yourself, don't see your own self-worth, and can't see past your loneliness, sadness, and shame, you are more likely to participate in irrational and reckless behavior, putting yourself and others in physical danger. An example might be driving too fast and weaving through traffic in your car while not wearing your seatbelt. It can also manifest as mental bullying, telling yourself how big a piece of shit you are and seeking an escape in substances like drugs and alcohol. If left unchecked, these kinds of thoughts and actions may lead you as far as contemplating taking your own life. The likelihood of actually going through with it increases if drugs and alcohol are involved, impairing your ability to think rationally.

Think about carrying a heavy suitcase or backpack around all day. How much better do you feel when you finally put it down and give your arms and shoulders a break? It's like the weight of the world has been lifted off you! You can take a deep breath, exhale, and collapse in a comfortable chair, finally unburdened from the heavy load. Emotional baggage has the same effect, weighing you down, creating stress in your life and affecting your mood. The longer you carry it, the more you get used to it. It doesn't mean it's not there, it's just sitting in the background, waiting for the next opportunity to rear its ugly face.

The point of all this is to say it's 100% OK to feel these emotions. There is nothing "unmanly" about it! You *need* to sit with them, feel them, acknowledge them, and work through them. It is normal and it is *human*. It can also be very uncomfortable and difficult. I understand if you don't feel comfortable sharing your emotions with everyone all of the time, and you don't have to. Telling another person about something you're ashamed of can be terrifying! You have to trust them enough not to laugh at you or weaponize that shame against you. However, it's critically important to find *someone* in your life to share these feelings with, whether it's a parent, a best friend whom you trust, or a mentor of some kind: a teacher, guidance counsellor, family friend or relative. There is *always* someone. Fighting a battle – even an internal one like this – is almost impossible on your own. It's much easier when you have allies fighting with you, even if all they do is listen.

If you don't have confidence in anyone around you, or you're just not ready to open up to someone you know, it's ok to seek out a professional therapist. Seeing a therapist has long been stigmatized because the implication was that something was inherently *wrong* with you – that you were crazy or something. A therapist is just another type of doctor. Mental health is just as important as physical health. If you break your arm or tear a ligament in your knee, there's no shame in going to a doctor to get help, right? People would think you were crazy if you *didn't* go! You go to the doctor to get the diagnosis, have surgery if needed, and return for follow-up appointments to measure progress until you're healthy again and it's no longer needed. Going to therapy is the same thing. Just because you cannot *see* the injury or ailment doesn't mean it's not there. You can't see asthma or heart disease either, but nobody would argue it's not worth being treated by a doctor. Therapy can be a great tool to help address and treat these challenges in your life. Just like a traditional doctor's visit, it doesn't last forever, and it doesn't mean you are weak. Don't be afraid to ask for help if you need it.

You have a limited capacity to hold everything in – like a bucket. If you've ever been in an old building when it's raining, you have likely seen random buckets placed in hallways and rooms where there's a small leak in the ceiling. The bucket does a great job of catching those drips and keeping them contained so the water doesn't spread all over the floor. The buckets have a limited capacity, however, so there must be a custodian or building caretaker who is paying attention to the water levels in those buckets and emptying them at regular intervals, so they don't overflow. If nobody empties the buckets, the water will eventually start creeping over the sides and creating a mess. Even worse, if a person walks by and accidentally or purposely *kicks* one of those buckets, you've got a real problem on your hands!

Similarly, when your emotional bucket is full, you need a way to empty it in order to allow it the space to slowly fill up again. If your bucket is constantly full, your emotions will spill over every time something new is added, causing you to lash out. Finding someone to confide in and be vulnerable with is an opportunity to safely empty your bucket. You can even tell that person that you're not looking for advice or their help in solving a problem. Tell them that up front! Let that person know that you just need to get some stuff off your chest. Having someone who will simply *listen* to you is a great way to empty your bucket and let the weight of the world fall off your shoulders. Give yourself permission to cry. You don't *have* to cry, but don't fight the tears if you feel them coming. Consider it your body's way of getting rid of these toxic feelings – like taking an emotional shit through your eyes. Just like that morning deuce, you'll feel a lot lighter afterward.

Don't believe the lie that men don't cry or show emotion! It doesn't make you weak and it doesn't make you any less of a man. Give yourself permission to acknowledge your feelings and express your emotions. As you get older, this skill will serve you well in all relationships. The ability to acknowledge and accept your emotions and allow yourself to be vulnerable around the right people will make you a better lover, husband, and father, as well as a better employee, manager, and business owner.

If you have read this far and are still holding firm to the belief that real men – *tough* men – don't cry, please go watch a documentary called "The Work." If you are still doubtful about the value and healing power of sitting with your emotions, feeling them, naming them, and expelling them from your body through tears, this documentary will show you just how powerful it can be. The film follows a group of men from everyday life, who volunteer to enter a four-day therapy program with inmates inside a maximum-security prison. These inmates are some of the baddest, toughest dudes you can imagine – the kind of men you don't ever want to meet in a dark alley. They are murderers and former gang members with multiple life sentences around their necks. They are in one of the harshest environments you can imagine, where being tough and emotionally isolated are required for safety. Over the course of this four-day program, these inmates and free men alike break down and share their shame, regret, fear, and guilt. They cry – some for the first time – and they begin to heal.

You too can begin to heal now, *before* the toxicity of those pent-up emotions puts you in a prison – whether it's an actual cell block or just a prison in your mind. I encourage you to feel, emote, and know that there is nothing unmanly about it.

Whatever path you choose in life, the ability to work through your emotions and release them will improve your quality of life exponentially. Find a time and place to take off that armor and be vulnerable. Go ahead and cry! You can always put it back on, carrying an empty bucket, before stepping out the door to face the world again.

>Love,
>Tom

Chapter 5

Lie #2: Who I am right now is who I'm destined to be

Dear Ivan,

When I was in 7th grade, nothing was going my way. I wasn't cool or popular. I didn't have many friends. Girls weren't interested in me. I didn't make the middle school baseball team … but a girl did. I wasn't even that good at academics. By my own assessment, I was at best one or two rungs from the bottom of the social ladder, and I'm pretty sure there were plenty of people who thought I was at the absolute bottom – if they even knew I existed at all.

By contrast, there was a kid in my class named Landon, whom I deeply admired. He was a good-looking guy with perfect hair and a killer smile. He was athletic and funny and constantly had girls swooning over him. I wanted to be him so badly! I would have given anything to trade places with him. I wasted far too much time fantasizing about what his life must be like and lamenting my own unfortunate circumstance. At that time, I was sure that I was destined to be a loser forever, and that thought was completely demoralizing. If this is my fate, what's the point of it all? Why bother trying harder in school or setting goals if nothing was ever going to really change?

Believing that whoever you are in this moment is who you are destined to be for the rest of your life is one of the most damaging lies you can tell yourself. You're all of what, 15 or 16 years old? You're probably less than 25 percent of the way through your life and you think that where you are, what you've achieved so far, and what other people think of you right now will define you forever? The thoughts you have at 15 – who you think you are, what's important to you, and the way you see the world will almost certainly change over time. From a scientific perspective, your brain hasn't even finished developing yet, so you cannot possibly comprehend everything that you will be capable of. If you really think about it, you've already come a long way!

As children, our minds work differently. Think about how you've changed over just the past few years. Do you remember what it was like before you learned to classify yourself or others as different, strange, or weird in a way that prohibits you from associating with them in public or social settings? Think back to when you were in elementary school. Did you worry about what clothes you were going to wear or if the other kids thought you were cool or not? Even if you did, I'll bet you didn't put as much thought into those things as you do now.

When I was a child, from kindergarten through at *least* third grade, I considered all other kids to be just like me: we were kids, and we were all on the same team. If you weren't a kid, you were a grown-up. It was just that simple. In my mind, being a grown-up was a terrible tragedy because it meant you couldn't play or have fun anymore and you were probably going to die soon.

In fact, I was so happy being a kid that I responded to turning 10-years old by literally freaking out. I had a pretty significant panic attack and mental meltdown on my tenth birthday. I sat in my room alone and cried. In my mind, I was being forced against my will to cross a symbolic threshold – having two digits in my age – which signified I was leaving childhood behind. I feared that I could not be a kid anymore, and I was horrified at the prospect that I would soon be joining the ranks of a new and scary classification: *teenagers.*

I was terrified of kids who were older than me, and teenagers in particular. It was probably a combination of something I'd seen on TV or in a movie, or maybe just stories I heard from my friends with older siblings, but I lived in constant fear that teenagers would try to beat me up purely for the sport of it. I didn't actually *know* any teenagers other than our babysitter, and she wasn't scary, but I remained terrified of older kids until the start of my freshman year of high school. I'll get into that later, but for now let's reminisce about those early years.

It is through the idealistic lens of childhood that I remember a very specific time when being a kid of a similar age was enough to gain entry to a social group. My dad was in the Air Force, so back when I was in first grade, we were stationed in Spain and living in base housing. I clearly remember the day when a little girl named Janae joined the class. It was immediately clear that she felt scared and very alone. Janae's father had just been transferred to our base, so she had been pulled out of her old school, moved halfway around the world, and forced to join my class in the middle of the year.

Imagine that for a moment – being six-years old and having your entire world pulled out from under you. Your grandparents, friends, favorite restaurant, favorite TV shows and even your old bedroom are left behind. Literally every comfort and constant that you've known in your life, with the exception of your parents and maybe your siblings, is gone. To top it all off, you get dropped into a foreign country where the only people who even speak the same language as you are here on this military base.

I remember watching this little girl walk up to the teacher's desk on her first day, vision blurred from a cascade of tears, voice shaking and gasping between sobs as if she'd just finished sprinting a mile. One word at a time, she communicated that she had no friends.

The teacher took her hand, turned, and addressed the class: "who would like to be friends with Janae?" I will never forget the look in her eyes. That poor little girl slowly turned toward a class of strangers with tears and snot running down her face, eyes darting from one student to the next, searching and begging for acceptance, hoping that someone – anyone – would agree to be her friend.

Within seconds, two other little girls stood up and said, "I'll be your friend." They walked to the front of the class, each taking one of Janae's hands in theirs, and took her back to where they were sitting.

This is the world of a child, and it goes a long way in showing that you are born with the innate understanding that companionship, friendship, and love should be offered to all. As you age, you begin building your suit of armor, forged by your life experiences. You create an underlying belief system that the way *you* see the world is the way the world actually is. This makes sense because your version of reality can only extend as far as what you have actually experienced. The more you experience and learn, the wider your field of vision becomes.

As you continue to make choices about the world based on your experiences, you begin to change. You assemble your personal suit of armor based on your beliefs and begin to project those beliefs outward onto the rest of the world and the people around you. The things you see and experience start to form the basis for your subconscious bias. That is, if you don't recognize what you see as being the *same* as you, you start to classify people as *different* and *other*. This is where social stratification begins, and we start categorizing the world around us.

A person who has qualities you admire and desire – like my classmate Landon – creates the classification of "cool," and you may start to look up to them. On the other hand, someone who acts in a manner that you personally find off-putting may be categorized as a "loser," a person to be avoided and possibly ridiculed to create separation between yourself that individual. Remember that all of this is based on *your* version of reality, but your version of reality is only one way to look at things.

Looking back now, I can see my evolution from "being a kid," where welcoming a newcomer like Janae was accepted unconditionally, to the point where I started projecting my own ideas of what the world *should* be, based on my experience and comfort levels, onto my classmates with much more scrutiny and caution.

By the fourth grade, my family was living in Arizona. I had a kid in my class named Zeke. He smelled like he hadn't taken a bath in weeks. He wasn't very smart and was a constant disruption in class. He wore the same clothes every day and the ends of his shirt sleeves were coated in a solid crust of snot from the constant wiping of his nose.

In the fifth grade, there was Jolene, a freckle-faced girl with unbrushed hair who talked funny. She was always the last person picked for the kickball team at recess and nobody wanted to sit next to her in class because she had "Jolene germs."

These characteristics deviated from what I considered normal and acceptable. I could also tell that many of my classmates – the ones who I believed were very much like me – felt the same way. We made fun of Zeke and Jolene when they were not around and developed fake maladies like "Jolene germs" as a way to unify ourselves against them. This kind of groupthink strengthened my resolve to reject them. As I said before, my reality, even though it was a reality shared at least in part by many of my classmates, was only one side of the story. It just so happened to be the *only* side I could see from my limited life experience and knowledge of the world.

Unbeknownst to me and my classmates at the time, Zeke's parents were from Mexico. I do not know if they were US citizens or undocumented, but I would guess the latter. I also do not know if Zeke himself was born in the United States, but those details are not important to me. Zeke's family was poor and didn't have the means to buy him new clothes. He was learning English as a second language, which is even more impressive to me after having lived in Spain for three years and never learning a word of Spanish outside of hello, goodbye, and the ability to count to ten. He learned slower than the rest of us because he had to decipher a language barrier that I took for granted.

Jolene's family was from Georgia. She spoke with a southern accent and used words like *y'all*, which many of the kids from Arizona had never heard. She brought lunch from home and it seemed like everything she ate had mayonnaise in it, which was normal where she came from, but we found it disgusting.

Zeke and Jolene were different from me, and while their differences didn't make them any less human than my best friend, Harrison, I began to pick up on subtle social cues telling me that associating with them would say something negative about me to the other kids in the class.

It's not that I had anything personal against them – neither one of them ever personally attacked me in any way – but the fear of being cast in the same light as them through my *association* was enough for me to keep my distance. I began to form a new truth – ultimately a dangerous lie – that I was *better* than them in some way. My choice to join the rest of the class in condemning them to a lower status was made based on my desire to avoid that status myself. I didn't recognize it at the time, but it was a subconscious act of self-preservation.

I never specifically talked to any of my classmates, not even Harrison, about *why* or even *if* they shared a negative opinion of Zeke and Jolene, I just went with it – part of a mass movement of unfounded belief that turned out to be a lie in retrospect. It took me many years to realize that simply being different does not make someone good or bad. There are many factors to consider, and it's critical to remember that there is always more than one way to look at a person, situation, or idea. Change is constant. Opening your mind to the possibility of change is a great first step when you're evaluating your beliefs.

If the armor that you develop to protect your beliefs and project your worldview on others is your own personal creation, and all people have their own thoughts and opinions, then you must conclude that everyone is wearing his or her own unique suit of armor. How you're judged by others is the result of someone else's personal truths and convictions that they cast onto you. What they see when they look at you through their lens often determines how they treat you. In some cases, what *you* see reflected off their armor back at you can influence how you judge *yourself* and influence how you behave around that person.

This last part is critical. In many cases, and I have to admit this is still true for me today, the way we interact with other people is actually a defense mechanism to protect us from exposing our true nature. Rather than share our truest self, we put on a mask and deliver a performance that we think the other person expects or *wants* to see. We create half-truths and outright lies about ourselves in an effort to gain the approval of others.

One of the things that I have never liked about myself is that I have several moles on my body. I have always found them repulsive: ugly, soft, brown lumps that serve no purpose and look like small turds clinging to my neck and torso. One mole in particular bothered me more than the others. It was on the back right side of my neck, and it was the only one that I couldn't cover with normal clothing. I hated seeing it in the mirror, and any time I was in public I felt like people were staring at it. It was almost as if it was calling out to them, "Hey, look at me! How gross am I? Don't you just hate this kid I'm attached to?"

I used to pull my tee shirts down at the collar in front so the back of the collar would rise just enough to cover it. When I was talking to someone up close, I would hold one hand over my neck as casually as possible to cover the mole, but you can only do that for so long before it gets awkward. I was miserable. As silly as it may sound, I was getting mentally exhausted because I had to remain vigilant about whether or not people could see this mole on my neck! I was so disgusted by this small piece of flesh that I honestly believed other people saw me as gross and disgusting because of it.

Finally, I convinced my mom to take me to the doctor to get it removed. I don't remember exactly how old I was, but probably my early teens. I remember sitting in the dermatologist's office waiting for the old, bald doctor to come in and cut this thing out of my life. My spirits soared as he walked into the room. Then, in a flash, I felt my throat go dry and my stomach drop all the way down into my scrotum. My palms got sweaty, and a wave of nausea washed over me as I watched a young, gorgeous woman walk into the room behind the doctor. She had caramel-colored skin and long, straight, shimmering black hair. She was a new doctor, and *she* was going to be the one removing my mole. I was sitting there with my shirt off – no armor to hide behind. She could see the mole on my neck as well as the one on my torso. Of course, she was extremely professional and did her job expertly, injecting the area around the mole with a numbing agent and then using a scalpel to extricate the grotesque mass from my body. She dropped my nemesis into a specimen cup with some liquid in it, placed it on a tray next to me, and closed the incision with four stitches.

My unblinking eyes were locked on that cup the whole time. The mole looked like a little chocolate cupcake with a pink wrapper, suspended in the liquid. I should have been elated, but I was angry. Even in its last moment, it had embarrassed me in front of a beautiful woman.

Even after I had the mole removed, I was still embarrassed by it. For many years, when people would ask me how I got the scar on my neck, I would lie and say that my brother had shot at me with a pellet rifle and just barely missed my carotid artery, nicking my neck instead. I went to great lengths to lie about the scar because I still suspected that people might find me gross if they knew its true origin.

To this day, I am still a little self-conscious about my remaining moles. Just last summer, when Annah and I came to visit and we were hanging out at the lake with you, your cousins, and the rest of the family, I was standing around with my shirt off when my six-year old niece pointed to the mole on my torso and asked, "What's that?" Annah was standing nearby, and before I could answer, she walked over and poked it several times. She looked at my niece and said, "it's a mo-lay mo-lay mo-lay mole!" in the kind of playful voice a parent might use when sneaking up to tickle their child. I felt my face flushing red with embarrassment. My niece scrunched her nose and asked a follow-up question: "Why do you have it?" That's a question I've asked myself for as long as I can remember, I thought to myself!

As Annah started explaining the basics of genetics and birthmarks to my niece, my thoughts turned inward. The whole situation gave me a strange feeling. My niece wasn't disgusted by me, she was only being curious, but the fact that she had pointed out this part of me that I had hated for so long brought back all those feelings from my childhood. I felt slightly uncomfortable and self-conscious. I also felt strangely validated. Someone had actually noticed and asked about the thing I had spent many years of my life trying to hide. The feeling soon passed, as did her interest, and the subject never came up again.

This example is only one of many, and it is a natural part of being human: being afraid of what people will think of you if they discover the parts that you don't like about yourself, whether they're physical or emotional. Though many people will never admit it, deep down we are all afraid that if people see who we really are, they will once again cast us down to that lowest rung on the social ladder. It can take a long time for those feelings to go away, and sometimes – as I learned – you may think they're gone, but they can resurface when you least expect it.

That example is a physical one, but for many people, their greatest fear or shame is not a part of the physical world and is not visible to the naked eye. When I was in college, I had four friends, each in a different circle of friends, who would all eventually come out as gay.

My friend Greg was the first. He came out to me during the first month of my junior year of college. It was a small gathering, just me, him, one other guy and three girls. The five of us were the first people he ever told. Coincidentally, he was also the first gay person I'd ever actually met. I mean, I'm sure I'd met plenty of gay people before without realizing it, but this was the first time that someone actually *told* me they were gay. I felt weird at first. It wasn't a disgusted kind of weird, like I felt about my moles, but more of a realization that my reality had shifted and things would never be quite the same.

It wasn't that I doubted the existence of gay people, but I had never been confronted with the reality of it. Until then, my understanding of what it meant to be gay was a disorganized mosaic of stereotypes and tropes that I'd pieced together from various representations in the media and homophobic comments from others in my social circles over the years. Without knowing any better, I believed that gay people were all physically delicate, limp-wristed, fashion savvy, hyper-sensitive men who gave off an effeminate aura and spoke with a lisp.

Greg violated several of these stereotypes. He dressed very similarly to the way I did. He was really into cars. He didn't speak with a lisp. Greg was like me in a lot of ways!

After the shock wore off, I was filled with gratitude that Greg felt comfortable and safe enough around me to share such a big revelation, which he had felt the need to keep secret until then. I didn't look at him or treat him any differently after that. It actually simplified some things. For one, I was no longer confused by his interactions with women. He would tease them in a friendly way that was completely devoid of sexual undertones, which I had never seen from another man. It was also clearly liberating to Greg himself. After receiving such a warm reception from our small group of friends, he found the confidence to be himself with everyone!

In terms of officially coming out, Greg was the exception. My other three friends were firmly committed to acting the part of a straight male. I cannot give you their reasons because I have never spoken with them directly about it. I do not know if they were still uncertain about their sexuality, if they knew they were gay but were trying to force themselves to be straight due to the expectations of their religious upbringing, or if they knew they were gay but weren't ready to deal with the potential fallout from telling their straight friends. I'm only speculating. It could have been something else entirely, and I'm sure it was different for each of them.

Of those three, I was the closest to James. He was two years younger than me, but we had a similar sense of humor and similar interests. We sang in an a cappella group on campus together and we hung out all the time. James dated several women and had sex with at least one that I knew of. He was tall, handsome, and stylish. He always looked like he'd stepped right out of a photo shoot for some fashion magazine. He was also an amazing athlete, a star on the swim team. He definitely had some mannerisms and tendencies that some may consider effeminate, but he frequently reminded our circle of friends he was *not* gay, and we did not argue.

Occasionally, when our a cappella group would travel to other schools to perform with the groups from that school, someone who didn't know us would casually say something in conversation suggesting that James was gay. It could be a harmless statement like, "You guys should stay for the after party! There's going to be a ton of girls there ... and guys." Like wolves protecting the pack, our group would rally to his defense, declaring in no uncertain terms that James was straight. As if to prove the point, I often saw him at the after parties making out with some girl. In my mind, I was 100 percent sure James was just as straight as I was.

Right before the end of school, about a month before my graduation, James and I were hanging out in his room like we often did. He was telling me about a conversation he'd had with his friend, Brad, another student who was already out as gay. I didn't know Brad personally, but I knew who he was, and I did not have anything against him.

"Brad thinks I might be gay," James told me.

Instinctively, as I had done numerous times before, I came to his defense. "You're not gay," I said to James, with a touch of disgust. "Brad just *wishes* you were gay!"

"But what if he's right?" James asked.

"Dude, you're not fucking gay," I reassured him. "We both know that."

That was how the conversation ended. James never actually told me that he was gay. We drifted apart after I graduated. I learned he was gay from a mutual friend a couple years later. As I look back on that conversation now, I realize that James may have been *trying* to tell me that he was gay. Did he make up the conversation with Brad as a piece of his armor? Was that story just a safety net to gauge my response before making himself completely vulnerable? Did my aggressive rejection of the idea that he could be gay prevent him from sharing his secret with me?

James was a great friend, and I would have done anything for him. In that moment, I was doing what he had conditioned me to do for the past couple years – defend his straightness against any suggestion that he was gay, even if he was suggesting it himself! If he had simply told me he was gay, I'm sure I would have been shocked, but I would not have shunned him or thought any less of him. It breaks my heart to think that he might have thought otherwise.

If someone as good looking, multi-talented and outwardly confident as James could be so ashamed of a certain part of himself, or afraid of the potential repercussions of revealing such a big secret, that he did not feel safe sharing it with his closest friends, what hope do any of us have of avoiding a similar struggle in our lives?

I have thought a lot about this over the years and continue to think about it often. Of all the challenges I have faced in my life – the fears and worries about how people would see me if they knew certain secrets about me – none have had the level of risk and the potential to reshape (and potentially ruin) my personal relationships on the magnitude that my four college friends faced in making the decision to come out as gay or remain in the closet. I cannot imagine how heavy that burden must feel or how violent that internal struggle must be. I empathize with anyone who is struggling with their sexual identity, and I encourage you to put yourself in their shoes. Consider how dramatically your life would change if you were standing at this crossroad. Keep that in mind as you navigate your own life and choose to be an ally for those who are walking this path.

We are all human. We all have weaknesses or *perceived* weaknesses that we will fight and lie to defend and hide. The bottom line, and what I really want you to take away from this, is that right now you are only beginning to understand who you are and who you will become.

In the years ahead, you will begin removing the armor you are wearing now. Some of it will be replaced with updated beliefs and some of it will fall away completely. I hope that you will find hope and joy in this thought. You will find new loves in your life. You will find people, places, activities, and foods – among many other things – that move you and bring you incredible joy. I am envious of where you are in your life right now. You have so many incredible moments ahead that you will want to live in forever, and experiences that you will always remember fondly. Yes, there are bad times ahead too, dark days that will push you to your breaking point. In the end, the good outweighs the bad by so much that when you look back on your life, as I am now, the bad memories fade while the good ones shine even brighter than they seemed at the time.

The truth is that you will *never* fully understand the world. I expected to have it all figured out by the time I reached my 20s, like there would be some kind of switch that got flipped when I became an "adult," granting me all the wisdom I had sought for the past 20 years. I'm much older than that now and I still haven't got it all figured out – I don't believe anyone at any age does. If you think about it, it's an impossible expectation. Every person will experience this life differently, so *your* truth will be different from everyone else's. You will have the opportunity to share your views and beliefs with others and should always offer them the opportunity to share theirs with you. Do this as often as possible. It's one thing I really wish I'd done more when I was younger: expose myself to new and different points of view. Other people's arguments may not always convince you to change your own beliefs, but some might! At the very least, you will leave these encounters with a better understanding of how those individuals see the world and have a better grasp of how they came to hold an opinion that is different from yours.

My life would be a lot richer today if I would have taken the time to talk to people with different experiences than mine when I was younger. You still have a chance to get an early start! Please ask questions of those who have "been there and done that." Learn from their mistakes so you don't make them yourself! I know you have so many questions about life and how to tackle the challenges you're facing. There is no shame in that! Stop feeling like asking questions makes you look weak, stupid, and incapable! What it really makes you is *smart*. If you can learn from someone else who has been through your situation, you can avoid a lot of the pitfalls that you will otherwise stumble right into.

Don't confuse inexperience with weakness. It's only weakness if you refuse to ask questions and plow ahead blindly, trying to learn everything for yourself. You don't have to reinvent the wheel – it's already been done. Ask the questions that seem stupid like, "Um, excuse me, but how did you *do* that?"

I promise that more times than not, the person you're asking will look at you and think to themselves that you are wise beyond your years and your inquisitive mind will lead you to great success in life. Why? Because chances are good that *they* were that idiot who tried to do it all by themselves. On the flip side, if the person you ask *does* treat you like an idiot, you've still learned a valuable lesson: that person is not going to be a positive influence in your life and you're better off seeking advice and asking questions of someone else.

My challenge to you is to learn from those who have come before you and already know how to do what you want to do. It will save you a lot of heartache, pain, time, and money! Seek out a mentor or a coach. Find someone who is doing exactly what you want to do and ask to meet with them. You can find a mentor who is working in the career that you are thinking about pursuing. You can find a mentor who is more knowledgeable about a hobby you are just getting into. You can find a mentor for just about anything.

Mentors can be incredibly valuable to your personal growth, not only with the questions you have and the skills you will learn about a profession or hobby, but with the situations you will face along the way. They can help you navigate difficult conversations and overcome obstacles that cross your path. What if you find a mentor and then realize that you are no longer interested in that profession or hobby? No problem! You gained a friend and some real-world experience while learning that you don't want to spend any more time on that particular path. Seek out a new path and try again. Perhaps your old mentor can even introduce you to someone in your new field of interest.

Who you are right now means very little in the big scheme of things. If life is a process of building a house, your current moment in time represents the hole in the ground where the foundation has yet to be poured. Think about that for a moment. You've done the work of clearing the land and selecting the build site. Some groundwork has been laid, true, but the most important steps – the fun stuff – is yet to come.

Whoever you believe yourself to be, or whoever others have convinced you that you are is irrelevant. It's just a label that you can peel off with a little effort. You will have *many* opportunities in your life to re-invent yourself into whoever or whatever you want to be.

As a military kid, I moved around a lot. Every three years or so, I had to start over from scratch. I didn't know a single person in my new town or school, and nobody knew me. For the most part, it sucked because I always had to make new friends. I was a very shy kid, so making friends wasn't easy for me. For whatever reason, I had created the lie in my head that I was unworthy of others' friendship, so I approached every relationship with timidity, expecting to be rejected. Today, I have exactly zero friends that I can say I knew from childhood and grew up with.

On the other hand, however, I now look back and recognize the good that came from it. I learned it's OK to start over and that a new beginning can change what was a terrible story into a great one. It's like restarting a video game. You're going through, level by level, and at some point in your journey, your game gets erased. What the fuck, right? You've got to start all over again – but this time it's a little easier, because you remember where certain elements are hidden, which paths to take and which to avoid. It's a bit like that.

If you are reading this right now, thinking your life is a waste, you're a loser, and this is just your lot in life, you're WRONG. You're so wrong you can't even begin to comprehend how big of a lie you've got yourself tangled up in. You will have plenty of opportunities to restart your video game, choose a different path, and try again, recreating a new story along the way. You have been given an incredible opportunity – the chance to live a full life of choices and experiences – and you've only just begun to scratch the surface.

Think about it – out of millions of sperm, *you* made it. In the most important race of your life, you WON. You found the egg. You broke through first. That's an incredible achievement, so you can't say you have never accomplished anything. If you consider that throughout history there have been gazillions of other sperm who started their race only to discover *there was no egg*, or wind up in a dirty sock or tissue, (talk about a let-down!) well, that makes you even more successful! Your presence here is a gift, so start looking at it that way and you'll eventually come to realize that no matter what is in front of you, you have already beaten the greatest odds.

I once heard life related in this way: At any given moment, you will find yourself alone in a rowboat on a wild sea. Waves cresting 15-feet high above you on both sides and your boat tossed around like a leaf in a hurricane. You wonder how you will survive this ordeal. However, when you have the perspective of looking back on your life from many years in the future, you will observe that the sea behind you is calm and there are but a few ripples on an otherwise glassy surface.

Life always feels most challenging in the present moment. After all, it's the only moment in which you can actually take action. This will always be the case because you cannot change the past and you cannot foresee what the future holds. You have only *this* moment, right now, to take action, which is why the waves seem so threatening.

Think back to your earlier years for a moment. Think of a time when you thought your life was on the line – a science project was due and you hadn't started it; you crashed your bike into the neighbor's new car and they called the police; you fell out of a tree and broke both arms trying to catch yourself as you hit the ground and spent the entire summer in double arm casts with your mom wiping your butt again like you were a baby – whatever your scenario was, at the time, it felt like the worst moment of your life, but in retrospect, you are probably laughing at how silly that seems now. The consequences of that moment that you were sure would end your life are mostly forgotten.

It is the same with this present moment in your life. Whatever challenge you are currently facing, unsure of how you will ever live it down and escape with your life and dignity intact, it will appear as a mere ripple on an otherwise glassy surface when you look back on it a few years down the road.

You may be thinking, "Fuck you, Tom! You don't know my life, what I've been through, *what I'm going through now*. How can you say how I'm going to feel in the future?"

Good question. I had the same thought when I was younger. *How can anyone know what I'm going through – this is MY life!* But here's the thing – I've experienced it firsthand. So have tens of *billions* of people who have come before us. You are not the only one who has won the most important race in life – we *all* have. Do you really believe that out of all the people who have ever existed, your problem is unique to you? Somewhere, sometime, someone has experienced the same thing you're going through now. There have been millions of different outcomes from the same situation based on where and when they lived, what their particular circumstances were, and the course of action they chose, but they survived, and so will you.

High school feels like a big deal right now, but in the grand scheme of things, it's just a steppingstone on your path to bigger and better things. Regardless of what rung you currently occupy on the social ladder or how you're treated by others, this is temporary. You *will* have a chance to start anew. You can join the military, go to college or a trade school, or move to a new town, state, or country! Those opportunities are available to you if you pursue them.

High school is a gauntlet we all must run, but once you come out on the other side, whether you emerge unscathed or beaten and bruised, the next step in your path can be a new beginning. Don't give up. Don't quit. Set goals. Make plans and take that next step each day in pursuit of the future you want for yourself.

    Love,
    Tom

P.S.

As you prepare to enter high school, you need to understand and believe that these next few years will not define you. No matter how you may feel in the moment, even if that "moment" lasts for a couple years, it is incredibly unlikely that any experience – good or bad – will absolutely govern the rest of your life. There is no amount of bullying, mockery, misery, or pain that exists in your life right now that can justify a choice to end it. Do not be afraid or ashamed of who you are right now. Each experience is a building block for who you will become and how you will ultimately impact this world and affect the legacy you leave.

This knife cuts both ways, so do not be too confident that you've got it all figured out. Oh, you're a great athlete with D-1 college programs already sending you scholarship offers? Cool. Oh, you're a music prodigy with your first demo in the hands of the record company execs? Cool. Oh, your parents have set up a trust fund so you will never have to worry about money? Cool. Like I said, this moment in your life will not define you. Life is full of highs and lows. If you are riding a high right now, by all means enjoy it! But please, remember that your current situation is not a promise of how the rest of your life will turn out.

The road of life is littered with the remains of promising athletic careers derailed by an injury or being "good, but not *good enough*;" one-hit or none-hit wonders who made great music but never played to the right crowd or fell apart due to personality clashes within the band; and wealthy individuals who lost it all due to poor money management and a lack of life skills because they never had to do anything for themselves until it was too late.

Everyone says, "well, that won't happen to *me*." It happens more often than you think, and it *can* happen to you. Regardless of which side of this equation you currently fall on, you can put your faith in this: life will get better and life will get worse. It is the nature of the waves – up one minute, down the next – but in the end, you will look back and see that those crests and troughs were never as significant as you thought in that moment. Take comfort in this. Life is good. It's worth living, regardless of your circumstances, and you only get one shot at it, so make the most of every moment and enjoy the ride!

Chapter 6

Lie #3: I should have it all figured out by now

Dear Ivan,

When I was in high school, I was confident I'd have my life's course completely mapped out by the time I reached my mid-20s. This self-imposed deadline added urgency and an underlying layer of stress to my daily existence. I felt if I didn't choose my path soon, I'd risk falling behind all my friends who already knew what they wanted to do. I didn't want to watch everyone else achieve their goals and dreams while I sat on the sidelines trying to figure out where I went wrong, or worse, realizing I never went anywhere at all.

I had a friend named Erik who thought he had it all figured out. He was going to be a doctor. He had been telling me since middle school about all the good he was going to do in the world of medicine. He had a crazy idea that he was going to develop a procedure to surgically implant gills in humans, allowing us to breathe underwater like fish, eliminating the need for SCUBA gear, and make *millions*. He was a *great* student – straight A's across the board – and a member of the honor society.

Many of the choices he made at that time reflected his desire to follow his chosen career path. He took Latin to prepare himself for the field of medicine and understand the root words of different diagnoses. He stayed in on the weekends and read medical textbooks instead of going to the movies and hanging out with me and the rest of our friends. He skipped weekend trips to the beach so he could study for the advanced-placement classes he believed he needed to get into a good college with a pre-med program. I admired *all* of this about him and wished that I was as confident in my career choice as he was. I wished that I had it all figured out too.

Do you have any friends or peers like this in your life? How does it make you feel to see someone else who is so sure of themselves and confident in the path they've chosen? Do *you* know what you want to do with the rest of your life? Are you an Erik, or are you a Tom?

I knew what I *wanted* to do. I wanted to play professional baseball and make a ton of money; marry my high school sweetheart and have kids early so I could play baseball with them before I got too old to throw a ball; buy a big house with a pool and own a boat and a small fleet of nice cars; have a couple different homes around the country so I wouldn't have to stay in one place all the time; and on and on. As much as I wanted this dream life, I had no idea how to get there or even really where to start.

I held onto this elaborate dream so I didn't have to constantly face the reality that I had no idea what else I could possibly do to be successful in life. By giving myself until my mid-20s to figure it out, I was essentially just procrastinating on taking any kind of real responsibility for my future. I was afraid of what might await me if this dream didn't come true. It was *unknown*, and that was scary.

By the time I reached my mid-20s, I realized I wasn't Major League material, and I still had no idea what kind of career I wanted to pursue. My high school sweetheart wasn't "the one," and I wound up breaking off an engagement in what turned out to be the greatest heartache of my life up to that point. I didn't have any kids and I struggled to pay my bills and still have some cash left over to have some fun on the weekends. In short, I woke up from my dream and found myself face to face with the reality I'd feared for so long: no real prospects, no direction, and no money.

On the bright side, I *did* get an awesome truck. No, not the 4x4 pickup with the oversized mud tires from my fantasy, but a used, rear-wheel drive, four-cylinder

Toyota Tacoma with hand-crank windows that I drove for the next 17 years.

One warm summer evening I found myself driving home from the beach alone. I was cruising along with the windows rolled down and the sun setting in the rear-view mirror. I was relaxed, enjoying the breeze, and contemplating life. It suddenly occurred to me that I had *nothing* figured out. Surprisingly, it wasn't scary anymore. In fact, it was *comforting* in a weird way. That was nearly 15 years ago. I'm almost 40 now and I still don't have it all figured out.

A funny thing will happen to you between where you are and where I am now. You will realize that you will probably *never* have it all figured out. Actually, I really hope we don't. I mean, what fun would it be? What adventure would be left in life if all the uncertainty was removed?

It may sound silly to you now, but you're going to realize that *not* having it all figured out is one of the best things in the world. It allows you to open doors that you would have never considered and some that you never knew existed!

Imagine standing at the entrance to a long hallway. There are hundreds of doors on either side, spanning the entire length of the hall. Each door has a sign with the name of a person, place, thing, or activity written on it. At the far end, way off in the distance, is one final door facing you with your current plan written on it. There's only one rule: once you walk past a door, you cannot return to it later.

I wouldn't be able to walk down that hallway without opening at least a few of the other doors. My curiosity and adventurous nature would get the best of me! I'll bet you feel the same way. You may open some of the doors, take a quick look around, close it and move on. You may want to spend a little time in some of the rooms. Maybe you'll open one and instead of seeing that person, place, thing, or activity, you'll see an entirely new hallway with even more doors to explore – a completely new path for your life that you'd never considered before.

Maybe you're not like me. You're more confident and self-assured in your plans. Maybe you'd charge down that hall toward your destiny without even looking at the other doors as you pass. What will you do if you get to that door with your current plan written on it only to discover that it's locked?

Not having it all figured out means that you still have hundreds of thousands of options to choose from and choices to make. Some will be easy, some will be hard, and some will *seem* easy but wind up creating the greatest challenges you'll ever face!

The thing to remember is that *not* having it all figured out means that your window of opportunity is wide open. On the other hand, having it all figured out means you have to walk a very fine line in pursuit of what you *think* you want right now. Your desires will change. Your life goals will shift in new directions and the fact that you left yourself open to these opportunities will prove itself to be an incredible blessing time after time. Go ahead and open some doors.

There's something about your teenage years – the bridge between childhood and adulthood – that challenges you. As a child, you firmly believe that your parents have it all figured out. I mean, you *have* to have it all figured out if you have kids, right? They've obviously cracked the code and discovered how to survive in the world as adults, and you believe that you will too – that once you cross a certain age threshold, a veil will be pulled back from your eyes and the keys to life will be miraculously handed to you. After all, other animals do this. Look at horses and deer for example – they can walk almost as soon as they're born! Their parents show them a thing or two, but they're essentially self-sustaining after their first year of life. They just *know* what they need to do to be successful as an adult!

Unfortunately, it's not that easy for humans. There are so many more complicating factors for us, and we develop much slower in many ways. It takes some of us more than a year to learn how to walk, for example, and even then, we're stumbling around and find ourselves on the ground more frequently than we'd like. It's actually a lot like that for much of our lives. While you may get better at walking, you're going to spend a lot of time getting knocked down by other elements of life that you hadn't expected or planned for.

As I got older, I passed the age that my mom and dad were when they got married. I was still single. I passed the age when they had *me*. I was still single. More importantly, as I crossed each of these milestones, I realized that I was not prepared – mentally, financially, or emotionally – to be married or have kids! It made me think back to that perception I had as a child – that my parents had it all figured out. The truth is they were just as clueless then as I felt now, but they made it up as they went along because that's all anyone can do! There is no pause button on life. You can't take a time out to consult the user's manual or draw up a new play.

That day I was driving in my truck I realized that there is no user's manual, and *nobody got the playbook*. It's all done on the fly because time stops for nobody. Every person you meet is going through life for the first time. Some are older than you and have more life experience as a result, but each of us is constantly learning as we go. There is no age, education, or career milestone you'll ever hit that will open a magical door to all the answers of the universe. Maybe we'll get those answers when we die, but until then, all we can do is put one foot in front of the other, take the next logical step, and see what happens.

Don't get me wrong, it's good to have clearly-defined goals and expectations for yourself, but one of the worst things you can do – especially right now – is grade your life and base your perception of success or failure on those goals and expectations. The problem you're going to run into is that you will begin to limit the choices you make in life based on the idea that, since you have it all figured out, there's no need to try anything outside that narrow path. When you limit yourself in this way, you will find yourself paralyzed when a particular door gets shut in your face.

Remember my friend, Erik? Well, here's how his story turned out: Erik did get into an Ivy League school. He started pre-med and did really well with all of the foundational classes and was on track to be an excellent surgeon. Then something terrible happened. Erik realized that he couldn't stand the sight of blood. It made him sick to his stomach and feel like he was going to pass out. He tried to overcome this issue but, unfortunately, he just couldn't do it. He had to drop out of the medical program and his dreams of being a world-class surgeon were over.

All of that effort, planning, studying, and working his butt off in pursuit of this goal led to a dead end. Erik had charged down that long hallway and the door at the end was locked. He'd sacrificed time with his friends and family – *opportunities and time he'll never get back*. He pursued medicine to the exclusion of nearly all other interests and wound up with nothing to show for it. In the end, it turned out that Erik *didn't* have it all figured out, even though it seemed like he did. This story is just one of millions like it. Life is funny like that. There's a saying that goes, "If you want to make God laugh, tell him your plans."

Now, it's not all bad news. Erik turned out just fine. After a couple years of searching, he decided to use the time he spent studying and getting impeccable grades to apply for a study-abroad program. He wound up at St. Andrews, in Scotland, and later attended Kings College, in London, where he used his knowledge of Latin to dive deep into the study of philosophy and religion. Today he *is* a doctor, but not in a medical sense. He earned his PhD in Comparative Religion and is now a professor at a university back in the United States. He loves his life, and I don't think he'd change a thing. Well, maybe he'd have spent a few more weekends with me at the beach in high school, but overall, his choices have led him down a path to success and joy in his life and his work, even though it looks a lot different than how he'd drawn it up.

The point of the story is this: whatever you think you want to do with your life right now, it will change. Some of it will change by choice and some of the changes will be forced upon you. This is true for every aspect of life, including romantic relationships, career goals, and family dynamics.

It's OK to change your mind about a girl you're dating, or even one you're engaged to. You'll probably experience what it feels like to be on the other side of that too, when some girl breaks your heart. It's OK to realize that your initial thoughts about your career field no longer interest you. You're probably going to change jobs and careers several times in your life. In some cases, you're going to be told that you're not good enough to make the cut, at which point you will have to decide if it's something you're willing to work harder for and improve your skills and abilities to meet the demands of the career you're interested in, or if you would rather pivot and take a new path. It's OK if you don't get along with your parents right now. These transitional years of your life are hard on everyone involved, but it doesn't mean that your relationship will remain cold, confrontational, and strained for the rest of your life.

With this knowledge, please take some time to relax, breathe, and enjoy what life is giving you *today*. Go fishing. Learn a new song on the guitar. Try a new hobby or sport that is interesting to you – even if it doesn't fit into your present idea of what your life will be. You never know when you'll get an opportunity to do these things again or how the experiences may affect your life down the road.

Stop worrying about getting it all figured out and, above all else, ***don't be afraid to fail***. I really wish I'd tried more things when I was your age, taken more risks, and failed more often. You will learn far more from the failures in your life than the successes.

For most of us, the root of our desire to have it all figured out is to *avoid* failure. I used to pass on opportunities to try new things solely based on the fear that I wouldn't be good at it and would look like a fool while trying. I wasted a lot of time being afraid.

For example, I didn't try snowboarding until after college, when I went with a group of friends to a small mountain in Pennsylvania, a couple hours from Washington, DC, where I was living. I only agreed to go because my buddy Sean had never been either, so we could look like fools together.

If you've never been skiing or snowboarding, there are different runs on the mountain that are color-coded based on their difficulty. The easiest slopes are called bunny slopes, where beginners are supposed to go to learn the basics. Green slopes are considered the easiest of the main runs, followed by blues, then blacks, and ultimately double black.

Sean and I had too much pride to bother with the bunny slope, so we jumped into line to take the chair to the top of the green hill. When you get to the top, the chair doesn't stop. You're supposed to push off and use the momentum of the chair to glide away from the lift. Having never done this before, we were ill prepared for the dismount. One of our more experienced friends had the foresight to get on the lift a couple chairs ahead of us and snap a picture of us getting off the lift for the first time. It's a great picture – Sean and I are splayed out in the snow like bowling pins that have just been knocked over, and there's a little girl who was on the chair in front of us looking back over her shoulder with disdain. It was perfect foreshadowing of what was to come.

Sean and I spent half the day on our hands and knees. The other half of the day, we were on our butts. Everything hurt. We had chosen to try snowboarding over skiing because we heard that it was harder to learn, but easier to get good at once you figured it out. Skiing, on the other hand, was said to be easy to learn, but really hard to master.

Just before the sun began to set, I managed to figure out some of the basics. I did a couple full runs of the green slope without falling and felt pretty good about myself. I thought I'd figured it out!

Not long after that, I moved to Colorado. I agreed to go snowboarding with some new friends I'd made and borrowed an old board from another friend. Having a few successful runs on the green slope back in Pennsylvania under my belt, and wanting to impress my new friends, I exaggerated my ability and experience a little bit. As a result, they suggested we ride one of the blue slopes to warm up and get our legs under us before really getting into the big stuff. I figured I was ready for it, so we hopped on the lift.

The ride up on the chair seemed like an eternity – I didn't remember it taking so long to get to the top before. When we finally got there, I got off the lift with little effort. Clearly, I had kept my skills. I made my way over to where my friends were strapping into their boards and peered over the lip of the hill. The ground dropped away at a steep grade, and I felt like I was standing on the edge of a 10-foot cliff! The mountains in Colorado made their East Coast relatives seem like ant hills! I suddenly felt nauseous and realized I'd made a big mistake.

I had no choice but to go. It's the only way down from the top of the mountain. I didn't so much ride down the slope as I rolled down. At every subsequent drop-off along the route, I fell over the edge like a man in a barrel going over a waterfall. When I finally came to a stop, I'd sit there for a while, terrified, catching my breath. My friends were ahead of me, and each time I fell they'd slow down and yell at me to get out of the way because nobody could see me from the top of the drop. Skiers and snowboarders were flying by, dangerously close to my head. Part of me wished one of them would hit me so I could get lifted off the mountain by the ski patrol and my nightmare would end.

Eventually, I made it to the bottom. I spent the rest of the day by myself on the green slopes, which were still much bigger and steeper than what I'd done previously. I almost gave up, but you can't move to Colorado and *not* ski or snowboard, can you?

I wound up going once more with a different friend – the one who let me borrow her old board the first time. She was patient and taught me a few new skills. It helped a lot that the day we went was right after it snowed and there were eight inches of fresh powder, which felt like gliding over a cloud and flopping onto a plush mattress when I fell. By the end of that day, I had truly figured out the basics and felt more confident. It only got better after that. I'm glad I didn't give up, because snowboarding is a lot of fun once you figure it out!

That experience taught me a lot about myself. Despite the bruises and embarrassment, I was persistent and committed to learning a new skill. I learned that I could do and achieve things by facing my fear, putting in the hard work, and overcoming failure. I have leaned on this experience many times since then to boost my self-confidence and steel myself to take on new challenges in all areas of my life.

Learning something new often means that you won't be good at it at first. Sometimes you just have to say, "fuck it," and go for it! Think back to the original example of walking. If you remained afraid of falling – constant and painful failure for months on end – you'd still be crawling around on all fours. Just like walking, you will go through a string of painful and challenging failures before you become successful at anything.

Think about a little kid swinging a baseball bat for the first time. They look like a drunk person stumbling around an open field trying to catch butterflies in a net! Swinging an external object creates forces on the body that can be difficult to control if you're not used to it. It takes time to acquire the balance and coordination to swing a bat correctly. It takes even longer to learn how to swing it effectively and make contact with another moving object! If you really want a good laugh, go watch a low-level adult softball league game. It's immediately apparent which of the players have played before and which ones have never swung a bat but have been pressured into playing for the office team anyway.

Of course, as a small child, your self-consciousness about such things is minimal, which allows you to try things like walking and swinging a bat without concern about the adults around you laughing at the spectacle.

Speaking of which, I have video of you when you were two-years old, dancing at my wedding! You wandered out into the middle of the dance floor and started bouncing around to the music. It was hilarious, and everyone formed a circle around you to watch. You loved the attention, and your excitement was contagious. You took that wedding reception to the next level and you didn't feel self-conscious about it at all! Do you think you'd bust a move like that in front of a group of strangers today?

Balancing the risk/reward of trying new things allows you to accept numerous failures in pursuit of ultimately learning a new skill. Remember learning to ride a bike? Maybe you were lucky and only scraped your knee. I fell off face first, smashed my front teeth in, and shaved the skin off my face from my cheek bone to my chin. My brother, Andy, ran into our neighbor's parked car and put a huge dent in the door. The neighbor called the police! In time, we overcame those challenges. In a few short years, we were riding at full speed and launching ourselves off of dirt ramps we built in the woods near our house. How simple does riding a bike seem now? Wasn't it worth those initial failures to achieve a skill you can enjoy for the rest of your life?

Many of the challenges you will face in life require that same mental approach, even though the skill may be completely unrelated. First time playing volleyball?

You may take a spike to the face. First time kissing a girl? Your lips will be so tight you'll look like a baby refusing a spoonful of mashed peas. First time taking a foreign language? You'll feel like your mind is going to explode and the only words you'll ever be able to understand are hello and goodbye.

BUT, if you never take those chances, never risk looking silly or feeling inadequate, you will never learn from those initial failures, which will make you exponentially better each time you get up and try again. If you never take those chances, you will miss out on weekends in the park playing pick-up volleyball with your friends. You'll miss out on the heart-pounding moments of that first kiss with all your future girlfriends. You'll miss out on the opportunity to travel abroad and experience the local culture on a deeper level than most tourists.

Go for it. Be bold and don't be afraid to fail. If you're worried about people laughing at you, remember that they're probably just as scared as you and are secretly wishing they had the guts to give it a shot. Remember the story I told you about my high school teammate, Jordan, the first time he tried tobacco? Sure, we all laughed at him, but a lot of that laughter was masking our own insecurities about whether or not we'd have been brave enough to do it, stupid as it was. I know that's how I felt.

Often you'll find that the people who have done something before and are better than you won't be the ones laughing. They know the courage it takes to try because they've been there and they've been the ones getting laughed at. They are far more likely to be sympathetic to your failure and offer you advice and guidance for the next attempt.

I experienced this time and again as a weightlifting coach. While they may look simple – especially when done correctly – the Olympic lifts of snatch and clean and jerk are extremely technical lifts that require lots of practice and repetition before you can lift any significant amount of weight. For the most part, I was self-taught. I watched a lot of YouTube videos and spent hours in the gym trying to mimic what I saw in those tutorials. One of the hardest parts for many people to learn is how to make bar/body contact to catapult the weight up above your head.

I was particularly interested in perfecting my snatch technique and I worked on it relentlessly. To perform the lift successfully, you pull the bar off the ground keeping it as close to your body as possible. After the bar passes your knees, you start to bring your torso into a vertical position by hinging at the hip and pulling the bar into your hips while simultaneously driving your hips under the bar and making contact with a jumping motion. When your hips make contact with the bar, the transfer of power puts upward momentum on the bar, causing it to rise slightly and float for just a moment, giving you time to pull yourself underneath it and catch it over your head – all in one movement.

One afternoon, very early on in my weightlifting career, I was working on this technique by myself in the back corner of the gym while a group class was getting ready to start a different workout about 20 feet away. I had about 135 pounds on the bar, and as I pulled it toward me, I thrust my hips forward with as much force as I could generate, just as I'd seen in the video tutorials. I was trying to hip-check that bar straight through the roof! The thing nobody had told me – and I had failed to consider – is that if your penis isn't tucked *down*, it's right in the contact zone of the bar.

That bar smashed into my dick like a hammer driving home a nail. I yelled in pain and dropped the weight, which crashed to the floor and caught the attention of the class. I was rolling around on the floor, seeing stars and clutching my crotch, certain that I'd just cut off my own penis. A few people came over to see if I was alright and I had to tell them what had happened. It was embarrassing, but at that moment, I thought I had bigger problems. After they were convinced that I wasn't going to die and returned to their class, I gingerly reached into my shorts, preparing for the worst. I was relieved to discover that everything was still attached. I pulled my hand back out, checking for blood, but found none. I made my way to the bathroom to visually assess the situation.

You know how it usually takes a day or two before a bruise shows up after you bump your knee or something? Well, mere minutes after the train wreck, I already had a dark purple stripe right across the head of my penis. I counted myself lucky to be in one piece, called it a day and went home.

I have since become quite proficient at the Olympic lifts, winning two state championships, and placing third at the Masters' National Championships. I have coached numerous athletes and taught them how to be successful lifters. I can look back on my early technique and the mistakes I made and laugh. As awkward and foolish as people feel when trying these lifts for the first time, I never make fun of them and always offer positive encouragement on the things they're doing right. I know how hard this sport is to learn, much less be successful at, and I admire the courage of anyone who is willing to try. I also tell every male I work with to make sure to tuck themselves away before attacking the bar!

Failures offer a great opportunity to learn to *laugh at yourself* – after the pain subsides, of course. This accomplishes two things. By laughing at yourself, you take the power away from others who may laugh at you. What they usually find funny is the look of frustration and embarrassment on your face when you fail. By laughing, you neutralize this ammunition. The other thing is that you will begin to learn not to take yourself too seriously. Let's face it, taking a volleyball to the face or a barbell to the dick is slapstick comedy at its finest! If you can appreciate that this learning experience may be funny to people watching, you can begin to find the humor in it as well.

Laughing at yourself also helps relieve the pressure you feel to immediately be good at whatever you're trying. As you laugh and smile, the muscles in your face tighten in a way that releases dopamine in your brain. Dopamine is the "feel good" hormone that you experience when you're happy, and it helps you relax. Try it right now. Go ahead, look up from this page and smile. You'll start to feel more relaxed and your mood will improve! By remembering this trick, when you get up off the ground laughing, you'll think to yourself, "that wasn't so bad, let's try it again," rather than "OMG, I can't believe I screwed that up!" The latter will have you tensing up and becoming even less prepared to take another shot at it.

Of course, taking a volleyball to the face is a little different than bombing on a first date or failing at starting a business, but the rules still apply. You may not be able to smile in the moment, and that's OK, but when you're alone later, try to find something humorous in the experience – something you can smile or laugh about to yourself – something *good* you can take from the experience and use to improve upon it the next time. It will go a long way in helping you overcome that fear of failure and humiliation and give you the guts to dust yourself off and try again if you believe it's something that is truly worth pursuing. Even if whatever you're trying winds up being a one-and-done experience for you, you can move forward in life with that memory and a funny story that came out of it. In some cases, your embarrassing moment may actually turn out to be an endearing moment to someone else.

Here's something about me that you may not know – I've always been very shy about talking to girls. I was afraid of being rejected and the embarrassment and self-loathing that comes with it. Back in my mid-20s, I went to Las Vegas for a work conference – my first time visiting the city. Since it was Las Vegas, and the city's slogan is "What happens in Vegas stays in Vegas," I decided to throw caution to the wind and actually try talking to some random girls over the course of the weekend. After all, if they rejected me, I'd probably never see them again.

It just so happened that on the night before the conference officially started, I saw the most beautiful woman I've ever seen in my life – ever. I remember walking down a hallway in Caesar's Palace with some co-workers. I saw this girl walking the other direction and I literally stopped in my tracks. I swear it was like I was in a movie. The world started moving in slow motion and I stared at her with my mouth agape. In that moment, it was like nothing else existed but me and her. I'm not exaggerating. That's exactly how it felt. I stopped walking and just stared. I was still too paralyzed by fear to make a move.

The next evening at the opening-night party, I saw her sitting at a table near the dance floor. After some encouragement from my co-workers, I did what I never thought I could do – and would never have done if I'd been back at home – I walked over and asked her to dance. I am not a good dancer, but I was throwing caution to the wind. We danced for a few songs and then went to sit back down at her table. After some small talk, she agreed to join me for a bite to eat the next night. I couldn't believe my luck! I had to play this just right – the hard part was done!

The next evening, we were walking out of one of the casinos and I had a full drink in my hand. Things were going great, and I was feeling confident. We walked through one of those automatic revolving doors, where you just keep walking and it rotates like a carousel. Well, it was a really big door, and with the way it was designed, it looked to me like there was a glass panel in the center of the carousel, so I put my arm out to lean against it – you know, to look cool and casual like James Bond as we were passing through. There was no glass panel. I don't know what I thought I saw, but I wasn't paying close enough attention. It probably had something to do with the fact that I couldn't take my eyes off this beautiful girl who was actually talking to me! I put my full weight into leaning on that phantom plate of glass and just fell over, spilling the drink all over myself. To the casual observer – and to this girl – it looked like I was walking along just fine and then tripped over nothing. Only it didn't even look like I tripped. At least that would be a valid excuse! No, I was walking along and just fell over like a tree going down in the forest – slowly at first, then gaining momentum until I face-planted into the side of this revolving door and slid to the ground.

I felt like a complete idiot – the exact opposite of James Bond – and she laughed at me like it was the funniest thing she'd ever seen! Back home, I probably would have thought the night was over and I'd never see her again. I'd have made some excuse – oh, I don't know, maybe *my clothes are all wet* – and high-tailed it out of there before she could make her own excuse to leave. After all, when the most beautiful woman you've ever seen in your life sees something so clumsy, how could she not turn and run? She could obviously do better than this soaking wet idiot who can't even walk through a door. Because I was in Vegas, however, and I had talked myself into being a little braver than usual, I got up and laughed about it with her.

We went on to have an amazing evening, walking, talking, dancing, and laughing until dawn. Miraculously, she found this unfortunate misstep to be incredibly *endearing* – particularly since I was able to laugh at myself and tolerate her poking fun at me for the rest of the night about it. This humiliating event turned into a highlight in one of the best nights of my life.

How does the story end? Well, we got married a year later. She is absolutely my best friend in the world, and we still laugh about that incident to this day!

Ironically – and I'll probably hit on this in another letter somewhere because it's *that* important – when you look back on some of the greatest failures in your life, you won't remember the bad parts as clearly as the good if you can take a bit of humor out of them.

I know you probably feel pressure to have it all figured out in one way or another. Maybe you feel pressure from your parents to act a certain way, get certain grades, and be successful in everything that you try. Maybe it's pressure from friends to like certain music, enjoy certain activities, and be obsessed with a particular sport. Perhaps you find yourself in a situation where you feel the need to lead your family, take care of your parents, and set an example for your cousins. Whatever the case may be, you are not ready to have it all figured out – and nobody expects you to. This pressure is one that you put on yourself.

Believe me when I tell you that there is a lot more going on in the world than you can even imagine right now. Once you really start looking, you will discover that the opportunities are almost endless.

One of the main things that I recall feeling pressure to figure out was a career path. All throughout middle and high school, people were constantly talking about what they were planning to do with their lives. This is taught to us at an early age. Think about it, when was the first time someone asked you, "What do you want to be when you grow up?" Kindergarten maybe? Back then the options seemed pretty simple: policeman, fireman, construction worker, farmer, soldier and maybe doctor. Your choices were limited to the known world around you, which was very small. What has changed?

Over time, your knowledge of the world expands, and new professions become possibilities: lawyer, teacher, banker, athlete, and movie star work their way into the mix. As you continue to learn and experience new things, your understanding of the world and its list of possibilities continues to grow. If you understand this concept and do some quick calculations about how much more you'll know and learn in the next few years, you'll realize how silly it seems to try and choose your ultimate life path when you've barely even begun to live!

Think about all the career choices you have in front of you now. How many of them were you aware of when you were in kindergarten? How many more do you imagine will become known to you over the next few years of your life? I guarantee there are *thousands* of jobs that you've never thought of that may pique your interest. Professional sleeper? Water slide tester? How about research scientist monitoring the protein changes in human blood to predict your risk of disease, and which medicines will work best to treat it based on your genetics?

These are all real jobs. If you doubt it, look it up! Try doing an internet search for "coolest jobs in the world" and see what crazy options you can find. The point is that you may think you know what you want to do when you grow up, but that idea is still based on your very limited knowledge of the vast array of options available to you. You don't have to have it all figured out now.

Here's an interesting statistic for you: studies show that about 80 percent of college graduates change their major at least once during their college career. After graduation, more than 50 percent will ultimately find a job in a field outside of their major. That's right! Most people who attend college pay a ton of money to go to school only to discover what they *thought* they wanted to do was actually wrong. Then they graduate and try to find a job only to discover that the only job they can get isn't even related to what they went to school for! What do you think that does to a person who thinks they have it all figured out?

Try as many things as you can and find the ones you really enjoy; then consider all the different ways you can break into that industry in a way that suits you. Let me give you three examples of friends of mine who have made their way into very interesting jobs that aren't often listed among career choices in the guidance counselor's office. These people didn't go to school with the goal of doing what they're doing now, but they created their opportunities by being open to taking chances and trying new things.

I have a friend named Paul, who grew up in a rural mountain town in Colorado. Throughout his childhood, his favorite thing to do was snowboarding. He spent as much time as possible on the mountain every winter with the goal of becoming a professional snowboarder. Over time he realized that there were a lot of people who were better than him – hitting bigger tricks, getting bigger air, and attracting far more sponsors. Rather than change his career path completely, he decided to see what else was available within the industry. He started working at a local snowboard shop, where he could share his passion and knowledge of the sport with tourists and others who were just starting out. As his knowledge of the different elements of the sport grew, he leveraged his outgoing personality to join a team that managed the brands for several snowboard companies. He travels the country, going to different conferences and expos, showcasing the biggest brands in the sport he loves. He also leads private trips for wealthy clients who pay him to take them to some of the best skiing and snowboarding sites in Colorado. He lives with them for the week and spends his days on the mountain, getting paid to do what he loves most: ride fresh powder.

Another friend of mine, Jermaine, went to college with no idea what he wanted to do when he graduated. His father had been a bodybuilder, so he had grown up around the gym and understood some of the basics of fitness and training. He decided to get his degree in Nutrition and Food Science so he could be a personal trainer. The core classes for his degree taught him about the anatomy and physiology of the human body. After he graduated, he used this knowledge to land a job as a tissue processor at one of the country's biggest suppliers of allograft tissue. What does that mean, you ask? Well, when you check the option on your driver's license to become an organ donor, you are essentially granting permission for your body to be shipped to this facility when you die. Jermaine's job is to harvest the organs, tendons and bones from the donated bodies and cut, shape, and sterilize them in preparation to be used in other living people. For example, when I tore the MCL in my elbow playing baseball and had Tommy John surgery, the doctor used a tendon from a place like this to tie my bones back together. Jermaine goes to work every day with a responsibility to respect the gifts that have been donated into his care. He gets calls from doctors all over the country requesting pieces of bone or tendon that have to be cut and shaped to the exact dimensions needed to fit their patients. His work changes lives every day, but that's not what he was thinking about when he chose his major.

Finally, my friend Justin is a nerd, a very quiet nerd. He has always been interested in electronics and discovering how things work. He went to school to become an electrical engineer with the goal of becoming a college professor. When he graduated, he started teaching electrical engineering at a local high school. Before long, however, budget cuts required the school to eliminate some of the extra classes it offered, including his. With a family to support and limited options available to him, Justin began working on a project that he'd been thinking about for a long time. He used his electrical engineering skills to create a device in his basement that dramatically changed the way scientists could use sensors to monitor temperature changes. I'm not going to try and explain it to you because I don't really understand how it works even though it's been explained to me several times! Justin began selling his new device to small, local companies at first, but once the word got out about his product, he began receiving requests from companies all over the world. Today, Justin is running a multi-million dollar business that he started out of necessity in his basement. He followed his interests without being sure where they would lead, and he ultimately wound up being more successful than he ever imagined. To this day, Justin will tell you that he *still* doesn't have it all figured out.

The point is this: regardless of what your interests are, there is a place for you in the world. You don't have to know *exactly* what you're going to do or how you're going to do it. All you have to do is take the next step in that general direction. Set clear, concise goals for yourself and make sure that you're actively moving toward achieving them.

Take some detours along the way, because you never know what is hiding behind that unopened door. It could very well be a path that you weren't previously aware of but find very compelling! It's OK to tell people that you don't know what you want to be when you grow up or what you're planning on doing after high school or college. If you ask any adult in your life, most will probably tell you that they wound up doing what they're doing through an unconventional path. Many, if they're honest, will tell you that they *still* don't know what they want to do with their life, but they're doing what they're doing now because it pays the bills. By beginning to explore a variety of options now, before you have bills to pay, you can begin to figure out what you *want* to do and set goals that help you take the next step in that direction.

What if you have *no idea* what you want to do or even where to start? I recommend starting with this question: What would you do with your life if you knew you were guaranteed to be successful? Do *that* ... and be prepared to fail. You can't let yourself down if you are aware that failure is a possibility from the start. Don't be afraid of it! Don't be afraid to try new things. There is so much in this world to discover, so please don't feel like you should have it all figured out right now!

    Love,
    Tom

Chapter 7

Lie #4: Failure is final

Dear Ivan,

    I've failed a lot in my life. Some were small, insignificant failures, like bombing a math test or letting someone down by not following through on a promise. Others were much bigger, like blowing my entire life's savings on an idea that crashed and burned, leaving me broke and jobless. The trajectory of my life looks kind of like a long-term projection of the stock market: lots of small ups and downs, a big spike here, a huge crater there, but trending slowly upward over the long run. This will likely be true for you as well.

    How does it make you feel to *know* that you're going to be a failure? Here you are, thinking about what you're going to do and be, how you're going to impact the world, and how successful you're going to become and I'm telling you that, at some point, you're going to be a major failure. If you focused on that single point, it would almost be enough to make you want to quit, right? I mean, if you're going to be a failure, why not just give up now? What if your personal stock market crashes and never recovers?

I guess it depends on the day you're reading this. Some days you *do* think you're destined to be a failure. Nothing is going right, you have no idea what you want to do with your life and the only thing you can think to do is lay on your bed and stare at the ceiling, hoping that you'll find the answers there, or at least that the voices in your head will shut up and let you just disappear into the nothingness for a while.

I still have those days. It's a struggle just to get out of bed. The reality that I have to face the world – face my fears and failures – is so daunting that I just want to throw my phone against the wall and lay there feeling sorry for myself. The only response is to get up and get after it. The world doesn't care about my feelings. It doesn't care about yours. The only way you will ever overcome these days is to sling your feet over the side of your bed and get to work. Get to work studying. Get to work practicing. Get to work … working. Whatever the case may be for you today, it's the only way you can take that next step.

Pro tip: don't give up. You're going to fail. Everyone fails. Everyone fails a lot, actually. You will fail so many times in your life it's sickening. Think about all the failures you've already experienced in your life: failing to get a hit in a clutch situation, failing a test, failing to do your chores, failing to follow a good piece advice you got, failing to ask out the girl you were interested in and watching her get scooped up by some jerk that's half as good as you are ... you've failed a lot. Whatever you do, don't give up, because giving up would be the ultimate failure. It's why I'm writing this letter to you – to caution you against being discouraged by your failures. Instead, use them as motivation and, in some cases, lessons to be carried forward.

These failures may feel monumental in the moment, but they are nothing compared to some of the failures you will experience later on down the line.

Let me share one of my biggest failures.

First, a little back story: When I was your age, I had an iron allergy. I was "allergic" to the weight room. I believed that if I lifted and trained with big weights I would get too bulky to move athletically and ultimately decrease my ability to perform on a baseball field. Talk about a huge lie that I believed! When I was in my mid-20's, I got into CrossFit and it changed my life. I did a complete 180 on the subject and began working out and training like it was my job. I found so much joy in my personal transformation, and the ability to help others achieve this transformation for themselves through coaching, that I came up with a great idea for a business.

The idea was simple: the majority of office workers in America are not in great shape. It happens to most people because they get so beat down at work and bogged down in after-work and general life obligations that the gym becomes a distant afterthought. Besides that, most people have no idea what to do at the gym once they get there. My goal was to eliminate those obstacles by bringing the gym into the workplace.

I quit my job and started a business to pursue this goal. I spent the next three years building a great website with the capability to track progress for each individual user using a variety of metrics. I wrote three years' worth of training programs and loaded them into the site. I wrote an entire email series – one for each week of the year – to address something in the field of fitness, nutrition, stress management, and happiness. I created what I thought was a foolproof method for inspiring people to be more active and think about their overall wellbeing while at work. I was going to be successful. I was going to help people and it was going to make me rich!

Ultimately, after three years, I was barely making any money – about half what I had been making at my old job, which also didn't pay well. I had also exhausted my savings by pouring money into the business to get it up and running. I had a handful of personal training clients, but my main objective of working with businesses had yielded very little interest. After a long heart-to-heart with some close friends and my *best* friend – my wife –

I decided that I needed to close down the business and go back to working a "real" job.

I fought it for a long time. Even though I could see the writing on the wall, I fought tooth and nail to keep doing what I was doing because I didn't want to be seen as a failure. I couldn't admit to myself that I'd failed. My pride and self-assuredness had kept me from seeing some very obvious problems with my business model and it wound up costing me my dream. It was a series of small failures that I hadn't recognized that ultimately led to the complete failure of the venture. I had no business experience, so I didn't understand the relationship between marketing and sales. I also didn't understand how the money worked. Most companies don't have cash lying around to spend on a program like mine, and I didn't think about partnering with insurance companies to help cover the cost until it was too late in the game. I didn't think about scalability, so the time I had to spend with each personal training client cut into the time I could spend doing the myriad other tasks associated with starting the business. Finally, I quit my job too soon. If I had stayed working at my old job until the business forced me to step away and take it over as a full-time responsibility, things may have gone more smoothly. In short, it was an *epic* failure.

Thankfully, I had a safety net. My wife never stopped working, so we were able to scrape by on her income while I flushed mine down the toilet. If it hadn't been for her, I'd have been homeless – couch surfing with friends until I could get back on my feet. In some ways, that would have been easier. My failure would have affected me alone, but instead, I carried the shame of letting her down and erasing *our* savings. My failure had a negative impact on her life too.

You will probably experience an epic failure of your own at some point. It will have you standing in front of the mirror for much longer than necessary, trying to convince yourself that you are not a complete loser while at the same time questioning your very existence. You will feel like you failed yourself, the people you were trying to help, and even the people you love. In my case, I didn't just fail once. I failed several times along the way! It's easy to see these failures in hindsight, but it is often very hard to see them in the moment. This is true of most failures. On the flip side, of course, if you're only looking for the ways you could fail, you'll never have the courage to take the next step. It's a very fine line that you need to walk in all evaluations of risk vs. reward.

Think about it from a baseball perspective: as a hitter, you run the risk of hitting the ball right at any of the nine defensive players on the field. You could also swing and miss, which could make you look silly. If you don't swing, you could get called out on strikes without ever really competing. Finally, you could foul a ball off your foot or get hit by the pitch, the second of which gets you to first base, but can hurt pretty bad depending on where you get hit.

If you only consider the potential for pain and failure, you'd never get in the box! So, what's the answer? Step in and give it your best. You may strike out or roll a weak grounder toward second base the first time around, but you'll have seen what the pitcher has in his arsenal. The next time up, armed with this experience and information, you may loop a fly ball out to the left fielder, gathering more information about how the pitcher has chosen to attack you. The third time up, you'll sit on that weak curve ball and hit it into the seats for a home run. That's how the game works.

The very *best* major league hitters have a career batting average of around .300, which means they get three hits for every 10 at-bats. That means they fail 70% of the time and are still considered *very successful*! Sometimes the hits come in bunches and sometimes there are long stretches where there are no hits at all. It all comes down to making the necessary adjustments, getting back in the box, and taking another crack at it.

Life is a lot like that. It is a series of constant trial and error. Each at-bat gives you more information that you can use to evaluate your strengths and weaknesses and make better decisions about how to approach your next attempt. You can choose to never risk failure and never climb into the batter's box, or you can accept that failure is a part of the game, you will fail more often than not, but eventually the hits will come.

Think about some of the greatest names in American pop culture – names like Walt Disney, Stephen Spielberg, and Jay-Z – some of the most successful and influential people in history. Did you know that Walt Disney got fired from his job at a newspaper because his boss thought he "lacked imagination and had no good ideas?" Stephen Spielberg was rejected from film school multiple times. If he'd given up, we wouldn't have *Indiana Jones*, *Jurassic Park*, or *Saving Private Ryan*. Then there's Jay-Z. As a poor kid growing up in New York, he couldn't get anyone to listen to his first album, let alone give him a record deal. He didn't let that failure hold him back. He sold his first record out of the back of his car and went on to become arguably the greatest rapper of all time.

Each of these men faced tremendous adversity and repetitive failure. If they had listened to their critics or ceased to believe in themselves, we wouldn't know their names today. Think about it – how much different would your life be if you never went to Disney World, saw the *Jurassic Park* movies, or listened to *The Black Album*? Even if you have never done any of those things directly, the ideas and innovations they sparked in other people's minds have created a spiderweb of theme parks, movies, and music that you *have* experienced.

Thinking about it another way, what might you have to offer the world that it will never get to experience if you give up before you can make it a reality?

What I've learned through these experiences is that failure isn't the end of the line. In some ways it's just the beginning. A quote from the movie *Rocky* comes to mind here. It's been shared far and wide in an incredible variety of contexts, but for good reason – it's exactly the message that resonates with anyone who's ever failed or felt overwhelmed by life, and it is timeless:

> Let me tell you something you already know. The world ain't all sunshine and rainbows. It's a very mean and nasty place and I don't care how tough you are, it will beat you to your knees and keep you there permanently if you let it. You, me, or nobody is gonna hit as hard as life. But it ain't how hard you hit. It's about how hard you can *get* hit and keep moving forward. How much you can take and keep moving forward. That's how winning is done.

Yes, it's just a line from a movie and life isn't a movie, but it is a philosophy that has proved itself true time and again. Right now, for example, I'm working out the details for my next business venture. I've gotten a taste of what it feels like to work for myself rather than for someone else and I loved it, despite the fact that it ultimately failed. My next venture may not be successful either, but it will have a much better chance of success thanks to the lessons I learned and the bruising of my ego from the previous failure. I know the home run is out there, so I'll just keep taking my at-bats as they come until I run into that hanging curve.

Keep your head up. Don't be afraid to fail. Recognize failure for what it is – a learning opportunity that has now equipped you with the tools to make your next attempt a more successful one. It doesn't matter whether you fail in sports, school, business, love, or finance. There is always an opportunity to learn from your mistakes and carry those lessons forward.

Everyone views failure differently. Even a shared experience can be viewed through different lenses. For example, a perfectionist can get a B+ on a math test and be absolutely distraught that he failed to get an A. However, someone like me, who is not the greatest mathematician in the world, can get that same grade on that same test and celebrate like I just won the lottery because my expectations were much lower.

Failure, to some extent, is relative. I'm not suggesting that you lower your expectations to the point that your failures all look like successes, but I am encouraging you to examine what success means to you and begin to comb through the wreckage of your failures more carefully and see what you can salvage from the experience.

It's also important to recognize the different causes of your failures. Sometimes you fail because you weren't good enough in that moment: you didn't make the varsity team, or you didn't get a lead role in the school musical because you weren't as talented as someone else.

Sometimes you fail because your success depends on someone else who has more power in that situation: you got rejected when you asked Susie to the dance because she had someone else she wanted to go with. Finally – and this is a really important distinction – *sometimes you fail because in the end, you just didn't care enough.*

Now, initially, that may sound harsh or like I'm suggesting that you're lazy, but it's not always a bad thing. You may think you know what you care about, but sometimes when the chips are down, you ultimately realize that the thing you *thought* you really cared about was actually just a peripheral interest you discovered you can ultimately do without because there are other things that you care about *more*.

When I was in elementary school, my family lived in southern Arizona for three years. During the summer, the daytime temperature was regularly over 100 degrees, but the nights were pretty comfortable. My brothers and I would pitch tents in the back yard and camp out. Even though it was just ten feet from the house, the experience was exciting, and we looked forward to it every year. When we moved to Virginia, camping in the back yard lost its appeal. I was in middle school by then, and it just didn't seem like a *cool* thing to do.

I joined the Boy Scouts when I was in 7th grade, hoping to rekindle some of that childhood magic. My younger brother, Mike, had recently graduated from Cub Scouts to Boy Scouts, and when I learned that he would get to go on real camping trips away from home without our parents, I decided I wanted a piece of that action! I had grand visions of hiking out into the wilderness, catching fish for dinner, and sleeping under the stars. I signed up and joined the same troop as my brother. I was excited to spend time with him and re-live those backyard adventures on a much larger scale.

I quickly learned that the Boy Scouts had a lot of meetings, and I *hated* the meetings. I saw them as a means to an end – a necessary evil that would allow me to experience the great outdoors. At meeting after meeting, week after painful week, the plan for my first trip unfolded. I learned that we would be packing hot dogs for dinner – so much for catching fish to eat – but that we would be roasting them over a huge bonfire, which I considered an acceptable compromise. In addition, Mike and I packed beef jerky and a pack of full-sized candy bars for snacks.

We shuttled out to the drop point in a big van and walked out to a small island that was connected to the mainland by a bridge, arms full of tents, pillows, food, and everything else we'd need. When we arrived, I realized that our troop was joining several other troops in the same area – so much for seclusion. Mike and I set up our tent with a third member of the troop, who was going to be spending the night with us.

We spent the afternoon learning how to make fires, which I really liked. The rest of the day was split between gathering kindling and firewood, lighting a fire, and then letting it burn all the way out so we could do it again. That afternoon, sitting next to one of the fires we'd built, Mike and I offered a candy bar to the other kid in our tent. Things were going well, and we were all in a good mood.

By the time dinner rolled around, everyone on the island reeked of smoke, and we were hungry. We collectively built a bonfire and sharpened sticks for the hot dog roast. Unfortunately, someone forgot to take the hot dogs out of the cooler to thaw, so we struggled to get the half-frozen wieners onto our sticks. Cooking a frozen hot dog over an open fire posed additional challenges. The outsides cooked quickly, but the insides remained cold. Mike and I were so hungry by then that we choked down the worst hot dogs we'd ever had in our lives: charcoal-black exteriors with a cool, firm middle. The night would go downhill from there.

After dinner, we all headed back to our tents to make one more small fire before bed. Mike and I had saved ourselves a candy bar for dessert. When we looked in our bag, however, we realized that our tentmate had already eaten them! He offered a half-assed apology and explained that he thought we had brought them to *share*. I didn't really know this kid, so I didn't want to fly off the handle and completely lose my cool. In a very passive-aggressive tone, I pointed out that we had already shared one with him earlier in the day. I tried to hide my rage, but I was still burning hotter than the embers in our fire when we extinguished it in a cloud of smoke and turned in for the night.

I was ready to go to sleep and hopefully wake up in a better mood, but this kid would *not* shut up about how many merit badges he had and his goal of becoming an Eagle Scout. I was contemplating how easy it would be to suffocate him with my pillow – and wondering if they had a merit badge for that – when he finally fell asleep. Relieved, I tried to get some sleep myself, but the overwhelming smell of smoke haunted my dreams. I first dreamt that our tent was on fire, then that the entire island was engulfed in flames, and finally that I was trapped in my bedroom at home while the house burned down around me. I woke up from each of these nightmares in a cold sweat, and finally just stayed awake until dawn.

When I got home from that camping trip, I immediately quit the Boy Scouts. Some of the other guys in the troop said I wasn't tough enough and didn't have the heart or commitment it took to be a Boy Scout. They said that I *failed* as a Boy Scout for these reasons. They were right! It stung because I hated being labeled that way and I hated to fail at anything. However, I now understand that my failure was not a result of not being good enough – I could make a fire just as well as the other kids – nor was it the result of someone else having control over certain variables of the situation. I failed because, in the end, *I just didn't care enough about it.*

If my goal had been to become an Eagle Scout, like the candy thief I'd shared a tent with (he eventually *did* become an Eagle Scout), I would have worked harder on activities to earn merit badges, embraced selling stuff door-to-door to raise money for the troop, and looked at the meetings as a privilege rather than a penalty. In reality, my goal was simply to go camping, and the version of camping I experienced with the Boy Scouts was nothing like what I'd imagined it would be. I would rather spend my time playing baseball and hanging out with my friends than go to endless meetings and bad camping trips.

From that failure, however, I salvaged what I enjoyed about the experience – walking in the woods and sleeping outdoors – and built my next experience around them. Several years later, I took another trip with my two other brothers, Andy and Mark. We spent three nights on the Appalachian Trail, hiking from Tennessee to Virginia, and carried everything on our backs. We cooked our meals over a small camp stove, which eliminated the smoke. We slept outdoors, not even in a tent, staying on high alert for bears and other critters that might wander into our campsite during the night. We saw only two other people the entire journey. It was at times both miserable and exhilarating, but it was everything I hoped it would be. We went on several more backpacking adventures together when I lived in Colorado – each time building on our failures from previous trips to make the next one even better.

If I had given up on my ultimate goal of camping in the great outdoors after one terrible failure, I would have missed out on some of the best experiences of my life.

I still look forward with great anticipation to my next adventure in the wilderness.

If you really want something, don't give up on it. Work through your early failures, learn from them, and use the lessons to increase your odds of success the next time. This is just as true in relationships as it is in any individual endeavor in your life.

Let's look at one of the most common failures in our country: marriage. I know that you are probably not thinking seriously about marriage right now, if at all, and you shouldn't. It's not a top priority for someone your age, but there's a good chance that you've at least imagined what it might be like, who you might marry, what she's doing right now, etc.

I'm sure you know several people who have had a failed marriage. I'd bet most people do! When a marriage fails, there are all kinds of reasons thrown around, with blame on both people, and friends on the outside are typically asked to take a side and choose who they will remain friends with. But what's the real cause? I don't think it's because either person doesn't care about the marriage. I mean, maybe that's the case at the bitter end, but it doesn't start that way. It starts because someone cares *more* about something else outside of the marriage. Maybe they care more about drinking, golfing, gambling, working late, indiscriminate sex with random people – the list of possibilities is endless!

If the husband cared more about the marriage than his desire to blow a couple grand in Vegas every month, it could have been saved. If the wife cared more about the marriage than spending 80 hours at work every week, it could have been saved. It all comes down to what is most important to you.

The first example is pretty self-explanatory, but let's look at that second example – the time spent at work. Isn't the work a good thing? Isn't she providing for the family? Maybe so, but if all that time away from family is causing a rift which could be mended by being at home more, then is it really worth it? She could take another job, maybe for less money and maybe doing something she doesn't enjoy as much that would allow her to spend more time at home. It still comes down to personal *choice*. What does she care *more* about? If she cares more about her career than her family, the marriage will fail, and that is her choice. If she cares more about the marriage than her career, the marriage can be saved with some decisions to change careers or not take that promotion. That is also her choice.

Some people would consider this a sacrifice. In order to choose one, you must *sacrifice* the other! It shouldn't be viewed as a sacrifice though – it's a choice between what you want more. Sacrifice is an interesting concept. It doesn't mean the same thing to everyone.

I was hanging out with a group of friends at a Veteran's Day barbeque one time. We discovered that one of the guys in our circle was a veteran and had served in Iraq. Like many veterans, it wasn't something he talked much about. Another one of the guys in the group, who had not served in the military, thanked him for his sacrifice. The veteran's reaction surprised me. He made it very clear that he did not consider his military service a sacrifice of any kind. He pointed out that he had *chosen* to enlist. Sure, he had risked his life, missed many holidays and celebrations with friends and family, and forfeited the carefree days of his early 20s, when he could have been out chasing girls and getting drunk with his buddies, to go looking for enemy combatants in the middle of the desert, but that was his *choice*. He asked us to never refer to his military service as a sacrifice ever again.

Sometimes your choice will be extremely difficult to make. You will need to differentiate between where you don't *want* to fail and where you absolutely *refuse* to fail. If you have two things that you really like, but you can only choose one, which will you choose? The one you like *more* of course! Even if it's only a very slim margin, you will still come out ahead, so where is the sacrifice? You won!

Start thinking about your failures this way and see if you can identify areas where your failures were a result of caring *more* about something else rather than being bad or *not* caring about what you failed at.

You failed a test? You *could* have aced it, but you cared more about video games than studying. You didn't make the football team? You *could* have made it, but you cared more about playing capture-the-flag in the woods with your friends than spending time in the weight room. All of these things add up over time. You failed to get into the college of your choice? Hmmm, in retrospect, maybe you should have cared more about that math test or making the football team.

Get in the habit of asking yourself what you *refuse* to fail at, knowing that you will fail at other things. When you decide what you will refuse to fail at, all of your other decisions must reflect that value. If you refuse to fail at getting into a specific school, for example, homework needs to take precedence over video games. If you refuse to fail at a sport, spending time in the weight room and on boring skill work must take precedence over spending every afternoon with your friends. Again, these are not sacrifices. They are choices that you are making freely. You can change your mind at any time, but you must realize that impulsive decisions like blowing off a study session or a training session can ultimately derail the thing you said you refused to fail at.

This may seem contradictory to what I said in my last letter – where I told you to open some other doors along that hallway. Don't get me wrong, you need to take the time to explore other paths and options, but you need to *plan* for it. You can study for your test and still make some time for video games. The problem occurs when the time you allotted for video games is up and you *choose* to continue playing instead of making the shift to studying. You need to learn to balance your time, create a schedule, and develop the self-discipline to stick to it – especially when it affects the things you refuse to fail at.

Of course, there will be times when things just don't work out. You can have excellent grades and a wonderful list of references and activities and still not get into the school you wanted. You can either stop there, or you can keep up your refuse-to-fail attitude and work that much harder during your first year of community college and transfer into the school of your choice. There are many paths to the same goal.

It's also important to remember that how we perceive other people's failures is often just a reflection of our own values. For example, someone who is 6'5" with great athleticism may care more about his preferred sport than he cares about math. This choice is based on his belief that athletics will be how he makes his living in the world. He will choose to care more about practicing the skills and building the physical capacity necessary to maximize his athletic potential than he does about a math test that he may fail because he *chose* to spend his time elsewhere. Conversely, someone who is 5'3" with a gift for mathematical theory may care more about his math test than his PE class. He may not be able to score very high in the physical fitness testing and fail that class because he *chose* to focus on learning more about math than spending his time preparing to do a max effort set of pull-ups. He made this decision because he believes that mathematics is his key to success in the world and that physical attributes will never be as important to him. Each is labeled by the other: the jock, the nerd. Each may be a failure in the eyes of the other, however, each has his own set of values and is prepared to accept failure in other parts of his life in pursuit of what he cares about most!

It could also wind up being just the opposite. The athlete could wind up getting hurt or just not being good enough to get paid to play sports. He may fall into a career selling cars and, over time, work his way into a management role, where he has to crunch numbers to figure out which cars need to be sold, how to incentivize his sales team with bonuses for selling those specific cars, and how to handle payroll. All of a sudden, that math test looks a lot more important in the rear view. The nerd could wind up in the middle of the pack at an elite institution, lose his passion for the subject and decide to take up horseback riding as a hobby. He could discover that he loves the wind in his hair and wants to race horses for a living. He gives up math to pursue a career as a professional jockey and wishes he'd worked a little harder at developing the requisite strength to keep up with the best in the world.

Life's funny – you never know how things are going to turn out. What you consider to be a failure today may not look like one in five years. Failure is not the end of the road – it's just a steppingstone to what's next. Don't put too much pressure on yourself to succeed and don't put too much emphasis on *not* failing. Everything is relative in the end, and you can get just as much out of one as the other, depending on how you look at it.

Failure isn't the end of the book. It's just the end of a chapter.

> Love,
> Tom

Chapter 8

Lie #5: Money is the key to happiness

Ivan –

Do you ever daydream about having a lot of money? Do you ever imagine how much easier and carefree your life would be if you had it?

I used to think about money a lot and fantasize about how much better my life would be if I was rich. Occasionally, I'd receive a scratch-off lottery ticket as a gift. Rather than scratch it off immediately, I'd keep it in my pocket for a couple hours – sometimes a couple days. I knew the odds of winning anything substantial were very slim, but the window of time between receiving the ticket and scratching it off was a license to escape reality for a while. Just the thought that I *might* have a million dollars in my pocket gave me the liberty to dream about what I'd do with it and how my life would change.

I don't "come from money" or even from a family that's ever had a lot of it. My dad grew up poor – his dad died when he was very young, and my grandma raised him and his brother and sister on her own at a time when women's salaries were far less than men's. My mom grew up in a family that always had enough, from what I know, but they were never wealthy or even "well-off" either.

When I was a kid, my dad was the only one working. My mom chose to give up her career as a nurse when I was born so she could stay home and raise me and my three brothers, so the budget was always tight. I don't mean to suggest that I didn't have everything I needed! I was very fortunate in that I always had food to eat and a house to live in, but my parents definitely chose more thrifty options any time there was a chance to save a dollar.

I can count on one hand the number of times I remember going out to eat. We never had a new car. They were always used and usually several years old. Let me clarify – I never had *any* car. My dad generously let me borrow his '88 Blazer when I was old enough to drive. That thing was 10-years old and took about five whole seconds to go 0-20 when you put the pedal to the floor. I didn't have my own vehicle until I bought a used truck my junior year of college.

My brothers and I didn't wear brand-name clothes. My mom took us shopping at discount outlets and second-hand stores and we wore shoes from brands that nobody had heard of. My dad cut our hair until middle school, when I finally convinced my parents that I literally could not survive in public with the utilitarian hack job he was notorious for. My parents didn't even spend money on themselves. I'm pretty sure my dad *still* cuts my mom's hair!

Were we poor? My answer is definitely no, but I guess it depends on who you ask and what they consider to be poor. I just accepted that we spent money on the things that we really *needed*, but my brothers and I didn't always get the things we wanted.

In retrospect, I think this was a very good thing for me and my brothers. Without the ability to buy anything we wanted, we had to use our imaginations to create new ways to play with the toys we *did* have and invent new ways to make old games more interesting. For example, we had a big bin of solid plastic cowboys and Indians that we used to play with indoors. Later, we repurposed them as targets, spending hours in the backyard setting them up in hard-to-hit locations and weaving elaborate backstories about the scenario we were about to bring to life. Then we'd build a small fort of our own on the back porch, using the picnic table and benches, and take turns using our BB guns to take out the onrushing armies.

We also played with our stuffed animals a lot. Each one had a name, a backstory, and certain characteristics that made them unique. When you have a large cast of well-defined characters, much like a soap opera, there is no limit to the scope and length of your storylines. With that said, playing with a stuffed animal has significant restrictions. For one thing, they're *stuffed* animals, so they can only move if you manipulate them yourself, and it can be a little embarrassing to carry them around in public after the age of six or so. Secondly, they're bound by the laws of physics, which means they can't change size or shape to work well with other toys. We solved these problems by creating a magical force that gave our stuffed animals the ability to become invisible and leave their physical bodies.

The magic was activated by touching a certain part of the armrest in the car or the correct combination of knots in the wood of our bunk beds. Using this magic, we could take one stuffed animal in the car with us, make them invisible when we arrived at our destination – running errands with mom or going on a family hike – leave the physical toy in the car, and allow our animals to run wild! Oh, the hijinks these rascals would get into! The magic also allowed them to change size, so at home we used our stuffed animals as pilots in model airplanes, conductors on toy trains and drivers in radio-controlled cars. They fought wars, robbed banks, and starred in just about any other scenario you can imagine.

The depth of our imaginary world was quite significant, and I can tell you more about it later if you're really interested, but I believe I've told you enough to make my point: *not* having unlimited money to buy whatever I wanted actually benefited me later in life. The development of my imagination and story-telling ability is the result of being forced to create new experiences with the limited items I had at hand. These skills have helped me sustain a curiosity about the world around me. They have helped me get jobs and excel in marketing roles where the goal is to *tell a story* about a product that makes someone else want to buy it. Just because you don't have money doesn't mean you can't make the most of your situation and develop other skills that will carry over later in life. Use the hand you've been dealt to build the unique tool set that will set you apart from everyone else down the road!

While the long-term benefit of my situation is clear to me now, it was no consolation to 16-year old me. I wanted stylish clothes, my own car, and the cash to take girls out on elaborate dates and buy them gifts. I fantasized about being rich because I believed these things would make me happier and more popular. However, my assumption that money itself was the key to my future happiness turned out to be completely wrong. I'm still not rich, and I may never be! I'm OK with that because I'm happy with what I've got. One of the most important discoveries I've made in my life – and the main point I want you to take from this letter – is that *money alone won't make you happy*.

Living in a society where having money seems so important, it's hard to believe that you can be successful and even comfortable with relatively little in your pocket. The key is to identify what is most important to you and prioritize your spending accordingly.

It took me a long time to realize that money isn't the key to happiness. In fact, it really came about out of necessity – I didn't have money and I still wanted to be happy! I want you to know that it's possible to be happy without it. You could even make the argument that you can be *happier* without a lot of money.

There is a lot of talk about socioeconomics when it comes to money – the "one percent," the upper, middle, and lower classes, and ultimately the poor. It is easy to assume that the more money you have, the happier you will be because you have less to worry about. This really isn't the case when you look at this philosophy in practice.

If you haven't learned about it yet, you need to check out Maslow's Hierarchy of Needs. The diagram is shaped like a pyramid and outlines the needs that people have, breaking them down into basic needs, psychological needs, and self-fulfillment needs. Each of these layers builds on the previous one. Just like any pyramid, you can't achieve the second layer before you build the base.

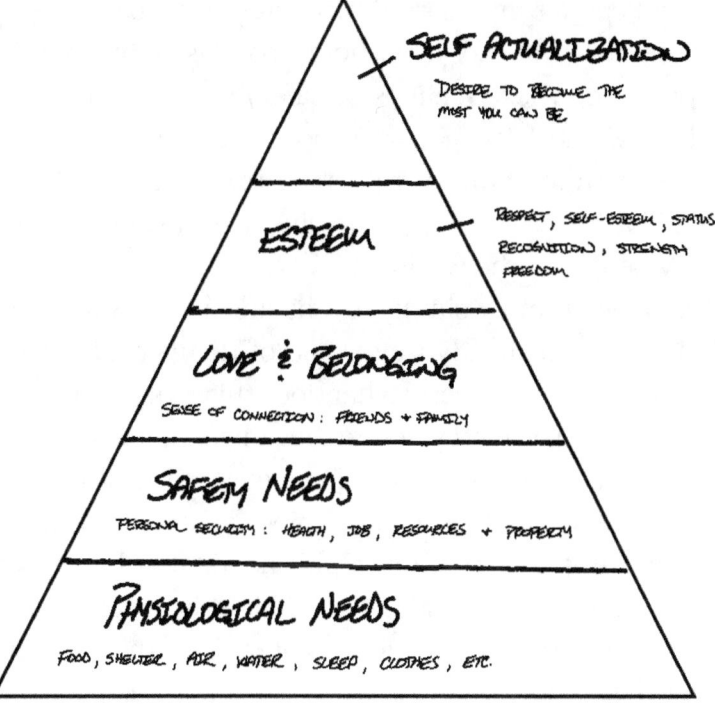

At the base of the pyramid are the basic needs – what you absolutely *must* have to sustain life: food, water, warmth, and rest. Without these things, you will die. Pretty cut and dry, right? One step above these physiological needs are the safety needs: safety and security. What does this mean for you? To me, it means a house, a room, or apartment – somewhere I can call "home base," where I can let my guard down, relax and recalibrate for the next day ahead. This home base is only effective in providing these feelings of safety and security when I also *believe* it is safe – a space that is mine alone or shared with my family or people I trust. Once you have those basic needs met, you're already doing better than many people in the world.

Imagine that – simply by having food, water, and shelter, you're already way ahead of the game. So, what else could you want, and what does this pyramid have to do with all that money you're dreaming about?

After your basic needs are met, the next level of the pyramid holds the psychological needs: intimate relationships and friends. Think about it, what makes solitary confinement such a horrible prison sentence? I mean, the inmates have food, water, warmth, rest, relative safety, and a fuck-ton of security. Their basic needs are met, yet some people argue that it's actually a form of *torture*!

The thing that makes solitary confinement so unbearable is the lack of interaction with others. Loneliness is one of the primary ingredients for depression and can lead to suicidal thoughts and worse, even when the basics for living are covered. The psychological need for interpersonal relationships cannot be understated. It's hard-wired into us – an innate part of being human.

Just above those friends and relationships are the needs of your ego: prestige, dignity, and a feeling of accomplishment. You know – the stuff that makes other people look at you with respect, if not envy. This includes things like getting good grades, making the team, getting the part in the school musical, keeping your room clean, rebuilding the engine in the truck and, yes, making a lot of money.

Your esteem needs are different from everyone else's, so keep that in mind. Your idea of success might be earning a huge salary and living in luxury while someone else's idea may be owning as little as possible and keeping their schedule flexible enough to travel when they want without being tied down by a house, dog, job, etc. Two people can have wildly different definitions of personal success and accomplishment, but it doesn't make either one more correct than the other. Pursue *your* preferred path, whatever it is, and don't worry about being judged by others or comparing yourself to them.

As you get older, you'll also realize that your own esteem needs will change and evolve. When I was your age, I needed the approval of others around me – I needed to be liked. That was the most important of my esteem needs – to be *liked*. It was OK if I didn't like someone else, but I still wanted that person to like *me*. It's a hard pill to swallow that someone out there doesn't like you for one reason or another. I mean, when you're such a nice guy, how could anyone *not* like you? The one way I was sure I could get people to like me is if I had money. They would like me, envy me, and possibly *fear* me to some degree. That's a lot of power!

The problem with money is that we can never seem to get enough of it. Regardless of how much you have, there's always a little voice in the back of your mind that asks, "but what if you had a little more?" Even though I have enough money now to live comfortably, I still hear that voice from time to time suggesting that if I had a little more, I could go on a better vacation or buy nicer stuff. Even if I'm not thinking about what that extra money could do for me *now*, there's an underlying fear that I could *lose* what I currently have, so I should be actively stockpiling more as a backup – just in case!

When you don't have a lot of money, you spend your time deciding how to spend what you do have and, hopefully, enjoying the items or experiences you're able to attain with it, appreciating how much work it took to earn it. For some people, this means simply fulfilling the bottom levels of the pyramid: paying rent and putting a hot meal on the table. They don't have the luxury of thinking about spending a week at the beach or a ski lodge in the mountains. Ironically, some studies suggest these people are often among the happiest in the world. A lack of options can be a blessing. Having fewer choices available simplifies things and can reduce anxiety and stress about making the right choice. A simple life can be a fulfilling life.

On the other hand, people who have a lot of money – more money than they'll ever need – are often preoccupied with getting more. At some point, money itself becomes the goal, rather than a means to *reach* a goal. Rather than enjoying what they have, some people live in constant fear that another person has *more*, and the only way to be happy is to get even more money than that person. They become a servant to their money, rather than the other way around. It can be a slippery slope and I imagine it's a miserable way to live.

There *is* a correlation between the amount of money you have and how happy you are, but the actual numbers may surprise you. In a 2018 study from Purdue University, using data from a Gallup World Poll, researchers found that the ideal base income to achieve emotional wellbeing is $60,000. Essentially, once you have enough money to comfortably fulfill your physiological and safety needs – the bottom two levels of the pyramid – additional money will not make you happier. In fact, the study also shows that when people earn more than $105K, their happiness levels *decrease*. These numbers are obviously going to fluctuate over time, but it goes to show that you definitely don't need to be a millionaire to be happy! Someone making $60K a year can be *just as happy* as someone making two, three, or ten times that much! Beyond that base threshold, finding meaning and purpose in your life is a much better predictor of happiness than how much money you make.

You might think that sounds crazy, so let's test it. I want you to try out my little "what if" game from when I was a kid: what would you do if you won the lottery? Let's say you won a huge jackpot of $500 million dollars. What would you do? Would you drop out of school? Quit your job? Buy a new house, three new cars, and relocate somewhere else in the country? Take a few months to travel the world? Take a few minutes to think about it and have some fun. Let your imagination run wild! What would you do if you never had to worry about making money again?

Money gives the *illusion* of happiness. From the outside, we all look at people with money and think about how we would feel if we had that kind of cash on hand. We think about all the great stuff we'd do, the trips we'd go on, and the toys we'd buy. How far does that really get you?

In this fantasy you're mapping out in your head, you're only thinking of the present and perhaps the immediate future – the next year at most. What happens after that? What happens when you don't have to go back to school or work and you're home alone with your cars and personal movie theater? What happens when everyone you know still has to work or go to school or both?

You live in isolation. You become lonely. Your life begins to lose its sense of purpose. You become the inmate sitting in solitary confinement. You just have a nicer cell.

After a month of doing nothing but relaxing, you will be ready for something else. Relaxing won't feel like fun anymore. After all, a vacation is only exciting and special because it's rare and temporary. If your life becomes one extended vacation, it will lose its exciting quality because it's no longer rare! You can sit on your plush couch or in the hot tub you had installed in your living room, binge Netflix, and get fat, but you will slowly begin to despise yourself. Loneliness has a way of doing that to a person. Why?

You will have lost some of those psychological needs – the needs for friendship and close, meaningful relationships. The people you used to hang out with will no longer have much in common with you. What are you going to talk about? You don't have to worry about your job, your car breaking down, the cost of healthcare, the price of food or gas, the state of the economy, or any of that. You have all the money you'll ever need.

We tend to think of money as a ticket to freedom – freedom from having to worry about the financial constraints of our current situation. Ironically, having a ton of money also has the potential to *take away* some of your freedom.

Think about the wealthiest people you know of: movie stars, pro athletes, music icons ... why do you think so many of them live in gated communities? It's not that they want to live in elite company and avoid seeing the scum of society blighting their pristine landscape. In many cases, it's more of a self-imposed prison! Living in a place with limited public access is the only way they can keep some expectation of privacy and semblance of a normal life. Think about it. Every time they go out in public, they've got the paparazzi following them, trying to take pictures of them doing something stupid, or looking fat, ugly, and ... *imperfect*. As soon as they're recognized, they're mobbed by throngs of people who all want selfies. No public space is safe. The only place they can escape the pressure and constant bombardment is within the confines of their gated community, insulated from the madness and insanity that people like us create for them.

Imagine living that way. Would you *really* enjoy that? You could no longer make the last-minute decision go to the movies with your friends on a random Friday night, or take an impromptu trip to grab a drink at your favorite coffee shop, or pop into your local grocery store to pick up snacks for the big game because that relaxing night out or 15-minute errand becomes a circus as soon as someone recognizes you, and you're the main attraction. You could no longer act a fool in public as we have *all* done with our friends when we're in a good mood and around *our* people! You have to be very careful about everything you say and do because the media is just waiting for you to slip up so they can tear you apart. Everyone has their phones at the ready. Everyone's recording. You are in a fishbowl, and the whole world is watching your every move. Think about everything you currently take for granted that you'd have to give up if you were famous. Is it worth it?

Let's say you're not famous, but you're still rich. We've already established that you would no longer have to worry about financial concerns. Does that mean all your worries go away? Not even close! That's when the fear will begin to set in. What happens if the money runs out? What happens if all of the *stuff* you've bought goes away? What if you have to actually go out and get a real job again? How embarrassing would it be to face your old friends and have them know that you blew it? You had it all, and now you're back in the trenches of life with them!

That fear is enough to make many wealthy people crave more. It drives them to get more at any cost. By isolating yourself in a cocoon of extreme wealth, you can become impervious to the challenges faced by most of the other people around you. Money creates a buffer between you and the realities faced by the common man. You can lose sight of "the greater good," and worry only about yourself. What happened to you? Back when you had no money, you were happy just to have a warm meal and a safe place to call home.

Money can tear apart all the greatest parts of your life. It can destroy relationships with friends, family, and community. It can harden you to the realities of life that the great majority of people face. It has the potential to make you see those with less money than you as less worthy and less valuable than you. Ultimately, you can begin to lose your connection to humanity itself because your point of view is so different from everyone else's.

Money can also disappear very quickly, especially in the hands of a novice who doesn't have a lot of experience with it and doesn't really understand how it works.

Did you know that 70 percent of lottery winners lose it all within a few years? It's true. Thirty percent – that's nearly one out of every three – will actually wind up bankrupt and worse off than they were before they won. This is true for many professional athletes as well. In both cases, you usually have people who come from modest means and are suddenly thrust into great wealth. It can be overwhelming. Everyone you know will seek a little bit of your fortune. Friends from childhood whom you haven't spoken to in years, cousins you didn't even know you had, strangers with business ideas they want you to invest in – it doesn't stop! When it feels like everyone around you has become a predator, trying to siphon off your money for their own benefit, how will you even know who your real friends are?

Many lottery winners actually look back and wish they'd never won in the first place. If you don't believe it, do a quick internet search for "broke lottery winners." You'll see that the prospect of all that money for nothing isn't always all it's cracked up to be.

I'm not saying that having money is evil or that rich people's lives are all doom and gloom. You can definitely do a lot of good with your money in your community, maintain close personal friendships with people on all rungs of the financial ladder, and live an extraordinarily fulfilling and happy life! I just want you to realize that money isn't the *solution* in and of itself.

Let's go back to Maslow's hierarchy and finish off the pyramid. At the very top is self-actualization. This refers to the achievement of your full potential – using your unique gifts to leave your mark on the world. For me, this includes creative activities like writing songs and stories, including this book!

If you're thinking about this pyramid as a check list, working through it in your head and checking off each of the levels as I discuss them, you're probably going to be stuck on self-actualization for a while. Self-actualization requires time, experience, honesty, and a lot of soul searching. It's a constant work in progress. As I mentioned above, self-actualization is the achievement of your full potential. If you truly believe you have reached your full potential at this point in your life, or that you're even close, that's a good indicator that your mind isn't even developed enough to fully grasp the concept. That's not an insult! It's a physiological truth that the male brain is not fully developed until age 25. How could you possibly believe you've reached your full potential before your brain is even fully developed?

All of this is to say that as you're reading this, I hope that you grasp the concept that your life as you currently know it will expand exponentially, with tentacles reaching in all directions, with different interests, pursuits, and emerging beliefs that will fundamentally change how you see yourself and the world around you over time.

This is something to celebrate! The path toward self-actualization will continue to stretch in front of you until the day you die. Even as you accomplish great things and achieve goals you set for yourself, there is always another step to take in the quest to realize your true, full potential.

Keep in mind that just because your brain is fully matured by age 25, it doesn't mean that all the answers will suddenly be revealed to you when you get there. What's more likely is that you will begin to realize just how little you actually know and how far you truly have to go. When it hits, this epiphany can be scary, but it's really the first *true* step toward self-actualization.

Have you ever been talking to someone older than you – someone with more life experience – and you got into an argument about a topic that you felt sure you were right about, but were unable to convince them to see things your way? This happened to me many times. Each time, I remember getting a little bit heated that this person couldn't see that I was right. Once my companion realized that I was too young to truly understand what I was talking about, they delivered a dagger: "you don't even know how much you don't know," which promptly ended the conversation.

I don't even know how much I don't know? What does that mean? What kind of response could I possibly have to that statement?

Years later, I still think about those moments and realize just how right they were! I don't remember the specific context of those conversations, but as I look back over how my life has unfolded after high school, it's clear that there are very few things that I was absolutely convinced of that have remained that way. There are things I've changed my mind on in the past year alone that had already changed drastically from what I believed in high school.

Self-actualization isn't a check box. It's a text field with no character limit. Don't look at self-actualization as something to be definitively achieved, but rather as a constant state of personal evolution and improvement! No amount of money can buy self-actualization.

To wrap it up, money is important to a certain extent. Once you get past the threshold of being able to afford the basics of food, clothing and shelter, the amount you earn will not dramatically increase your happiness and, past a certain point, can even contribute to your emotional and psychological downfall.

Always pursue your goals and dreams! Having money is not a bad thing as long as you understand what it can do and what it *cannot* do. If you are able to make a lot of money, do it! If you are fortunate enough to get rich, consider working with a good financial advisor to help you sustain your money and insulate you from catastrophic losses, so you don't have to constantly worry about it. Rather than seeing money as the ultimate goal, choose to see it as a tool to help you *achieve* your end goal: a life full of meaning and purpose.

Whether you wind up rich, poor, or somewhere in between, don't base your value and self-worth on the amount of money you have. More importantly, don't try to measure your happiness by the amount of money you have or pursue more money with the illusion that you will be happy when you get it. It's a false idol that can lead you down a very dark path. You can be successful and create a happy, fulfilling life worth living without a huge bank account.

Love,
Tom

Chapter 9

Lie #6: The more friends I have, the better

Ivan –

Pop quiz: without thinking too hard about it, how many friends would you say you have right now? 10, 20, 50, 100? More?

As I shared in my last letter, the most important consideration in my life when I was younger was whether or not people liked me. It didn't matter how well they knew me or if we ever hung out outside of school. I based too much of my self-worth on how many people liked me – and I counted each of them as friend.

Funny, but true: if you look at my 7th grade yearbook, I highlighted the names of every person I counted as a friend. I recently looked back at it as part of this project, and it was actually pretty sad. I highlighted the kids who rode my bus. I highlighted the kids in my classes who never spoke to me, but also were never *mean* to me. I even highlighted several of the "popular" kids, who definitely weren't my friends, but didn't pick on me.

At the time, I thought when I looked back on that yearbook in the future, I'd have forgotten so much about that part of my life that my future self – me *now* – would think I had a lot more friends than I actually did. Yes, as absurd as it sounds, I was so concerned with how many people liked me that I legitimately thought I could trick *myself* into misremembering how uncool and unpopular I was, and how few friends I truly had.

I know you count lots of people as friends, but I'm writing this letter to tell you that all friends aren't created equal. There's a big difference between *good* friends, casual friends, and acquaintances. It's very important that you learn this sooner than later.

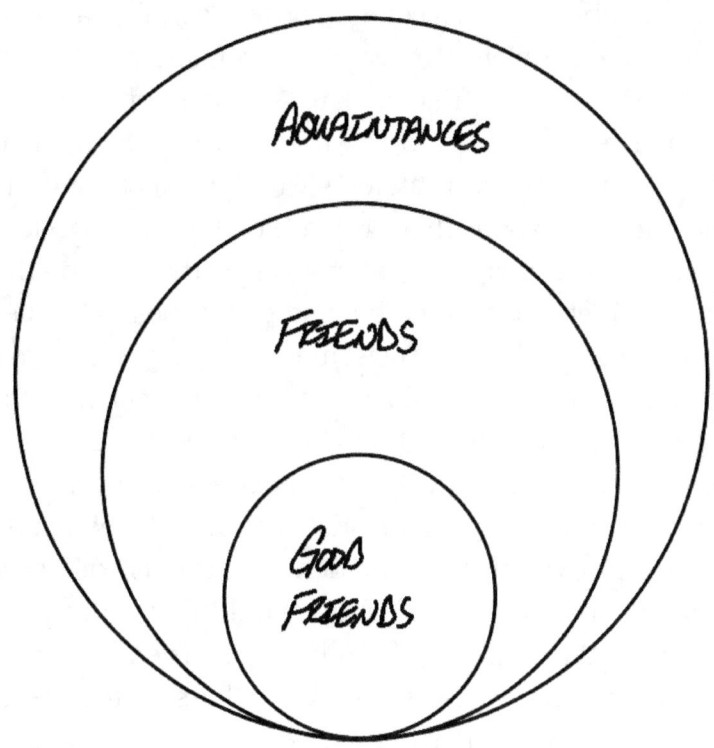

Let's start with the largest circle: acquaintances. Acquaintances include all of the people you know – actual friends, social media "friends," and enemies alike. These are the kids you go to school with, your teachers, and even the kids from other schools whom you know through extracurricular activities like sports or other social groups and clubs. An acquaintance is someone you wave to in the hall or see at a big party but don't really know that well. Most of the kids I highlighted in my 7th

grade yearbook were acquaintances. Basically, anyone who isn't a complete stranger is an acquaintance.

Then you have friends. This segment of your acquaintances includes people whom you know a bit more about, share common interests with, and feel comfortable talking to about those things you have in common. These are the people you hang out with most of the time – sometimes all together and sometimes as smaller groups broken off from the same circle. They know you and like you, and you share a mutual appreciation for one another's company, thoughts, and ideas. You share more personal details about yourself and the way you see the world with your friends, but you still keep most of your armor in place so you don't run the risk of losing these friends if they find out certain things about you.

Finally, there are good friends. A good friend is someone you are very close with. Most adults count themselves lucky to have two or three good friends. Some have a couple more and many have fewer than that, and with good reason. A good friendship, like a marriage, takes work to maintain. Right now, at this point in your life, it's relatively easy to have a larger group of good friends. Your responsibilities, on the whole, are not all that great. You have school, some chores and maybe a part-time job. You are limited only by these commitments in the amount of time you can spend nurturing your friendships, and school doesn't really count because you get to spend time with some of your good friends there. As you get older, and more responsibilities creep into your life, your circle of good friends will start to shrink because the amount of time you have to spend with them will be reduced as more commitments eat into your free time.

In high school, I probably had at least 10 people whom I considered good friends – mostly guys, but with a few girls sprinkled in too. Once I graduated college and had a full-time job, my group of good friends was whittled down to about six – mostly college buddies, several of whom I lived with. When I moved to Colorado and eventually got married, that pool became even smaller: about three. Most of my time was split between work and spending time with my wife, leaving less free time for those friendships.

Eventually, my wife and I started making friends with other married couples, and now I count seven men in my life whom I would still drop anything for if they needed me – not counting my brothers. While I say I have seven good friends, none of them went through high school with me and none of them live very close either. The closest one is a three-hour drive and the farthest is a four-hour plane flight across the country, so if you ask me how many close friends I hang out with regularly, the answer is actually zero. The number of good friends you have in *your* life will fluctuate over time as well.

Good friends are the people whom you can truly be yourself around. They won't be afraid to challenge or confront you when they think you're in the wrong, but also will not hesitate to come to the rescue if you call them in the middle of the night. Over time, these select few will also earn your trust to the point that you will begin to remove more of your armor in their presence, risking a bit more to reveal your true self to them. These are the people you seek out to confide your deepest fears and greatest problems in. They are the ones you trust to keep your secrets and not judge you for your shortcomings and weaknesses.

Your *best* friend is the one you will share everything with – not just which girls you like or that you cheated on your math test. Your best friend is who you will talk to about arguments and conflict within your family, worries about your financial situation, and your thoughts on hot-button topics like social issues, politics, and religion.

Your best friend can change over time too. I have had several in my lifetime, but my situation is a little unique in that I moved around a lot and constantly had to make new friends. In kindergarten, I had Justin, who had an awesome toy collection. In sixth grade, it was Harrison. We spent countless days together exploring the Arizona desert, playing video games, and talking about the girls in our class. My freshman year of high school, it was Mark. He and I were inseparable, but he moved to Michigan after that first year. Mark and I still keep in touch, and I will always consider him a great friend. After Mark left, it was Chuckie. We both played saxophone in band and talked about life's problems in great depth. In college, I felt like I had a couple best friends: Connor and Dave. We're still really good friends to this day. When I moved to Colorado, I met Tim, who was just like me in so many ways it was almost as if we were twins. He's another one who stood the test of time and whom I would do anything for. Finally, there's my wife, Annah. She knows more about me than anyone ever has, and I know she'll love me no matter what. I would literally trust her with my life.

There is a lot of gray area when it comes to friends and acquaintances. It's hard to draw a solid line between the two, and some people will fade back and forth across that line for as long as you know them. Some will drift out of the picture completely. Your good friends, however, will stay with you wherever you go.

One of the big misconceptions I had at your age is that having more friends is a status symbol and the more friends I had the cooler I was or the more swagger I had. It was important to me that I had a lot of friends. I needed affirmation from others to believe that I was a good person and people liked me. What better way to gauge that than by the number of people who sign your yearbook, right?

As you get older and gain the benefits of hindsight and experience, you're going to learn that most of the friendships you have now are actually very shallow. That's OK! You don't have to worry about this right now, but just keep in mind that it's normal to drift apart from people over time and it doesn't necessarily have anything to do with you personally.

This also speaks to the value of having a few good friends. The most popular kids may seem to have a ton of friends – everybody likes them and wants to emulate them. Maybe this is you and maybe it isn't.

If this describes you, Mr. Popular, think about how many of those people you would actually trust to keep your secrets. If you got in trouble, who among them would stick by your side and either cover for you or share the blame, and who would point the finger at you to get themselves out of trouble? Who would drop whatever they're doing to come help you out if you called with a flat tire on the side of the road and who would say they're "busy," and then go back to binge watching some show on Netflix? If the tables were turned, who would you defend? Who would you drop everything for? It may not be obvious to you now, but over time you will begin to recognize your true friends – the special people in your life.

If you find yourself on the other side of the spectrum, with very few friends, who are the people you really enjoy being around? Chances are, these are the people you'd do anything for and expect them to do the same. These are the special people in your life.

Sometimes you may consider a person to be *your* best friend, but they may not categorize you the same way. When the people you trust let you down and show you they're not who you think they are, it can be a rocky landing. Take my best friend from high school, Chuckie, for example. We hung out almost every day for three years. We talked about our classes, the girls we were interested in, where we wanted to go to college, and what we hoped to do with our lives after that. Despite our close friendship, Chuckie and I still had our fights.

In our junior year of high school, Chuckie told me he liked Annie. Unfortunately, I also liked Annie and Annie liked me. We had already been seeing each other secretly, not wanting to make a big deal of it in our circle of friends because we'd been "just friends" for so long. I think Chuckie took it pretty hard when we officially started dating and felt like I'd stabbed him in the back and stolen his girl. He never said anything to me directly, but he did talk to some of my baseball teammates in one of the classes he had with them.

One afternoon at practice, they told me that Chuckie was talking shit about me and had called me a "pansy." He had validated that comment by telling them some of my personal business that was meant to stay between me and Chuckie. I honestly can't remember what he told them, but I was irate. My supposed best friend was spilling secrets and talking shit about me to the guys I wanted to be accepted by the most – my teammates!

These events happened to coincide with the annual production of the school musical, in which I had a leading role. Chuckie was in the pit orchestra – the band that plays the music for the production. After baseball practice, I had to go get dressed up for the final rehearsal before opening night. After I got my costume and makeup on, I went to confront Chuckie in the auditorium. I walked in through the backstage entrance and saw him at the front of the stage, unpacking his saxophone.

"Hey, Chuckie!" I yelled, "You think I'm a pansy, huh? Why don't you say it to my face?"

As I started walking toward him, Chuckie put down his instrument and ran out of the auditorium. I chased him up the stairs, out the doors, and down the hall, where he ducked into the men's bathroom and locked himself in a stall. It was well after school hours, but I can only imagine how ridiculous we looked: me, dressed in red velvet capris pants, a shirt that was basically a blouse, stage makeup, and a cap with a feather in it, chasing Chuckie, a band nerd in his button-up white-collared shirt and black tie, into the bathroom and threatening to kick is ass while yelling, "who's the pansy now?!?" It was absolutely absurd.

We worked it out and remained friends after that, but I had seen a side of Chuckie that I didn't know he had. I chalked it up as a one-time thing. Surely, chasing him into the bathroom had made my point – don't fuck with me, Chuckie.

A few years later, after college, Chuckie asked me to be a groomsman in his wedding. I had recently ended my seven-year relationship with Annie. We had been together from junior year of high school, through college, and our first year after graduation. We broke up about six months before Chuckie's wedding, and I was finally starting to think about dating again.

One of the bridesmaids at the wedding was a cousin of the bride. She was devastatingly beautiful, with brunette hair past her shoulders, green eyes, and an olive complexion to her skin – the kind of girl that I thought was far too pretty for me to talk to. She was younger than I was – I think she was 18, and still in college, while I was about 23 and done with school. During the picture session after the wedding, we flirted briefly, and she playfully asked me to save her a dance at the reception.

I was really nervous. For one thing, I had just come out of a long relationship, and I hadn't talked to another girl with any kind of romantic undertones in a long time, much less one who was out of my league in terms of looks. For another, her whole family was there, and I didn't want to come off as some creep who was trying to pick up their daughter at a wedding! I avoided her during the reception, and we never got that dance. As things were wrapping up after we'd sent the bride and groom on their way, she walked up to me, looked me square in the eye and said, "you never asked me to dance." I immediately felt terrible, both for letting her down and for missing the opportunity. I apologized and gave her my email and phone number and told her I would make it up to her and we could reschedule that dance for another time.

I did follow up with her. We emailed and texted for a few weeks after the wedding, which was all we could really do because she lived in another state. We were both interested in writing and recording music, so we would send sample tracks back and forth and had even discussed her coming to visit so we could record a song together in the little studio I'd cobbled together in my bedroom – just a nice microphone connected to my computer. She must have told her cousin, Chuckie's wife, about our developing relationship, because one day out of nowhere she told me that she probably shouldn't speak to me anymore because I wasn't the person she thought I was. I was caught completely off guard and couldn't understand what she could possibly be talking about.

Chuckie had told her I was a "player," a womanizer who used women for sex and threw them away. Nothing could have been further from the truth, and Chuckie knew that, but she didn't. I couldn't say anything to convince her otherwise. I can only guess that he was still bitter that Annie had chosen me in high school, and he wanted to sabotage me in any way he could. Again, I was really angry. This was the second time Chuckie had shown me who he really was, but I couldn't chase him down this time.

I saw Chuckie once more after that. He and his wife were visiting Colorado and asked me to join them for dinner. We had a good time and laughed about old stories from high school, but my guard was up, and I didn't offer any new information about my life since we'd last seen each other. We didn't discuss the events that transpired at the wedding. I haven't spoken to him since, and it wouldn't bother me if I never do again. I'm no longer angry with him, and I'm thankful for the high school memories, but I'm also comfortable letting go of this friendship because I know it has no further value to offer.

As you push through the storms that are an inevitable part of life, it will become clearer that having a lot of *acquaintances* means a lot less than having a few really good friends. This is why it's so lonely at the top. When everyone wants to be your friend, it gets harder and harder to pick the few real friends out of the crowd. With this in mind, is it really so important to reach that level? My advice is to spend less time worrying about how popular you can become and more time thinking about who's going to be there to help you clean up the mess after the shit hits the fan.

With that said, you still have to choose your friends wisely. It has been said that you are the sum of the five people you spend the most time with. This means that the five closest people to you stand to have the strongest influence on your life. Think about your circle of friends for a minute. You probably share some of the same interests and hobbies. You likely have certain phrases, handshakes, or inside jokes that are unique to your group. This is all well and good, but there can be a dark side to this as well. How do you and your friends speak about women, for example? What about people of a different race, religion, or sexual orientation? The wrong group of friends can cast you in a light that you don't agree with and give you a reputation that you don't want.

It's one thing to see a beautiful woman and talk about her good looks and certain features that you think are attractive. You may even have some more explicit thoughts in your mind – that's OK, it's part of the hardwiring of being a straight male. It's something else to use derogatory language to demean her and make her seem like an object rather than another person. I've experienced both scenarios, both of which occurred well after high school, but they are stories that could have easily happened when I was your age and that you may encounter.

There have been many times when I was out with a group of my friends from the gym and seen some beautiful women. There may be a quiet comment from one of the guys to the rest of the group about her legs or her butt – we can all appreciate a beautiful member of the opposite sex – but then it gets put in context of, "I wonder how much she can squat." The conversation moves on to something we find interesting – weight training and physical fitness.

On the flip side, I've been hanging out with a group of acquaintances – guys I played baseball with – when a similar scenario unfolded. Unlike the group of friends from the gym, one of the baseball guys shouted at her, "Yo! What up girl?" Getting no response, he turned back to the group and said loudly, "I bet she likes it dirty." Several other guys in the group laughed.

How do those two scenarios make you feel? How would you react? Which group of "friends" would you rather spend time with? This isn't a comparison of guys who like to work out and guys who like to play baseball

– with different people in the mix, it easily could have been the gym guys making degrading and sexist remarks and the baseball guys speaking respectfully.

Personally, I prefer to hang out with the guys who know where to draw the line and maintain an appreciative, but respectful approach. That's where I choose to spend my time. These are the guys who continue to help shape me into the man I am, and whom I help shape into the men they are. In scenarios where I'm hanging out with the second group, in this case at a restaurant after a game or at a tournament in another city, I do my best to separate myself from the kind of comments that I would never make and that I personally find reprehensible.

Sometimes I spoke up in those situations. Sometimes I'd say something to the offending teammate – tell him how much of an ass he was making of himself, and me by association – but not always. In some situations, after wrestling with the emotions of hating what was said and not wanting to be associated with it, and weighing the social cost of being seen as a guy who can't take a joke and just be "one of the guys," I chose to keep quiet. Even well into my adult life, I struggle with these scenarios from time to time. You will too if you're not already!

I have made big gains in the last few years. I'm much less concerned now than I used to be about what people will think of me if I say what I'm thinking and feeling. It's still not easy, but I can sleep a lot better at night when I know that I've stayed true to who I am and what I believe in. It all goes back to that early letter about what it means to be a man and how you define that role for yourself.

Choose your closest friends wisely. I'm not saying you need to go through your social media accounts and get rid of a bunch of people. You have plenty of time to meet and get to know plenty of people in the years ahead. I'm just letting you know that over time, the best of them will rise to the top and you will benefit greatly from having them in your life.

Spend the most time on these friendships because they will be the most rewarding in the long run, regardless of how many friends you have now. Hundreds, if not thousands of people will come into your life, stay for a while, and then leave. Some will go without you noticing and some you'll have to throw out the door yourself, but ultimately, having two or three really good friends is a great place to be.

>   Love,
>   Tom

Chapter 10

Lie #7: I am special

Dear Ivan,

I am not special. I'm just another guy trying to make my way in the world like everyone else. It took me a really long time to reach this conclusion, and it was an uncomfortable trip. I spent a lot of my younger years thinking I was special and expecting other people to recognize it and treat me accordingly. I just *knew* I was put here for a reason. I was meant to do great things, and until I figured out what my true purpose was, I expected things to be handed to me simply because I obviously deserved them.

This miscalculation warped the way I saw the world and reacted to my circumstances. When things didn't go my way – I didn't make the team, win the prize, or generally get what I wanted – it wasn't my fault. I harbored anger and resentment against whoever denied me what I felt was rightfully mine and didn't recognize that I was special. Even worse, my victories – the results I *truly* earned – were diminished because I felt like I deserved them, and anything less would have been unthinkable.

My eyes weren't fully opened to reality until after I graduated high school and the "real world" started kicking me in the balls repeatedly. Over the years, I've had many experiences that have reminded me that I'm not special and I've actually learned to appreciate them! Most are small reminders, like when you find yourself sitting in the waiting room at the doctor's office 30 minutes after your scheduled appointment time. Every once in a while, however, one will sneak up and slap you in the back of the head to really drive the point home.

When I first moved to Denver, I worked part-time for Major League Baseball's Colorado Rockies as a member of their game-day promotions staff. My job was to throw tee shirts into the crowd and manage the in-game events, like a hot dog decorating contest or a fly-ball catching contest to win prizes from different sponsors. I also helped escort the mascot around the stadium for different meet-and-greet opportunities. One day, a fan approached us after we'd already thrown all of our tee shirts for that game and asked if we could bring up another shirt for her since it was her birthday. I wished her a happy birthday but told her we had to move on since we were on a tight schedule and had to go set up for the next promotion. She persisted, emphasizing that since it was her birthday, we should grant her wish. Of course, we had no more tee shirts to give, so we moved on, leaving her on the concourse, upset on her birthday.

Once we were off the concourse, one of the full-time staffers made a comment that really stuck with me. He said, "people need to understand that in a stadium of 50,000 fans, on any given day there are at least 100 people who are also there celebrating their birthday. *I'm sorry, but you're just not that special.*"

When he said that, I felt the slap of reality on the back of my head. He was right. If you divide the stadium capacity of Coors Field, about 50,000, by the 365 days in a year, you get 137. There is no way that we could cater to 100+ individuals at every game just because it's their birthday.

Listen, there's no easy way to say this, so I'm just going to come out and say it: you're not special either.

I'm really sorry to break it to you. I know your mom tells you you're special all the time, but it's just not the case. All moms think their kids are special. It's basically rule number one of motherhood. Ok, let me back up just a bit here – you *are* special to your mom. But here's where you're going to have to draw the line: not everyone thinks you're special. In fact, there will be a very small group of people in your life who think you are special. Those people will be the people you love and maybe your very closest friends. Outside of that very exclusive group, you're just another guy.

This can be a hard pill to swallow, especially when you think highly of yourself. The fact of the matter is that by sheer force of numbers, we can't all be special. Consider a colony of ants. There are hundreds, maybe thousands of them! Each one plays an important role in supporting the colony, but if you look at them from the outside, you just see a bunch of ants, all doing the same thing. Or, how about the human equivalent: the army? Think of all the soldiers that make up the United States Army. They all have mothers who think they're special, but when it's time to go to war, the powers that be see them only as numbers. If we held back all the "special" soldiers to keep them out of harm's way, we'd have nobody left to do the fighting. In this context, you can begin to see that this lie, just like all the others, is all a matter of perspective.

A few years later, I felt the slap of reality again, but this time it caught me straight across the face. Annah and I got married on the front porch of her parents' house in Indianapolis. It was a great day, surrounded by family and friends. The weeks and months leading up to the wedding were awesome. We had several small celebrations with different groups of friends and co-workers and were showered with gifts and well wishes. We definitely felt special!

We decided to spend our honeymoon on the Hawaiian island of Maui, which was incredible. Coming off our grand tour of celebration, we figured we would continue to be honored as newly-weds and take advantage of the hospitality and free-upgrades commensurate with our status. On our first night out, we went to a luau – a traditional Hawaiian cookout that was built around religion and royalty, complete with hula dancing, island music, and the whole deal – a meal celebrating a king! I had booked our reservation months in advance, so we had prime seats right in front of the stage and were first in line for the buffet. We felt special!

Just before the show started, the hostess got up on stage and thanked everyone for coming. She then announced that there were several couples in attendance who were celebrating that evening. She asked all of the couples on their honeymoon to stand. *Wait, what? ALL of the couples on their honeymoon?* Half of the audience stood. After a round of applause, she asked everyone who was celebrating an anniversary to stand. The other half stood. We all looked around at one another, clapping. In that moment, I was once again dragged back to earth with the realization that I was not special.

One of the greatest problems with people in general is that we *all* think we're special to some degree. We're different, sure, and we all have little quirks that make us unique, but unique is not the same thing as special. Think about it this way: you take a dump just about every morning and they're all unique, but you don't value any one of them more than the last, right? It's just more poop in a bowl. I know you think your poop *smells* better than the next person, but that's only because it's yours. People are the same way. We all like to *think* we're better or more important than the next guy, but that person feels the same way about you.

We all think of ourselves as uniquely good at something, which is true in most cases. You're better at some things than other things. You're probably better than most other people at one or two of the things you are best at and care the most about. There may be someone better than *you* at those things, but it still doesn't change the fact that you're better than *most*.

Take my brother, Mike, for example. With almost no formal training at all, he can play just about any instrument you put in his hands, and he's an incredible songwriter. He has a genuine, innate gift for music – a gift that can't be taught. He is a very special musician and I love being around him and listening to him create songs and melodies out of thin air. When we were in high school, however, we worked in the deli at the Langley Air Force Base commissary. At the deli, nobody cared that he was a savant with the guitar. They just wanted their ham and cheese.

Like I said, this is a two-way street. I remember one time when Mike and I were working the closing shift at the commissary, which is when all the service men and women come in after work and it's a mad house at the deli counter. At five o'clock, the flood gates opened and there was a line at least 20 people deep waiting to take a number at the counter and place their order. We already had 15 orders stacked up, which I was working to fill while Mike took new orders. The wait grew to about 30 minutes, since we had to cut all of the orders fresh, and I was the only one working the slicer. People were free to finish their other shopping while waiting and come back to pick up their deli order on the way out.

While we were scrambling to process orders as quickly as possible, a general in full uniform stepped to the counter, already slightly annoyed that he had to wait to take a number. He placed his order and Mike told him it would be about 30 minutes. The general looked at Mike like he was wearing a clown's wig instead of a deli cap and asked why he had to wait. Without breaking eye contact, Mike gestured with his thumb over his shoulder at the long list of orders already being processed and calmly explained that we were filling the orders as quickly as we could, but it would take us that long to get though his number in the line.

Now, this was a man who was used to having his every command obeyed immediately without question. To every other servicemember on base, he was *special,* and he knew it. But Mike and I weren't in the military — we were just a couple of high school kids who happened to work at a military installation. Honestly, if I had been the one taking orders rather than filling them, I probably would have pushed the general's order to the front of the line based on his status, but not Mike. I watched with a mixture of concern, admiration, and amusement as the general's face turned darker and darker shades of red. Finally, he slapped his hand on the top of the counter and snarled, "Do you know who I am?!?" Mike looked up from another order he was taking and casually replied, "You look to me like someone who is about to wait 30 minutes for his deli order," and went back to work. To Mike, that general was no more special than the airman who just got out of basic training.

Everyone *wants* to be special to some degree. You may not admit that to yourself easily, but on some level, if you search deep enough and are truly honest with yourself, you believe you've been put here on earth to do something special. You're *meant* for something great. In most cases, what you are really seeking is for *others* to think you're special – for them to notice you and celebrate you for being awesome. This is human nature. By the same token, everyone wants to *know* someone special, so they can say, "I saw that guy way back when, and I knew he was special!"

Ms. Andrews was my seventh-grade pre-algebra teacher. When she handed back tests, she called all the students who got an A up to her desk, one at a time, to hand them their results. The look on her face has always stuck with me – the way she looked at those kids with adoration. Without her saying a word, I could read her thoughts: "This one is *special* – he's going to be a real blessing to the world, and I helped him get there!"

I'm sure the reason I still remember that is because I was jealous of those kids. I was (and still am) terrible at math and there was no amount of studying that was going to get my name called in that class. I knew for sure that when it came to math, I was *not* special, but

I *wanted* to be! I wanted to stroll to the front of that classroom, chest puffed out with pride, feeling the envious eyes of my classmates on my back as I graciously accepted my test from this woman and slowly returned to my seat with a satisfied smile. I wanted to feel like more than just another deadbeat middle schooler. Sitting there watching my peers triumphantly accepting their perfect scores, I was sure I was destined to have a minimum-wage job for the rest of my life because I sucked at math.

I saw a similar phenomenon a bit later on. In college, I got a part-time job at a mid-sized newspaper, where I worked covering high school sports. Some of the full-time writers seemed to idolize the local kids, projecting them to be future stars in the NFL, giddy over the idea that they'd be able to say, "I saw them play in high school and knew they were special." The thing is, looking back now, none of those kids made it. Same thing with the kids in my math class. I haven't kept up with all of them, but I guarantee that those kids who got A's on their tests are not all CEOs raking in millions of dollars.

We spend far too much time as a society searching for "special" and idolizing it when we find it.

Here's something to think about: what happens when you *do* find someone or something special if it's not you? What did Ms. Andrews get? Did she get to spend her evenings telling her husband or her cats that she once handed a test back to some great entrepreneur? Maybe. What did those sports writers get? Did they have a good story for their buddies at the bar about how they saw some NFL stud rush for 300 yards in a high school game? Sure. But what did it really *get* them? Nothing. For some people, deciding another person is special is actually a bad thing. It reinforces that they are a nobody by comparison. It is a constant voice in their head reminding them they haven't accomplished nearly enough in life, and they've missed their own chance at greatness.

On the other hand, what do you get if you *do* turn out to be special? You may look at your idols and see fame, fortune, and great success, but behind every one of those images is a flawed human being, struggling with their own fears, problems, and self-doubt.

Many professional athletes live their lives in a constant state of pain. There's the physical pain of pushing their bodies to the limit day after day, breaking bones, spraining ankles, and taking drugs to mask the pain so they can push themselves further, doing untold damage to their long-term wellbeing. Then there is the emotional pain of handling life on the road away from family and the financial pain that comes with every sibling, cousin, and long-lost relative trying to borrow money while they try to figure out how to invest for the future.

I know you may not believe me, because it's rarely talked about at your age, but in 2009, *Sports Illustrated* did a study of former NFL and NBA players. It showed that after only two years in retirement, 78 percent of NFL players were either broke or struggling financially. Within five years of retirement, 60 percent of NBA players were broke. These guys were on top of the world, but a few short years later, the great majority of them have nothing to show for it. Think about it – most of these guys are still in their 30s or early 40s at best when they go broke – they still have most of their lives ahead of them – but they're back to where they started.

This is true of the music industry and Hollywood as well. Not only do many of these guys lose their fame and fortune after they're finished, but many of them are suffering while they're still in their prime. Who is at the top of the mountain right now? When you think about success in music, you eventually get around to Kanye West. The dude is super rich, super famous, and is successful in both the music and fashion industries. If you listen closely to his lyrics though, he will give you a peek behind the curtain. Consider this excerpt from a feature on Young Jeezy's record, *Put On*:

> *They say, "Damn, Yeezy Yeezy, you don't know us no more?"*
> *"You got that big fame, homie, and you just changed on me"*
> *You can ask big homie, man the top so lonely*
> *I ain't lyin*
> *So lonely, I ain't lyin!*

Other artists share a similar sentiment. When you are that rich and successful, it's really tough to tell the difference between your true friends and those who are just sticking around for the money. Even if you're not doing it for the money, the top can be a very lonely place.

I have been lucky enough to meet Travis Mash, a two-time world champion powerlifter and former world record holder. Travis has shared his story of pursuing his goal of becoming the world champ and what it cost him. He trained hard, with incredible determination, in pursuit of this singular goal. He missed major life events, including his friends' weddings, because it would have interfered with his training. He was so focused on his goal that he became blind to everything else around him, even to the point of choosing training over his relationship with his family.

Travis ultimately accomplished his mission, becoming world champion and setting a new world record in the process. You would expect this to be the happy ending to the story, but this is actually where it takes a downward turn.

Travis had been chasing this goal for so long and had imagined the way he would feel so many times in his head, that the actual accomplishment of his dream felt like a letdown. There were no parades, no fanfare, and almost no national media attention. At the end of the day, Travis Mash stepped off the podium and went back to his hotel, just like every other competitor.

In the days and weeks that followed, he found himself feeling lethargic, sometimes sickly, and constantly in pain. He initially believed that this was simply his body's reaction to the intense training he'd been engaged in, but when it didn't subside, he went to see a doctor. Travis couldn't believe the diagnosis: he was *depressed*. How could that be? He had achieved his goal, broken a long-standing record, and been crowned a world champion! How could he possibly be depressed?

Reality rarely measures up to expectation. You can build grand visions of success in your head and imagine how incredible you'll feel when you achieve your goals – when you *become special* – but this expectation is a mirage. Travis had sacrificed relationships, experiences, family time, and more in pursuit of this goal, but when he achieved it, the feeling of success didn't measure up to the expectations he'd created in his mind. This sent him into a spiral of depression. Despite being seen as special by the other competitors and spectators in the crowd that day, and despite owning a new record and world championship title, the top proved to be a very lonely place.

Travis's story doesn't end there. After diagnosing the lie that had fueled him for most of his life – that being a world champion, being *special*, would fulfill him and give his life meaning – he changed course and became a coach. Rather than focusing on himself exclusively, Travis now spends most of his time with his wife and family. He coaches younger athletes and prepares them for competition on the world stage in various sports while sharing his cautionary tale with them. He is now more fulfilled in his life than he ever felt as a competitor at the top of his game.

Here's what I want you to take away from this: rather than spending your time worrying about how special some other kid seems or what you can do to make yourself seem special to others, I want to you to start focusing on being *you* and doing what you love. Live for *yourself* and create a healthy balance between pursuing your goals and staying engaged in the present moment.

What really makes life special is living in a way that makes you happy. Constantly trying to be special can be exhausting and, in the big scheme of things, doesn't mean very much. By pursuing what makes you happy, without the expectation that reaching your goals will fulfill all of your dreams, you will enjoy your life a lot more and you won't spend as much time *wishing* you were something or someone else.

If you can remember this as you go through life, you will mitigate how much stress and anger you carry with you. If you go into every situation with the belief that you are somehow superior to others and that you deserve special treatment, you will be disappointed more often than not.

You may be thinking that it sounds impossible to be happy without being special. It's important to realize that being special is all a matter of perspective. Each one of us has a select group of people whom we consider special, but that group is different for everyone. How about this classic example: "your mom" jokes. We can tell them and laugh at them, but as soon as someone directs one at your own mom you go on the defensive and maybe get a bit angry. Why? Because *your* mom is special to you. You don't really care about someone else's mom the same way you care about your own.

You don't have to actually *do* anything to be seen as special by a select few people in your life. Your presence is special enough. For those people, you will be special regardless of how you live your life and what you choose to do with your time and career. If you've ever watched a show about prison, for example, every time there is a scene showing the visitation room, it's full of family and friends with tears in their eyes. Even though their loved one has done something bad enough to wind up in jail, they are still special enough for those people to spend their time visiting.

You can waste a lot of time and energy trying to be special. You can also experience a lot of anger and resentment if you go through life expecting everyone to treat you as though you're special. The fact of the matter is that you cannot control how others see you. It's impossible to be liked by everyone. Think about someone famous whom you admire, literally anyone. If you do an internet search of that person, or even just check out their social media feed, you won't have to look very far to find someone who dislikes them. There's a good chance that someone in your own group of friends thinks they're garbage! The mere fact that someone is famous is often enough for someone else to despise them, whether it's because that person stands for something they don't believe in or purely out of jealousy. Being special to the masses isn't all you think it is.

As I mentioned above, most of us want to be special because we think it means that we'll be liked by *all*. That's what I thought when I was your age. If I was liked by everybody, I'd be happy! For me, and I suspect this is true for many others, happiness was inextricably linked to the need to be special. I could not see how one could exist without the other. Happiness was the main goal I was seeking when I dreamt my big dreams and created extravagant lifestyles in my head.

Rather than go through all the trouble and heartache of trying to be special, why not just be happy instead? As it turns out, that's not as simple as it sounds.

Why is it that happiness seems like the hardest thing to grasp in the world?

It's always amazed me how many times in my life I've caught myself thinking, "when I achieve X, I'll be happy," or "if only X would happen, I'd be happy." When you start to depend on external variables to determine your happiness, you're truly in trouble.

When you have a thought like this, ask yourself a very important question: "Why?" *Why* will accomplishing a certain goal make you happy? *Why* will buying a new thing make you happy? *Why* will you be happy if a certain thing happens to you? If you take this exercise seriously and you're honest with yourself, you'll probably have to think for a while about the reasons that certain outcomes will make you happy. Regardless of the reason you ultimately settle on, they're all misleading.

Let's start with achieving a goal. There is nothing wrong with goal setting. In fact, you *need* to do it otherwise you'll lead a very unstructured life with no direction. However, goals should be viewed as steppingstones rather than the ultimate source of your happiness. Think about any goal you've ever achieved. How did you feel? For me, achieving a goal usually leads to one thought: I want more! If you are constantly seeking more, how could you ever be happy?

Think about Travis, the world champion powerlifter. He was sure that the world championship would secure happiness, but he wound up in a state of depression! If he had instead looked at that goal as a steppingstone on the *path* to happiness, he probably would have enjoyed the accomplishment a lot more. Viewing the achievement of your goals as steppingstones allows you to find happiness in those moments without believing that you've reached the end of the road. The end of the road can be a dark place because you've put all of your energy and expectations into that moment. It has no choice but to let you down because it means you have nowhere left to go!

Think about writing a paper for your English class. When you've spent several hours researching and writing something that can feel like a waste of your time, you are ecstatic when you finally finish! But what's really going on? You are celebrating reaching a *steppingstone*.

You are happy because you have achieved your goal of completing that paper, but you still have to take the exam, pass the class, and move on to the next grade. The completion of the paper was not the end of the road, just a steppingstone, a mile marker on your longer journey. Just about every accomplishment in life is that way, so if you can learn to see them as such, you won't suffer the same disappointment Travis did. There will always be one more pound to be lifted, one more touchdown to be thrown, one more championship to be won, and one more dollar to be earned.

Set goals. Achieve goals. Celebrate and enjoy the moment, allow yourself to be happy with your success, then keep going. It's not the end of the road, so don't expect the heavens to open up and all of your wildest dreams to come true. The road ends when you die. Until then, live in each moment. The space *between* the steppingstones is some of the most incredible time you'll have on this earth, so enjoy the struggle, embrace the suck, mourn your failures, and celebrate your successes, but don't put all of your energy into believing that happiness only occurs when you reach a pre-determined goal. It's just a steppingstone to what's next.

How about buying a new toy? Why do people stand in line for hours, or sometimes days, for the release of the next iPhone when they already have a perfectly functional phone in their hand? Why do people spend hundreds of dollars on new clothes and shoes when they've already got an entire closet full of things they hardly wear? It's because they *think* it will make them happy.

In reality, as soon as that new purchase is in your hands, you've got a few hours, maybe a few months of joy before it's no longer the best thing out there. As soon as a new phone launches, or someone drives up with a nicer car, or the new fall fashion lineup hits the rack, people begin to seek happiness in the next best thing. This is no mistake!

Marketing companies understand this concept, known as the *hedonic treadmill*. At its root, hedonism is the doctrine that pleasure, or happiness, is the highest good. The hedonic treadmill, therefore, is the idea that people will continue to seek pleasure and happiness through buying things that they believe will make them happy, but as long as the market continues to put out new and perceptively *better* things, people will continue to buy in search of happiness without actually going anywhere. Thus, people who seek happiness in *things* will ultimately be let down in the same way that people who chase goals will be. Each new purchase is merely a steppingstone on the way to buying the next great thing in a never-ending loop.

The dark side of the hedonic treadmill, of course, is that you can blow through a lot of cash by constantly buying things you don't actually need. Will a new phone *actually* make your life better? Or will it just give you a few upgrades to your existing phone that you really won't use all that much? Is it *really* worth spending hundreds of dollars on those few upgrades, or would you be better off saving that money for a big trip with your friends? Seeking happiness in *things* is just as much a fool's errand as seeking happiness in achieving a certain goal. It's just another step on the path, and if you think otherwise, you're in for a big letdown.

Finally, don't base your happiness on something for which you cannot control the outcome. Easy example: you'll be happy if your team wins the Super Bowl. This idea may seem silly to a lot of people, but for others, it definitely rings true.

When I was living in Denver, I noticed that the city had a remarkably different vibe on Monday depending on if the Broncos won or lost a game the previous day. Some people are so engrossed in the exploits of other people on TV, playing a game, that they let it impact their own personal happiness, even though they have absolutely no way to influence that outcome! One time, I was watching a game with a friend of mine and the Broncos blew a fourth quarter lead and lost the game. He looked at me and said, "Well, I guess I'm going to call in sick tomorrow. My boss is always in a terrible mood when the Broncos lose, and I can't stand to be around him." How crazy is that?

The Broncos won the Super Bowl in 2016, after not having won it since 1999. The city went crazy. There were fireworks going off in every neighborhood, people celebrating in the streets and the energy level was as electric as I'd ever seen it in the 10 years I lived there. There was a huge parade and tens of thousands of people flooded the streets to celebrate their heroes. It was incredible. At the end of the day, however, it was over. Just like that, things returned to normal, and life resumed. What did those die-hard fans get? Did their lives improve in any way? Not really. They got the chance to buy a shirt commemorating the victory, but nothing else really changed for most of them. Was that one moment of happiness worth the 17 years of depression leading up to it? Would you trade 17 years of your life – in your case, perhaps your *entire* life – for one day of joy over something you had no real part in?

The funny thing is, the athletes themselves understand this better than the fans. The players – the ones who actually impact the outcome of the games – realize that a loss isn't the end of the world and, in most cases, isn't even something to get upset about. Have you ever watched a post-game interview with a player whose team just lost a game? The reporter will typically ask something like, "how demoralizing is a loss like this?" The player will often respond with something like, "well, we did some things wrong, but there were a few good moments. We'll learn from this experience, build on it for next week and put this one behind us." Even in a championship game, when the whole season is on the line, many players won't get overly emotional about a loss. Sure, it's good to learn from mistakes and remember how it feels to fail – that's what drives you to get better – but it's not a be-all, end-all event. The players realize that each game is merely a steppingstone on the path to something more.

Sports is just one example, but there are many others: I'll be happy when my boss gets fired and I get a raise. I'll be happy when I win the lottery. I'll be happy when I get a girlfriend. I'll be happy when…. The list goes on and on. Once again, these are steppingstones along the path of life. If you rest all your faith and hope in the outcome of a scenario that you have limited or no control over, you are essentially *giving up control of your own happiness*.

So, what's the answer? You want to be happy, but there's no real formula for it!

Here's my advice: Don't chase happiness.

Happiness is defined as the state of being happy. The state of *being* happy. It's not a *thing* that you can hold and touch. It's a state of *being*.

I recently read a book called *The Subtle Art of Not Giving a F*ck*, by Mark Manson. In it, he makes a very keen observation. All the self-help books out there that claim to help people find happiness are missing the point. They give advice on ways to get happier and lay out frameworks for defining happiness in your life. If you're constantly in pursuit of something, however, you're never really there. In short, there is nothing you can do that will result in your ultimate happiness – it's a moving target. Even if you achieve it briefly, it will always escape again.

The key is to learn to be happy – to achieve that state of *being* – in your everyday life.

As I'm writing this, for example, I'm on the back porch of a house that I'm renting – it's not even *my* house! I'm sitting on some cheap patio furniture on an overcast day with a cup of coffee doing something I love: writing. I'm content and happy with my life despite the fact that I'm not rich or famous. I'm not special to the rest of the world, but I'm loved by my family, content in my day-to-day life, and overall, I'm *happy*. I've stopped putting all my hope and expectation into believing that things and experiences will make me happy. Sure, I still pursue those things and experiences, and I'm often happy when I achieve them, but I have stopped expecting them to fulfill my dreams. In this mindset, I am able to enjoy and appreciate each steppingstone before moving on to the next one.

Don't get me wrong, 15 years ago I would have read those words and gotten depressed. Fifteen years ago, I was sure I needed to be special. In order to be happy, I needed to be someone whose name was known around the globe! I was tired of the Ms. Andrews' of the world looking at *other* people with adoration in their eyes. I was tired of hearing gray-haired sports writers pinning accolades on high school seniors who were running over freshman half their size. I wanted to *be* the guy they talked about. I wanted to throw 95 miles an hour, play Major League Baseball, and then become a successful businessman traveling the world closing deals and vacationing on my private jet and 100-foot yacht. I wanted to be *special*! I didn't realize that by thinking in those terms I had already forfeited control of my own happiness by making it dependent on variables that I could not influence or change.

I don't think there was a singular defining moment for me. I didn't wake up one morning and realize that I wasn't cut out for those things. It was more of a slow realization over time that I wasn't happy with where I was in life, I hadn't put in nearly enough work to accomplish any of those things, and the even greater realization that accomplishing those goals I thought I wanted wasn't going to fulfill me anyway. I knew I had to start making changes to the way I looked at my life and the way I measured my success. The biggest change that I made, which has continued to work without fail is practicing one key thought.

Gratitude.

For me, practicing gratitude has broken down walls of anger and resentment that have festered beneath the surface of my life for a long time. It is very easy, especially living in a country like the United States, to forget how good we have it and how small most our troubles truly are, relative to others.

Practicing gratitude is as simple as taking a moment to pause and think about where you are and the problems you're facing, then put them in context. For example, you may be thinking that it's unfair that your friend got a car for his 16th birthday, while you only got a card from your mom with $10 in it. You still have to ask to *borrow* a car if nobody else is using it. FML, right? Instead of feeling envious of your friend and resentful of your own situation, be grateful your family has a car you can borrow and the money to insure an additional driver.

Suppose you get permission to borrow the car to go to a concert you want to see. You and your friends try to get tickets online, but it's already sold out. You can still be grateful that you can go out with your friends to do something else rather than working some part-time job at a fast-food joint on a Saturday night because you need to help support your family.

Suppose you have to work at a fast-food joint on a Saturday night to help your family pay the bills. You can still be grateful for the roof over your head and food on the table to eat.

Suppose you don't have enough to eat, and your family doesn't always make enough money to make ends meet. You can still be grateful that you have each other and there are food pantries where you can go to pick up a little something to hold you over until the next paycheck comes in.

Suppose the food pantry is out of donations and you're going to go hungry for the next few days. You can still be grateful that you live in the United States instead of some third-world country where you could be sold into slavery as a child and never know what it's like to make a decision for yourself or have the opportunity to change your lot in life and determine your own future.

The list goes on. Regardless of where you are in your life, if you live in this country – or any developed nation for that matter – you are already better off than most people in the world. I'm not saying that everything is *fair*. I recognize that injustice, discrimination, and oppression are realities in every society. However, regardless of where you find yourself in the present moment, you can find a way to put your problems into perspective. You can begin to see the gifts and blessings that are abundant in your life that you never noticed because you were too busy complaining or wishing you had *more*.

It can be hard to do, especially with so little life experience at this point in your journey, but finding joy in the little things around you will soften you to the anger and resentfulness that are currently present in your everyday life. Let go of the little things that don't matter. Stop focusing on being special and thinking about all the things you *don't* have and focus instead on what's good in your life. Take time to appreciate those things and be grateful. As you make this a consistent practice, you will find that happiness will become more abundant in your life without trying to chase or catch it.

You may not be "special" to the world at large, but you do have special qualities and gifts that set you apart and will make you special to certain people in your life. Be grateful for those gifts and those people and be at peace with the knowledge that you can be happy without having to be special.

Love,
Tom

Chapter 11

The truth of the matter

Dear Ivan,

Hopefully my last nine letters have helped you see some of these perceived "truths" for what they really are: a bunch of bullshit. It's time to change gears. In the pages that follow, I'm going to share some *real* truths with you. I hope that you will consider these next letters carefully and approach them with an open mind and an open heart.

This is *my* truth. It is what I have lived and experienced as real. Some of the stories I tell and points I make in the following letters may challenge your current beliefs and understanding of the world. Some may insult or offend you. You may doubt my point of view or reject it outright. That's fine. It's expected.

Use the tools you learned in the previous letters to think critically about the message and see what resonates when you take off your armor. There is no one to judge you but yourself. Give yourself space to think about these truths and consider how they can be applied in your life. You may have not yet experienced some of the things I write about. Other topics will be so fresh and present in your life that you haven't had the time or space to think about them objectively.

These next letters are intended to provide some guidance for the *now*, as well as the future. This is the shit I *wish* I knew in high school, not just to help me through those four years, but to help me see the bigger picture beyond graduation. I hope these letters help you understand what is happening around you at this time in your life and how much – or how little – it will actually shape your life moving forward.

Some of the information will be immediately relevant in your life and some will become more relevant over the next few years. Bookmark this page and revisit these letters from time to time over the course of your journey. As your life experience broadens, you may find that your understanding of these next letters evolves. Topics and stories that seem irrelevant or unrelatable to you at one point in time will suddenly make perfect sense and provide comfort and guidance at another point, so keep that in mind as you go.

Let's start talking truth!

>Love,
>Tom

Chapter 12

The truth about sex and pornography

Dear Ivan,

Alright, let's talk about sex. I'm going to go out on a limb here and guess that you opened the book straight to this chapter. Am I right? I know that's what I would have done! It's cool, man. Close the door and lock it if you want. You don't want your mom to catch you reading this chapter because that will lead to a very uncomfortable conversation! Yes, I'm definitely laughing at you right now because I've been where you are, and I know what you're feeling. Settle in and let's have this very personal conversation.

Regardless of what else is happening in your life at any given moment, sex is never far from your mind. Am I right? I know you're turning a bit red right now. The room is getting warmer, and you can feel your heart beating in your ears because you know it's true. You're also looking around to see if anyone is watching you, as if they know what book you're reading and what the words say. You don't want them to uncover your dirty little secret! Don't worry about it man, it's not dirty and it's definitely not a secret. It's normal to be curious about this topic.

I have been obsessed with sex from, well, pretty much the very beginning. When I was in kindergarten – or maybe even preschool – my mom was using flash cards to teach me the parts of the human body. She'd call out a body part and I'd point to it on myself. I don't remember exactly how it happened, but at some point, I learned that girls don't have penises. That blew my little mind. "If girls don't have penises, then how do they pee?" Legit question from a kindergartner. Awkward situation for a first-time mom.

After that mind-melting revelation, I was dedicated to learning what a girl's "privates" looked like. This proved harder than expected. Apparently, most kindergarten-age girls aren't as curious about the anatomical differences between themselves and their knuckle-dragging counterparts as we are. Who can blame them, really? When they see one moron run headfirst into the slide because he wasn't watching where he was going, and across the playground another takes a six-foot fall and lands in a heap under the jungle gym because he thought he could hang from his feet like a monkey, they probably assume they're the superior beings and whatever differences we have, we can keep! Needless to say, "I'll show you mine if you show me yours" didn't go over as a seamless transaction.

I learned about sex at a much earlier age than most. In 2nd grade, I had a female classmate who lived in the apartment above my family. She had a sister who was 16, pretty much the age you are now, and going through the same changes. She knew about sex and shared some of her knowledge with her little sister, who then shared it with me. My classmate also agreed to the "I'll show you mine if you show me yours" offer, which was an incredible milestone, but it generated more questions.

Of course, getting my sex education second hand from another 2nd grader rather than my parents or anyone else with actual experience had its shortcomings, but this was a *covert* operation! I learned that sex meant a boy and a girl getting naked and rubbing their bodies together. This seemed logical, but it still lacked some critical details. Of course, at that age, you take what is given to you as fact, no matter what.

Later, I learned from this same friend that rubbing your bodies together sometimes included putting your penis *inside* of the girl. Whaaaat? Stop the world – how does *that* work? Does it accidentally fall in there or something? That seemed like an unlikely scenario. How could you get that limp little earthworm in your pants into another person? Do they make a shoehorn for something like that? It seemed like a lot of work. Wouldn't that hurt? New mission: learn physics and unravel the dynamics of penile implantation.

As a good older brother does, I shared this revelation with my younger brother, who promptly went to our mom and dad to fact-check what I'd said. What the fuck? That was supposed to stay between us, bro!

Mom and dad called me over and asked where I got my information. After revealing my source, they confirmed the basics were true, but offered no further elaboration on the process. I'm sure it was very uncomfortable for both parties, and I couldn't wait to get out of there! They ended the short conversation by offering to answer any questions that I had – now or in the future. Cool. Thanks guys. Definitely not taking you up on that one.

Mortified that my parents had learned of my immense sexual knowledge, but afraid to ask the real questions I had, my miseducation continued in the 4th grade. I happened to be party to a conversation some of my classmates were having about sex. "Why does sex have to smell like tuna fish?" one of them asked. "Why can't it smell like bananas or something?" That's a direct quote. I'll never forget it. I didn't know where these guys got this information, but again, I believed it. I could now build upon my knowledge base: a boy and a girl get naked, rub their bodies together, sometimes your penis accidentally falls in, and it smells like tuna fish. Sounds like a good time ... I guess?

For all the time I spent thinking about sex and theorizing with my buddies about it, most of it remained a mystery until 5th grade, when I discovered that the school was going to be offering "sex education" class for 30-minutes at the end of each school day for a week. Finally! Something worth learning would be taught at school! I was too embarrassed to ask my mom and dad to sign the permission slip, but I got it done by burying it in a stack of homework assignments that *cough* needed to be signed. In retrospect, I'm absolutely sure they read it and knew exactly what they were signing, but at the time, I thought I was pretty sneaky.

I don't remember many details about that class, other than we were separated from the girls, who had their own class. The majority of the time was spent on one slide – the female anatomy. I was captivated, along with the rest of the boys in the room, by the diagram showing the cross-section of a vagina, uterus, Fallopian tubes, and ovaries. It was nothing like I'd expected. It didn't look anything like what I'd seen in my show-and-tell sessions with my friend in 2nd grade, and it changed the way I looked at girls forever.

While it was interesting, it didn't offer the information I was truly interested in. On the next-to-last day, the teacher put out a shoebox and suggested that anyone who had a question that they didn't want to ask out loud write it down and put it in the box. This was it! This was my chance! At the end of that afternoon, I took a pencil and a piece of paper and carefully crafted my question, writing with my left hand to disguise my handwriting: "HoW dO yOu HaVe SeX?"

The next day, the teacher went through the slips of paper one by one. The questions ranged from easy like, "Will I grow hair all the way up my penis?" to more complex queries like, "What if you accidentally pee in a girl?" and, "What if you accidentally put your penis in the wrong hole since there are three?" Tough questions to be sure, but not *my* question. The teacher looked like he was being grilled by the FBI about a suspected terrorist plot. Poor guy – I'm sure he didn't expect 5th graders to have questions of this caliber. His answers to these questions were, "Probably not," "You won't – just trust me on that one," and "Don't worry – she'll let you know." Fucking genius. This guy was great at avoiding real answers. He had a real future as a politician.

Finally, he got to *my* question. He read it aloud, struggling through my left-handed block letters, and the whole room went silent. All eyes were on him, anxiously awaiting this answer. We were finally going to get the step-by-step instructions on how you actually *have* sex! It felt like an eternity before he finally spoke. He started a couple different times, but paused, looking helplessly around the room. There was nobody to rescue him. In the end, he simply gave us a re-cap of the anatomy that we'd discussed and talked a little bit about the development of a baby after the egg was fertilized. We all left, crestfallen.

The point of this elaborate backstory is this: there is no blueprint for sex. It's a mystery to *everyone* at the beginning. Moreover, while all of us were interested in how to have sex, we missed a lot of the real important information, like what was happening to our bodies, why we were growing hair in new places, and why we were "peeing the bed" at night, just a little bit, but it made our underwear crusty.

Sex is a very confusing topic. I know you have a lot of questions, but you may not know who to ask. Let me share a few thoughts with you that will hopefully help answer some of them.

Let's start with pornography. What is real?

I was introduced to pornography around the same time I was playing show-and-tell with my 2nd grade classmate. Actually, calling it porn is probably a stretch. My dad was interested in photography and had a subscription to a magazine dedicated to the hobby. In one issue, I stumbled across an article titled, "They Still Shoot Nudes, Don't They?" I didn't know what nudes were, so you can imagine my surprise and elation when I saw the accompanying images. They were very tasteful, artistic photographs, but they were naked women – and you could see their boobs!

My elation quickly turned to panic as I re-read the title. *Who are THEY, and why would they STOP shooting nudes? This is the best thing EVER! Please, please, please let them keep shooting nudes!*

Fearing that I may be clinging to one of the last relics of a bygone era in which people took pictures of naked women, I hid the magazine in my bedroom. I shared a room with my brother, so I showed him the pictures too. I couldn't keep something this exciting to myself, nor could I risk getting caught with it and not having anyone else to blame it on.

It was too good to last. A day or so later, when I thought my dad was outside, I walked into our bedroom and found my brother playing with some toys.

"Where's the magazine with the naked ladies?" I asked him. He looked up from what he was doing and froze, eyes wide and mouth agape, looking over my head. I turned around just in time to see the back of my dad's head as he passed our doorway, walking down the hall. He didn't stop, or say anything to us, and I hoped that he hadn't heard me. When we got home from school the next day, however, the magazine was gone. I searched the house multiple times, but never saw it again.

Shit. I hope they keep shooting nudes, whoever they are! Godspeed, gentlemen. Godspeed!

I lamented the loss of that magazine for the next five years. Then, in 7th grade, a friend of mine found a dirty magazine at a construction site near his house. *They did it! They kept shooting nudes!* And these weren't the tasteful, artistic nudes from a photography magazine either! After that, I spent hours combing over every construction site I passed, trying to find a magazine of my own.

For most young men, 7th-9th grade is about the time you hit the next real milestone in your sexual awakening: the first time you realize how things *really* work. It's a memory you'll carry with you forever.

By my freshman year of high school, between late-night internet browsing and the pooling of resources with friends at school, I had amassed a small collection of illicit photos. One evening, I was sitting in my room, looking through the treasure trove that I'd successfully managed to hide from my parents and listening to some loud music. That little earthworm in my pants had grown exponentially – like one of those little dissolvable capsules that you drop in water and watch the sponge inside it turn into the shape of an animal and expand to 10 times its original size. That in itself is amazing. Then I realized that it felt *good* to touch it. If some is good, more must be better. Then, eventually, it's unbelievable, amazing, incredi...*blah*! Whoa! What was *that*?!? Holy shit! I did it! It worked!

Learning to masturbate is a lot like learning you can start a fire with a magnifying glass. I wanted to get up, throw my hands in the air and yell, "I have made fire!" Then fear set in and I realized that, holy shit, it's dinner time and I have a mess to clean up and evidence to get rid of!

Of course, after that initial panic attack, all I could think about was doing it again ... and again. Just like when I discovered the power of the magnifying glass, and all I wanted to do was burn as many things as I could, this new-found activity consumed most of my daily thoughts and set my imagination ablaze.

I had very conflicted feelings about all of this. Masturbating felt so *good*, and it didn't cost any money! It was the most fun you could have for free! At the same time, I felt guilty about it, like I was doing something wrong and dirty. I went through peaks and valleys – alternating between periods where I jerked off multiple times a day and periods where I tried not to do it at all. During the times when I was trying to be "good," I always wound up having wet dreams. This was even worse, because I didn't want my mom asking questions about why I was changing my sheets so frequently.

Regardless of how you're raised and what community and cultural values are taught to you on this subject, you can't escape nature. As you enter into sexual maturity, your body changes. Your hormones don't give a shit what your church or culture has to say about it. It's going to start producing semen like crazy, and it's going to escape in one way or another. It's not a switch or a faucet you can turn off.

Imagine you're filling up a water balloon and the faucet gets stuck in the on position. You can pull the balloon off the faucet and release some of the water in a controlled manner – masturbating – or you can leave it on the faucet and see how far it can expand. The longer you leave it on the faucet, the more the water pressure builds in the balloon. In real life, this can become painful

– it's what's known as "blue balls." Ultimately, the balloon will burst, and you'll experience a wet dream.

Masturbating is *normal* and it's healthy. You don't need to feel bad or guilty about it. In addition, masturbating is the best way to experiment with what you like and don't like, which will make sex with another person a lot more enjoyable later on.

One thing you do need to be aware of, however, is the material you use when you masturbate and how it can potentially lead to a *negative* impact on your sex life in the future.

The advent of the Internet arguably did more for sex education than anything else in history, and not necessarily in a good way. You no longer have to find a girl willing to take turns dropping trou to see what the female anatomy looks like. The world of sex is at your fingertips on demand. It seems like you have to try *not* to find porn! You no longer have to use your imagination to find your X-rated entertainment and you can spend hours in your room practicing your craft.

Here's the thing about internet porn – or any kind of pornography – most of it isn't real. I mean, yes, the people you see are actually having sex, but it's not an accurate representation of what sex really is. Most of the sex you will find online is about as real as a WWE wrestling match.

As a kid, I used to watch these huge guys slamming their opponents into the mat, hammering them with elbows and metal folding chairs and throwing one another out of the ring. This was all presented to me under the guise of "wrestling." These guys are monsters! How can they continue to get up from hits like that? I believed it was real until I considered trying out for the high school wrestling team and realized that what I'd be doing was really quite different. Talk about a letdown! You want me to wear *what*? You expect me to let another dude wrap his legs around my head and break the cartilage in my ears as we roll around a sweaty mat? Where's my sweet headband? Where are the chairs?

Looking at it another way, if real sex is like your actual high school experience, then pornography is like Hogwarts from the Harry Potter series. There are a few common themes: there are boys and girls, they go to classes together and have awkward social interactions outside of class, but that's where the similarities end. You don't have classes on how to cast spells, there are no monsters lurking in the girls' bathroom, and floating stairways and the magic sorting hat are all made up. It's a *fantasy*.

If you didn't *know* that Hogwarts was a made-up place and it was presented to you as the reality of high school, how would you know any better until you got there? You wouldn't! It's the same with sex. If you are watching porn as a means to inform yourself on what sex looks like, how it works, and how you're *supposed* to do it, you're in for a big letdown when you discover that reality is far from what you were led to believe.

The people in the pornography business are *performers*, just like the WWE wrestlers. They map out a scenario, some more outrageous and unrealistic than others, and then go *perform* it. The positions they use are designed to get the best camera angle, not to provide the most pleasure. The sounds of "pleasure" are mostly fake.

Spoiler: most girls don't scream and moan the whole time, but that doesn't mean they're not enjoying it or that you're doing it wrong. Do you scream and moan while you're jerking off? In addition, most porn is made for men, by men. Because it's a fantasy, they make it look like *all* the girls are into it, *all* the time. Depending on the genre you see, you may be led to believe that girls like being tied up, slapped around, strangled, having penises rammed down their throats while they gag, and any number of other situations that result in them being treated as an object for male domination and pleasure.

If this is how you approach sex – thinking this is reality – you're going to be terrible at it. Most women have no interest in any of that stuff, certainly not in an abusive way. If you think the way to make a woman orgasm is by using your dick as a jack hammer and pounding away as hard and fast as you can, you're going to be disappointed when you fail, and even more disappointed in the performance review she gives to her friends.

Moreover, watching porn can be detrimental to your psychological health and self-confidence. Remember, you're watching professional performers! When you watch a Major League Baseball game and you see some monster hit a 495-foot home run, do you think that you're inadequate because your longest is only 350 feet? Of course not! He's a professional! He's got genetic gifts and athletic ability that he's leveraged into a career as a professional hitter. Even among all the other professional ball players out there, there are very few who can hit a ball that far. It's the same thing with porn. The guys in the industry just have a different genetic gift. They are the exception, not the rule. However, if you're watching porn to learn about sex without considering this perspective, you're going to feel really inadequate when you look at what's in your hand versus what's on the screen, among other points of comparison.

There's a hidden side to the porn industry, just like professional athletics: many of these guys use performance enhancing drugs. There are penile injections – literally sticking a needle in your dick – that help them keep erections longer. In some cases, they can hardly feel anything at all after a while, which is part of the reason they can last so long. Where's the pleasure in that? Sometimes the production crew will use a pump and fake jizz to make that high-volume, high-velocity finishing shot because the performer is literally worn out and too tired to do it for real. Just like the WWE guys who use hidden razors to cut themselves to make that chair to the face look bad ass, there are tricks to the trade that you are unaware of as a casual observer. It's not real.

So, if porn isn't an accurate representation of sex, what *is* real sex like? How do you know when you're ready to try it? What can you expect?

I'll save you the suspense. The first time you have sex, it's probably not going to go very well.

While sex is a basic instinct, it still requires practice. Yes, I know that you've been practicing regularly on your own, but that's a controlled environment. Everything is literally in your hands. When it comes time to partner up and actually perform in front of an audience – even an audience of just one other person – the game completely changes.

Think about the first time you did *anything*. How did you feel the first time you tried to ride a bike on your own without training wheels? How about the first time you dug in to take an at-bat in a live baseball game with someone other than your coach pitching to you? What about when the curtain came up on opening night of your school musical and you were standing alone in the spotlight? Or how about the first time you tried to merge onto the highway when you still had your learner's permit?

In all of those scenarios, you had plenty of practice before the actual event. You spent hours with someone walking behind you, holding the seat of your bike so you wouldn't fall. You had weeks in the batting cages and at practice with your own team. You had rehearsals and dry runs to make sure you knew your lines. You spent hours in the parking lot practicing accelerating, braking, and using your turn signals.

Despite all of this practice and preparation, you are still nervous, a bit shaky from the adrenaline, and maybe a little nauseous when it comes to that first ride, first at-bat, first scene, and first merge. You feel vulnerable and a little bit *naked*. It can also be incredibly exhilarating! Why? Because suddenly the *consequences* are real. You have performance anxiety! Someone else can see you, judge you, and potentially embarrass you. It's the same with sex, only perhaps even more so.

When it relates to sex, this combination of excitement and terror, resulting in performance anxiety, can manifest in many ways. Some guys get so hypersensitive that they cum before they can even get their pants off. The anticipation of what's about to happen can be so mentally stimulating that just kissing and touching is enough for their body to fire off the first shot before the game ever really gets started. Other guys can get so worked up thinking about what they should be doing, how they should be acting, and trying so hard to get it right that their mind takes them out of the moment and they can't even get hard – or they fall flat before the big release.

My experience was the latter. It was the summer between my junior and senior year of high school. My girlfriend, Annie, and I had been dating for a few months, and we had been really good friends for about two years before that. We had talked extensively about sex, and both of us were ready to try it. Annie's parents had gone out of town to visit her older sister and she had the house to herself. We had done plenty of making out in various stages of undress in the preceding months, we both knew this night was going to be *THE* night.

I stopped by a convenience store on the way to her house to buy condoms, which was another terrifying experience. I browsed around until all the other customers left and I triple-checked to make sure I had enough money before I brought them up to the counter. I imagined the cashier getting on the loudspeaker and saying, "attention in the store, this virgin doesn't have enough money for condoms. Can anyone spare fifty cents?" My heart was racing, and I was sweating when I finally checked out. Nothing happened. It was just my own insecurities manifesting in my head. It was a harbinger of things to come.

When I got to Annie's house, we ate dinner and started watching a movie, but quickly decided that we could skip the formalities since her parents weren't there and just take the party upstairs.

I'd been in her bedroom before, back when we were just friends working on a school project together, but this felt very different. Even though we knew her parents were hours away, every time a car drove down the street we peeked through the blinds to make sure they weren't coming home early or had laid a trap for us and were preparing to catch us in the act.

Eventually, the moment of truth came. It was the first time either of us had stood in front of another person completely naked, and it elicited all of the feelings I talked about before: a bit light-headed, heart pounding, slightly nauseous, but not in an about-to-puke way.

We made out for a bit and then decided it was time for the main event. We moved over to her bed and she laid on her back, looking up at me. This was also the first time I'd ever tried to use a condom. I unrolled the first one and tried to put it on. That did *not* work. It was like trying to put a wet tube sock on your foot by just holding the open end and trying to cram it in there. Annie looked at the instructions on the box and eventually helped me figure it out, but by that time, the anxiety and change of focus had started to let some of the air out of my balloon.

Pro tip: when you use a condom, you don't unroll it all at once. Unroll it just a little bit and gather the tip in your fingers and then put it on your penis like a little hat and use your other hand to roll it all the way down. If you're really nervous about how this works, practice it by yourself during one of your "training sessions" in your room. If nothing else, practicing by yourself first can help mitigate some performance anxiety since you'll already know how to suit up when it's time for the real thing.

Once we got the mechanical intricacies of the condom figured out, the next challenge was actually making an entrance. Trying to find her vagina with the latex-coated tip of my penis while laying on top of her and leaning on one arm for support was like trying to feel my way around a room I'd never been in before while wearing a blindfold. Once I thought I'd found it until she said, "nope, not there." It was just like my 5th grade sex ed teacher had said! It felt like an eternity, and all the while my anxiety about being "good at sex" and making the first time special were eroding my erection.

We finally figured it out, but it didn't last very long. It was her first time too and it was a bit painful for her. I'm not sure how long we kept at it. A minute? Maybe two? Between my slowly deflating penis and ego, and the discomfort on her face, we decided we'd had enough fun for one night.

Neither one of us had an orgasm. Neither one of us thought it was amazing, although technically it *was* the best sex either of us had ever had. Regardless of this less-than-ideal outcome, we were both ecstatic! I drove home that night in a trance-like state. I had finally done it – my 10-year quest for sex, which began as a kindergartner, had finally reached its end.

For as terrible as it truly was, it was a special moment for both of us. We had literally bared all of ourselves to another person for the first time and we had survived. It was an amazing *emotional* experience and it left us both with a strong desire to do it again. Over the course of our relationship, it just got better and better – with *practice*.

That's the reality of your first time right there. You cannot expect to be God's gift to women your first time out. Don't be ashamed of it. This kind of thing is *normal* and should be expected rather than feared. If you know what worst-case scenario to expect, it won't be so intimidating.

On that note, I'll offer you a valuable insight – if you truly want to be a great lover, *ask her what she likes*. If you are trying to impress a girl by taking her out to a nice dinner, you'd ask what kind of food she likes first, right? Apply the same philosophy! In addition, learn to use your hands and mouth. Your penis is primarily for *your* pleasure and making babies. While intercourse might feel good for her, it's not always the ultimate source of pleasure and it can be difficult for many women to reach orgasm that way. If you are skilled with your hands and mouth, you will be much more successful in ensuring she has a pleasurable experience, and it will alleviate some of your anxiety over whether or not your penis is big enough. Ultimately, penis size matters far more to *us* than it does to women, especially if you have the extra skills to satisfy her.

If you do it right – and by right, I mean choosing a partner and a time that feels right to both of you – you can still expect your first sexual experience to be magical and amazing regardless of how terrible it may be in retrospect.

Now let's step beyond the physical and look at what *really* makes sex an incredible experience: the emotional connection.

To start off, let's get one thing out in the open: not everyone in high school is having sex. It may *seem* like it, but a lot of it is bluster and exaggeration.

Early in my junior year of high school, I came home one day and found my brother, a freshman, in his room, visibly upset. This was uncharacteristic of him, so I knew something must really be wrong. When I asked him what it was, he told me that he'd just learned that one of his best friends had sex for the first time.

The reason he was so upset was that he was under the impression that *everyone* was having sex but him! In his irrational state, he stated that his friend was doing it, I was doing it ... everyone was doing it but him!

At that point in my life, I wasn't doing it either. I wasn't even dating Annie yet. My brother believed I must be having sex because I had become fairly popular, started for the varsity baseball team, and was dating a girl named Chelsea, who was on the cheerleading squad. The truth was that I hadn't even kissed Chelsea yet! I told my brother this and it made him feel a little better, but then I addressed the real issue: why did he care that his friend had sex with this girl? I knew who she was, and she wasn't someone that me or my brother found attractive at all. I asked him if *he* would have slept with her and he said, "of course not!" So then what's the big deal, I asked him? I joked that, all things considered, he was actually *ahead* of the game, and we both had a good laugh about that.

The moral of the story is this: just because you *can* sleep with someone doesn't mean you should. Sex is one of those things that will follow you around. Who you choose to sleep with is a big decision and shouldn't be taken lightly. Let me repeat that: just because you *can* doesn't mean you *should.*

I'm not going to give you the spiel about sexually transmitted diseases or try to scare you with pictures of peoples' genitals covered in sores and warts. Sure, that stuff is real, and you should definitely protect yourself from these physical risks. Wear a condom and don't be an idiot. Pay attention in sex ed when they teach you how to put one on and take it seriously.

The real damage I'm going to warn you against is emotional – the stuff they don't really talk to you about in sex ed, especially as young men. You can recover from most STDs. They may be painful or inconvenient for a time, but most of them will clear up with the right medical attention. Emotionally and psychologically, however, your decisions can carry much more significant and long-lasting consequences.

When people talk about the emotional consequences of sex, they tend to talk about it exclusively from the female perspective, but we are human too. We have feelings too. We experience emotional consequences just like women do – we just have a much harder time admitting it and talking about it. As men, we tend to bottle up our emotions, to not show weakness in any way, especially when it comes to relationships with women.

That's an unfair standard, and I want you to know that it's 100% OK to have these feelings.

Time for another thought experiment: if you were sitting next to an acquaintance and you noticed a $20 bill hanging out of her purse, you could easily grab it while she wasn't looking and she'd have no idea that you'd taken it. You'd conveniently have an extra $20 in your pocket and maybe you'd feel pretty excited about that for a little while. Later on, however, you'd probably feel bad about taking it, right? In this scenario, you have the option to return the money and apologize. If you're really feeling guilty and too ashamed to own up to what you did, you could even make up a story about finding the $20 on the ground and later wondering if she may have dropped it – giving her the opportunity to tell you that she had, in fact, lost that money and *thank* you for returning it.

Casting that same scenario in a sexual context, there's a good chance that you could wind up really regretting the decision to sleep with someone purely out of convenience. Unlike with the cash situation, however, you can't give it back. Once you've made the decision to have sex with someone, you can't go back and undo that decision. You're stuck with it – the potential guilt, feelings of uncleanliness, a slight nausea in the pit of your stomach – forever. Choose wisely. You will have plenty of opportunity in your life to meet people whom you really care about and actually *want* to sleep with.

Going back to the story about me and my brother, it's important to note that others can *assume* a lot about you based on circumstantial or even completely fabricated evidence. My brother *assumed* that I was having sex with Chelsea just because we were both good looking, popular people. That isn't always the case! I spent a lot of time on a school bus driving to and from baseball games. There were plenty of conversations on that bus about sex, but the truth is that a very small minority of the team was sexually active. There was a lot of storytelling, and a lot of the guys were content letting others believe the rumors, but in reality, they were just as clueless (and sexless) as the rest of us.

In high school, sex is a lot like fishing: partially-true or completely false stories exaggerated to epic proportions. "You should have seen the size of this monster I caught! It was at least three feet long and weighed about 15 pounds! It nearly pulled me out of the boat trying to reel it in. I lost my sunglasses and everything! It's too bad I forgot to take a picture." Guys will tell big stories about it, and some tend to get more far-fetched as the story is spread and re-told, but with nobody there to witness it, how can you ever know if they're telling the truth? Regardless of whether some other guy is having sex or not, you shouldn't let it affect the way you make your personal decision. As I mentioned before, it's a big decision and it should really be something you think a lot about before deciding to do the deed.

You may not be ready for sex, or you may not *want* to have sex yet and that's completely fine too! Some guys are committed to saving themselves for marriage. If that's the way you want to go, I encourage you to stay true to yourself and strong in your convictions. There is nothing wrong with this approach and it's not a reason to make fun of someone. I had several good friends in high school, and many more in college, who fell in this camp. Did I think any less of them? Of course not! Well, maybe one guy, who claimed that he'd never even masturbated. That kid must have changed his sheets at least three times a week!

At the same time, however, I would sometimes feel personal guilt and shame when I talked to my friends who were in the celibacy camp. I felt pressure to suppress or reject my own desires and wished that I shared their chaste ideals. It's normal to feel this way. You want to be like your friends, whom you respect and share common interests with, but just as you shouldn't make fun of them for their decision to bottle up their hormones and instincts, they should not diminish you or judge you for making a different choice. Again – and I can't state this enough – everyone is entitled to his own feelings, emotions, and standards in this department.

In my opinion – and this is just *my* opinion – I think it's important to have a couple of different partners before you get married. I'm not talking about sleeping with anyone who will open their legs and running your body count up into the hundreds. I'm talking about healthy relationships that offer you an opportunity to grow as a person and gain real-world experience and knowledge. I realize that this goes against a lot of the teachings that you may be exposed to, and the religious establishment in particular, but here's why I feel so strongly about this.

You are living in a much different time than any other point in human history. In the age of the Internet, with the ability to get information, buy a new toy or just about anything with a few taps on a screen, we have become a culture that expects instant gratification. Not only that, but we are also a culture with very short attention spans and a consumerist attitude of throwing away perfectly good options in favor of something we believe will make us even happier.

This extends beyond material goods and, in some cases, into relationships. I think part of the reason the divorce rate is so high is that people are in the habit of finding the next best thing. The screen on your phone cracked? Don't replace it, just buy a new one! You got some mud on that new pair of white sneakers? Order a new pair online and they'll be here in two days. Tired of the relationship you're in? The sex isn't as good as it once was? You don't feel like working on your relationship to fix the root cause? Don't worry about fixing it, just get a divorce and start over!

If you get married without ever experiencing sex with another person, there's a chance that you will wake up one day and wonder what else is out there. Are you missing something? Is this as good as it gets? Now, I'm not going to go too deep into the marriage conversation because you're way too young to be thinking about that. However, I do believe that if you eventually decide to go that route, marriage should be forever. If you make that commitment to another person, you should be bound to honor that promise despite the problems and challenges that come with it. The value in sleeping with more than one person in your life is that you will realize that there is a significant difference between sex with someone you kind of like, and sex with someone you deeply love. The difference is significant, but unless you've had both, you'll never truly understand it.

I bring this up because I had these feelings and concerns when I got engaged to my high school sweetheart, Annie. We dated from our junior year of high school all the way through college. She was the first and only girl I'd had sex with up to that point. We got engaged a little more than a year after we graduated college. I was about 22-years old and living in a suburb of Atlanta, where she was getting her master's degree at Georgia Tech.

I had changed, and so had Annie. You will too! The difference between who you are, or who you *think* you are, in high school, and who you discover yourself to be in college and beyond are often very different. Those years will be the most transformative of your life. By the time I asked Annie to marry me, I already felt that our paths were diverging. I was becoming interested in working out and getting stronger, still aspiring to play professional baseball. I followed current events and had opinions on what was happening in the world around me. Her interests were different, and the time we spent together slowly became stale and our conversations more and more hollow.

The closer I got to the wedding date, the more intense the feelings of fear and anxiety became. I slowly awakened to the fact that I was no longer as interested in Annie as I used to be, but I was still desperately holding onto the *story*. I wanted the *story* of being able to say that I married my high school sweetheart and we lived happily ever after, but I ultimately realized that that was a horrible reason to get married.

I was also paralyzed by the thought that I might only have sex with one woman in my entire life. When I would go out with friends, I would often look at the buffet of gorgeous women around me and wonder if I was missing out. I often fantasized about what it would be like to go home with someone new – specifically, what the sex would be like. This fear continued to grow in me and was the catalyst that ultimately wound up driving me to break off that engagement. For me, the heartbreak and excruciating emotional pain of breaking an engagement that would have committed me to her for the rest of my life was a better option than going into a marriage with these feelings of "what if" that could have led to me being resentful at best, and unfaithful at worst. I was young, but even then, I knew I did not want to live my life with those heavy emotions looming over me.

I had sex with a few other girls after that – not very many at all actually – but enough to realize that while everyone is a little bit different, the real ingredient that made it amazing was love. I had loved Annie, and while sex with the other women I dated after we broke up was pretty good – sometimes even great – it didn't fulfil me the way it had when I had been in love. Therefore, when I met Annah, the woman who eventually became my wife, I was 100% confident that I could commit myself to her forever and not feel like I was missing out on anything. We've been married more than 10 years now and I have never questioned whether or not I was missing out on sex with anyone else because a greater force anchors the roots of our relationship: love.

With that, let's push beyond the physical realm and I'll tell you the truth about love.

Love,
Tom

Chapter 13

The truth about love

Dear Ivan,

I want to give you some insight on the L-word. Love is a complicated topic, and it goes much deeper than your relationship with whoever you're dating right now. Love has more levels than all of your favorite video games combined, and it moves in all directions, ebbs and flows, in and out, up and down. It is the most complicated of emotions and can often be mistaken for anger, fear, or pain – all of which can piggyback on the base emotion of love.

Is it heroism that drives one soldier to risk his life by running toward danger in an effort to rescue his friend who has been hit by enemy fire? Yes, but at the base of that heroism is love.

Is it fear and worry that keep your parents up at night when you go out to a party? Yes, but at the core of those emotions is love.

Is it sadness, pain, and anger that cause you to cry at the funeral of a friend or family member who was killed in a car accident? Yes, but at the root of that trio is love.

Love is a word that is often thrown about with carelessness. It has so many shades and variations that it can be difficult to pin down a person's intent or meaning when they use it. What does it mean, for example, when someone breaks off a relationship by saying, "I love you, but I'm not *in love* with you?" It doesn't make any sense! Over the course of your life, you will learn that your interpretation of love may differ from someone else's – even when it's used in the same context – which can be confusing, painful, and infuriating at times. Love is not always sexual in context. Love can drive you to do some seemingly impossible things and push you beyond the limits of what you believe you are capable of.

I'm going to try and explain love to you in a way that will help you see it in many forms. I'm going to share something with you that I learned from a small men's group I was a part of. I was fortunate enough to find this group through a church I was attending at the time, but it was hardly the church group you imagine. We did discuss the Bible, but not in the traditional sense of reciting scripture or discussing what someone meant when they said a certain thing. It was more of a *life* group.

Personally, I have always been skeptical of religion, believing it's been the *cause* of conflict and chaos in the world more often than it's been the solution. I've kept that healthy skepticism. This group accepted me, questions and all. Each of the men in my group had his own story. The group ranged in age from a few years younger than me to some who were old enough to be my dad. We met weekly to discuss life – the way we had lived it in the past, the way we were trying to live it now, how Jesus had lived his life, and how we could live as close to that example as possible. The group included men who were the sons of pastors; men who had led adulterous lives and left multiple failed marriages in their wake; men who had found God at a young age and literally preached from soap boxes on street corners before questioning their beliefs and moving to the other side of the spectrum, questioning God's very existence. It was an incredibly unique opportunity for me to learn much about life through the actions and experiences of men who had been there and done that. In short, this men's group was more of a mentorship for me than a Bible study. Make no mistake, I *love* these men and I have no shame or hesitation in saying it.

Before you try to dissect what I mean by "love" in that context, let me get back to my original point and share the big lesson that I learned from one of the elders in the group. One night, sitting around a fire and sipping whiskey in someone's back yard – exactly how you imagine a church group, right? – one of the men commented that we, as a society, have simplified love. We've boiled its many forms down into one four-letter word to encompass all of its potential meanings, leaving us to interpret another person's intent when they use it. Luckily for us, he continued, the ancient Greeks had another way. They had *six* different words for love to help interpret the context.

You may think that six words for love is a little excessive, so let me frame it in a way you might grasp more easily. Imagine you're hanging out with your buddy, and he says he's hungry. You ask him what he wants to eat, and he simply replies, "food." What does that mean? There are so many things he could be talking about. Maybe he means pizza rolls and potato chips, but it could just as easily be a T-bone steak, grilled medium rare, with a side of sautéed mushrooms. What if he has an allergy to certain foods that you don't know about? You don't want to give him something that might cause him to spend the rest of the afternoon on the toilet or in the hospital! What if he only eats a certain brand of peanut butter? What if his religion has restrictions on certain foods? These are all potential variables that could make a confusing situation into an embarrassing one in a hurry! As a result, we've come up with a variety of ways to *classify* food that can help us narrow it down. You could ask if he wanted something salty or sweet, meat and cheese or just chips and crackers. The classification system gives you more options to express your desire for food than just the word itself.

It's the same with love. As it is, we have made a mystery of one of the greatest truths in the world – that love is the answer. Love is ultimately the answer to everything. Since we have just one word, however, that creates confusion. If you tell someone that you love another guy, does that mean you're gay? Maybe and maybe not – it depends on the *type* of love you're talking about. If someone says they love tacos, does that mean they want to have sex with a meat-filled flour tortilla? Hopefully not, but you can't rule it out if you don't know what type of love you're dealing with.

The Greeks laid out six different types of love: *ludus, eros, pragma, philia, agape,* and *philautia*. We'll go through each of them. My hope is that you'll start to appreciate the broad scope of love and begin to understand it in a deeper way.

Let's start with *ludus* – a joyous and *playful* love. This version of love is likely your first real experience with love. Think about the girls that you were especially drawn to early on. For me, it was Jenny in the 3rd grade. I thought she was the prettiest girl I'd ever seen. I would constantly stare at her in class and try my best to sit near her every chance I got. When our class went on a field trip to the zoo, I saved her a seat next to me on the bus. My head started spinning a little bit when she sat down next to me. I saw an opportunity to make my move and I took it! I don't know where my courage came from – it definitely isn't a characteristic that stayed with me – but I tapped her on the shoulder and asked her if she wanted to know a secret. When she leaned over toward me, I planted a kiss right on her cheek. I still remember that surprised and confused look on her face – like someone had given her a gift when it wasn't her birthday. At least *I* thought it was a gift!

Ludus is also at play when you see young kids playing "boys chase girls" or some other similar game on the playground. If you ever played this as a kid, you undoubtedly chased the person you were most attracted to, even if you didn't intend to do anything about it if you actually caught them.

Think about the girls you flirt with, chase, and spend time thinking about outside of class. *Ludus* is something that you may have heard called "puppy love," an infatuation with something or someone that you just want to be around and play with. *Ludus* is the "butterflies" in your stomach when you're around that person. It makes your heart beat faster and your palms sweat a little.

Ludus stays with us throughout life. It's also the love and joy you feel when you're out with friends having a good time. There is no sexual desire there, just the joy of good company while doing something fun, like going to a house party and making a fool of yourself in a circle of friends who won't judge you for your antics. Maybe there's some flirtation involved with some of the girls you find attractive, but it's not the romantic love in the sense that we imagine it when we use the word love in day-to-day conversation.

It's important to keep *ludus* in your life. It keeps you young at heart. When you see your parents at a party with their friends, sitting around talking and laughing – that's *ludus*. You will be there some day – at that age – and if you have *ludus* in your life, you will be much happier.

If *ludus* is the playful love, then *eros* is the next step. *Eros* is the most common connotation of love in today's society. *Eros* is rooted the idea of sexual passion and desire.

I went to my first school dance at the beginning of my 8th grade year. Isabel was a super quiet, but pretty girl, with long dark hair, an alluring smile, and glasses. She had been home-schooled up to that point, so she didn't know many of the other kids. This was great news for me because I was not very popular in my middle school years, and she hadn't had time to figure out that I wasn't cool.

I fully intended to stand in a corner in the dark by myself all night and just watch what everyone else was doing. I think Isabel had the same idea, but the girls around her had other plans. When the last slow song of the night came on, one of them came and grabbed me from the sidelines and dragged me over to her.

For a moment, we just looked at one another, then I put my hands on her hips and she clasped her fingers together behind my neck, and we started turning in slow circles, arm's-length apart. My heart was racing. I couldn't believe this was happening! The elation of my first slow dance soon turned to horror as I realized that I was getting an erection right there in the middle of the dance floor. There was nothing I could do about it – I couldn't take my hands off her hips to adjust myself because she'd notice. What would she think if I started grabbing my crotch while dancing with her! My penis played the role of a psycho in a straitjacket, raging against the restraint of my underwear and screaming to be released. I was pretty uncomfortable by the time the song ended.

If you haven't had that experience yet, don't worry, you will. I learned a valuable lesson that night: always make sure your little guy is well adjusted and has room to grow *before* you start dancing! The only thing that saved me from mortal embarrassment was the fact that we had about six inches of space between us, so she didn't feel anything poking her in the stomach.

I never danced with Isabel again, and we didn't get into any sort of romantic relationship, but the excitement of *eros* immortalized that experience as one of the highlights of my young life.

I got my first real kiss toward the end of 8th grade. I had a huge crush on this girl, Jamie, who was dating some other guy. However, her best friend Rachel was single, so I pursued her instead in an effort to spend more time with Jamie by association. I was never crazy about Rachel, but I was happy to have a girlfriend by any means possible. Rachel and I had chorus class together, and there was another guy in that class, Carl, who had a serious crush on Rachel.

One day at the beginning of class, before the teacher was ready to get started, Carl asked Rachel if she had ever kissed me. She said she hadn't, but she definitely would. This was news to me. I was in this thing to get closer to her best friend Jamie, and our relationship to this point had been strictly note-writing and handholding. I hadn't considered that there might actually be a greater opportunity here. As I was thinking this through in my mind, Carl pulled out his wallet and said, "I'll give you a dollar if you kiss him right now."

The three of us were sitting on the risers along the side wall of the classroom. By this time there were about 20 other kids in the room, milling about, waiting for class to start. As I was doing the calculus in my head about the possible outcomes of such a proposition, Rachel said, "OK," with the confidence of a bully who was about to take someone's lunch money. She spun to face me, grabbed my face with both hands, and gently kissed me on the lips.

I was stunned. It felt like the room started to spin, and I thought I might fall out of my chair. I recovered quickly, although the top of my head was still a little tingly, and I looked over at Carl. Our eyes met briefly, and I could tell he was just as stunned as I was. I think we both realized the power of a kiss in that moment. Rachel had a satisfied smirk on her face as she reached over and grabbed the bill from Carl's hand.

I had a lot more confidence and experience by the time I reached 11th grade, but confidence and experience don't change the intensity and excitement of *eros*!

Brooke was a senior – the class above me – and she had asked me to the Sadie Hawkins dance. We had been in several classes together over the years and I had always found her attractive. I was taken by surprise when she had asked me, and I was excited to be going with someone a year older than I was. Unlike the 8th grade dance with Isabel, where we had been clumsily thrust together for the last song, Brooke and I had gone out to dinner with a group of friends beforehand and had danced together all night.

By the time I dropped her off at her house, the sexual tension of the evening had been building for hours. I got out of the truck, walked around to the passenger side, and opened her door. We stood in the driveway in silence, faintly illuminated by the porch light. I held her in my arms, and we looked into one another's eyes, hearts beating fast, letting the anticipation build to the point where we felt like we might explode.

We had never kissed before, and we weren't dating, but the feeling was magnetic – our faces were so close that it was impossible to pick one focal point. Her eyes were darting back and forth between mine until she gently closed them and raised her chin toward me, gently parting her lips, and we kissed. All the tension that had been building over the course of the evening came roaring forth in that moment, and we made out in her driveway for several minutes before her dad started flicking the front porch light on and off.

As I said at the beginning of this letter, there are many levels to love. I hope these three stories have illustrated that there are multiple levels *within* each of the different types of love as well! *Eros* started with that awkward first dance, leveled up to a first kiss, and ratcheted up even higher with a steamy make-out sesh. Of course, the apex of *eros* is sex, but I think I covered that pretty well in the last letter.

Eros is that feeling you have at the beginning of any new relationship – the excitement and desire you feel just thinking about the other person. It's the reason you write notes in class or text them minute-by-minute updates of your day. It causes you to get lost in daydreams about spending time together, planning elaborate dates and spending too much money on silly things like flowers and cards. It's that euphoric feeling that you would do *anything* for them! *Eros* is intoxicating – you can't keep your hands off one another! It's one of the greatest feelings in the world and some people will go to great lengths to experience it again and again.

Despite how it's depicted in movies, however, *eros* is not everlasting. That incredible passion and desire will diminish over time, regardless of who you're with. When you've lost that feeling of *eros*, you can grow tired of spending time with the same person. You begin to long for that desire and passion that existed at the beginning of the relationship. This can lead to a breakup, allowing you to experience *eros* all over again with someone new.

This is normal at a young age and perfectly acceptable. In fact, I highly encourage it! Meet and date a variety of potential partners – it's the only way to learn who is truly a good fit for you. However, it can become a problem if you believe that love should always feel like this. What do you do once the initial blaze has died down and all that remains are glowing embers? If you allow that fire to go out, you will be starting from scratch again, which can eventually become a cycle of heartache and longing to find "the one" as you get older. If you understand that there will never be a single person who will keep that blazing fire of *eros* lit forever, then you have to learn to transition to *pragma*.

Pragma for the ancient Greeks was a more mature love – the deep understanding that develops between couples who have been together for a long time. I'm not talking about a six-month long relationship. I'm talking about years. Five, 10, 25 years. Think about the modern word *pragmatic*, which means dealing with things sensibly and realistically in a way that is practical. If *eros* is the crazy, passionate, irrational love of a new flame, then *pragma* is learning to stoke those embers and keep that fire burning for the long run.

Pragma doesn't have to be boring, although I know it sounds that way! There are plenty of times in a long-term relationship when something will happen that throws gasoline on your fire and those flames of *eros* will rage as hotly as they did in the beginning. It could be a special night out, a once-in-a-lifetime vacation, or some other catalyst, but the ability to live, love, and *stay* in love during those periods of glowing embers is what will define true love for you. There will be times when things get dark and cold, and you feel like those embers are on the verge of going out completely. You will have to work to rekindle that flame and bring it back to life. When you hear people say that marriage is a lot of work, this is the work they're talking about.

Do not be in a rush to find *pragma*. You are young! Enjoy the times of *eros*, meeting new people and experiencing new things. The key is to make sure that you evaluate each experience for what you enjoyed and what you didn't. Like every life experience, each new relationship is an opportunity to learn. Some will be good, and some will be bad, but each experience will prepare you to meet the person you want to have in your life forever – if you choose to go down that road.

People often get in trouble by confusing these two types of love, *eros* and *pragma*. They are still in that *eros* phase of love when they decide to get married. In my opinion, this is part of the reason the divorce rate is so high in our country. The passionate, physical clutches of *eros* are strong enough that you can overlook some of the things that *should* be telling you that someone's not a good fit. Once *eros* fades, people realize they don't have as much in common with one another as they originally thought, and that's when the problems really start.

Here's a reminder from the last letter: sex isn't everything. Good sex, even *great* sex is not enough to build a marriage on alone. *Pragma* requires an understanding of another individual outside of the bedroom. You have to find someone whom you enjoy spending time with – going on hikes, making meals, sharing deep conversations about things that are important to both of you, watching stupid movies, doing chores and yard work – all the tasks and monotony that make up the bulk of your time spent together. You have to ask yourself, in essence, if you could *never* have sex with this person again, would you still want to spend time together? If you can answer that question with an honest yes, then you've got something to work with.

So, what about that thing I said in the beginning about loving the guys in my men's group? That's *philia* – the deepest bonds of friendship and brotherhood formed between the ancient Greeks fighting alongside one another in war. You've heard Philadelphia called "the city of brotherly love," right? It's not spelled exactly the same, but the root of the word is there: *Phila*-delphia. That's where it gets its name and its tagline.

In my case, I formed these bonds with my men's group on multi-day backpacking trips and hunting expeditions in the Rocky Mountains of Colorado, sharing the most vulnerable parts of ourselves – our shame and self-doubt, our fears, and our short-comings as men – with the others in that group around the campfire without fear of judgement or repercussion. *Philia* is about showing loyalty to your friends and sacrificing for them if necessary.

Going back to my letter about friendship, these aren't your social media followers. These are the select few whom you allow to know you on a deep and personal level. These are the few friends that you would do anything for without asking questions. How many friends like this do you have? Who do you love enough to say this is true for?

I have a very small handful of friends (not including my *actual* brothers) who fit this description. There are certain people who, if I needed them, would drop what they were doing and either hop in a car or book a flight to be by my side if I needed their help. Even though we are separated by distance, there is something about our shared experiences and the commonalities we have in the way we see and understand the world that have formed stronger bonds than most. I would also drop everything to be there for them. The point is, your closest friends are not always those who are in closest proximity to you. However, when you ask yourself who would be there for you no matter what – you can find them easily enough.

Asking this question to yourself may also cause you to rethink the friendship of some others whom you had previously considered to be close friends. *Philia* is reserved for those special few. You will be fortunate to have a handful in your lifetime and you will know them when they appear.

There's more. I know it feels like we've covered it all! Friends, family, crushes, lovers … who else can you possibly love? How about literally *everyone* else? *Agape* is selfless love – a love that is extended to everyone, whether you know them or not. The love that you extend to all of humanity purely out of the fact that you are also a part of humanity.

This sounds like some new-age, hippie bullshit, and I totally get that, but I assure you that its origin is ancient. If I had to bet, I'd wager that it originated before the Greeks put a name to it. This is the kind of love that is seeded deep in your heart. It's the love that you feel for your community, your hometown, and your country. *Agape* has been referred to as the highest form of love.

Agape shows up when you pull over to bring gas to a stranded motorist or help them change a flat tire on the side of the road. It's there when you give a sandwich and a blanket to a person living on the street, recognizing their humanity and their need, rather than judging them for mistakes you *assume* they've made to put themselves in this position. It is the love that moves you to comfort a grieving person whom you do not know, embracing them and crying with them as though their loss is your own.

Agape is the common bond of love that ties humanity together. Regardless of whether you speak the same language, live in the same country, or believe in the same god as another person, it does not make them any less human. It is a shared understanding of the human condition and a willingness to reach out to help – *to love* – someone who is going through life just as you are.

Have you read John Donne's poem, "No Man Is an Island?" I had to memorize it one year for a high school English class and it's always stayed with me. Recently, however, I've begun to think about it in a deeper context. In particular, the line, "any man's death diminishes me, because I am involved in mankind." Those words are heavily weighted – that because you are a part of mankind, any death, pain, or struggle by another person is also yours to bear. It doesn't mean that you need to drop what you're doing and fight everyone else's battles. There isn't enough time or energy for that. However, we all need to express more empathy – the ability to understand and share the feelings of another – to see the world through their eyes, learn to love one another as people, and help where we can.

We all exist for a very brief period of time, and it just so happens that this moment, right now, is the *only* moment that we will all ever have together. In the time it took me to write that line, and again in the time it took you to read it, someone was born and someone else died – maybe hundreds or thousands of people. The world is always changing and evolving, but if we don't use the time we have to share the common experience of humanity and love one another, what's the point?

Agape is the opportunity to do something for someone else without any expectation of being repaid. A selfless act to benefit someone you know – or even a stranger – will fill you with more joy than anything you can do for yourself.

Think about the adage that is often said around Christmas: "it is better to give than to receive." Giving isn't limited to physical things. Giving love, giving a listening ear, giving kindness costs you nothing, but will return abundant joy. Try this in your life. The more love you give, the more you will begin to see love in places you never expected.

One night, my senior year of college, I drove over to the store to get some ice cream for movie night. When I pulled up, I saw one of the store employees in the parking lot, crying hysterically. When I asked what was wrong, she told me she had been made to work late and missed her bus. She had been on her feet all day and now had no way home. I offered to give her a ride and wound up driving more than an hour out of my way, round-trip, to drop her off at her apartment. She offered to give me gas money, but I knew she needed it far more than I did. The relief on her face when I refused the money, and the huge hug she gave me, were payment enough.

Another time, when I was living in Denver, I noticed an older gentleman struggling to carry two armloads of groceries along an icy sidewalk on a busy road. I pulled over and asked if I could give him a lift. I loaded his bags in the back, drove him home, and helped him carry them inside. He thanked me graciously and explained that his daughter lives with him and takes care of him, but she was currently out of town on a business trip.

I'm not telling you these stories to pat myself on the back or make you think I'm a perfect human being. Honestly, my initial reaction was annoyance when I learned how far I had to go to take that woman home. In addition, I'm sure I've passed up plenty of opportunities to help others in similar situations because I was lost in my own world and didn't even notice they were there. I'm telling you these stories now because I felt *amazing* afterward – better than any financial reward or gift could have made me feel. Helping a stranger in need can be one of the most rewarding experiences you'll ever have.

If everyone gave just a little more – showed a little more *agape* – in their daily lives, imagine how it could change the world. You can't control what other people do, but you sure can control your own actions. The next time you see someone in a place where you think you can help, do it. Don't expect anything in return. In fact, refuse any repayment or compensation of any kind. See how you feel. See how they react. That's the power of *agape*.

Finally, there's *philautia*, or love of the self. This is the counterweight to *agape*. I've saved it for last because I think it is the most important.

Maya Angelou once said, "I don't trust people who don't love themselves and tell me 'I love you.' There is an African saying which is: 'Be careful when a naked person offers you a shirt.'"

Before you can truly love anyone else in any real capacity, you must first learn to love yourself.

Most of us are pretty good at emotionally beating ourselves up, coming up with reasons why we're not good enough for any number of things. I still struggle with this, and I've detailed many of my struggles in the other letters in this book. I'm only writing this letter to you after a significant argument with myself over whether or not it is worth it. Will you even read it? Do you care what I have to say? Will you make fun of me or tell me it's garbage?

Ultimately, I decided it doesn't really matter in the end. I'm writing this for you, but I'm also writing it for *me*. Regardless of whether or not someone thinks my ideas are stupid, or if they even read them at all, I will still love myself for the effort. I see value in this endeavor and I'm going to put it out there with the hope that it will also help you learn about yourself and the world around you in a productive way.

Just because I had an argument with myself over this project doesn't mean that I don't love myself or believe in my own self-worth. Quite the contrary. There are a lot of things I love about myself. I think I'm good-looking, charming, funny, strong, emotionally stable (most of the time), and a joy to be around. I really hope you think these things about yourself as well! Some may call this *hubris* – excessive pride – but as long as you don't expect everyone else to agree that you are all these things, it's not. There's a difference between loving yourself and expecting everyone else to love you the same way.

If you *do* expect others to think you're all of these things all of the time — that you are the most amazing man in the world — then you will suffer from the dark side of *philautia*. This dark side shows itself in people who are completely self-centered and driven to obsession over themselves at all costs. Whether it manifests in the way they look or the amount of money they have, these "look at me" types are missing the point. The idea of *philautia* is to love yourself enough to be confident in who you are, regardless of how you look or how much money you have, and being secure enough in that to love *others*. The ability to appreciate who you are despite your flaws and faults — and they are numerous, as are mine — opens the doorway to the other five types of love.

That last part is critical to understand. Of course you have flaws and faults. Everyone does. It's also true that everyone is their own worst critic. Even the people who love themselves above all else. Secretly, they want something more — to look better, have more money, be more famous — every time they look in the mirror, they think it's not enough. The sad truth is that none of those things will ever satisfy them the way that experiencing the other forms of love will.

There is nothing so wrong or unlovable about you that can prevent you from truly loving yourself. Every "imperfection" you see that you deem unlovable is merely an obstacle that you've put in your own way. Learning to love yourself through your perceived imperfections is a real challenge. It requires you to stop caring about what you think other people will think and listen only to yourself. When you think about the things you don't like about yourself, what are they?

As I've mentioned in great detail in other letters, I didn't like the moles on my neck and torso when I was younger. I used to try and cover them whenever I was in close conversation with someone so they wouldn't see them. At the same time, I had friends who had moles on their faces, misshapen fingers, webbed toes, and other physical imperfections. It didn't stop me from being friends with them or loving them, but I'm sure they secretly hated those parts of themselves too.

I used to hate that I am so empathic. I *still* cry at Disney movies ... and love stories, stories where the dad or dog dies, stories where broken relationships of all kinds are mended. Ok, I cry at a lot of movies. So what?!? A lot of people wear their emotions on their sleeve. It can be an endearing quality!

Why do those things that you are so self-conscious about affect you in such a negative way when you see those same qualities in others but don't judge them for the same "flaws?" What sense does that make? Love yourself. Above all else, love yourself and don't let anyone else push you back into that dark place of questioning your worth. Putting someone else down is just a weak man's way of trying to feel better about himself.

The root cause of these negative feelings about yourself is fear. You are ultimately afraid that these things you don't love about yourself will make you unlovable to those around you. One way to begin conquering your fear is to face it head on.

Since we're talking about all these classical words for love, this seems like a good place to reference a Roman philosopher named Seneca, who is still widely revered for his work in Stoicism.

Consider this thought from Seneca: "We are more often frightened than hurt; and we suffer more from imagination than reality."

We are *frightened* of what we *imagine* others may think, and we *fear* how that will make us feel. One of the things Seneca did to address this fear was to put himself in the exact situation that he was afraid of. This doesn't mean put yourself in physical danger, but rather to challenge yourself to experience the thing you fear and see if your imagination lives up to the reality.

For someone of Seneca's status in ancient Rome, being dressed in fine clothing was a necessity. To be seen publicly in anything less would be extremely humiliating. To face his fear, Seneca would occasionally dress in clothes befitting a peasant to walk around the city. In spite of his worry that people would laugh at him – and surely some people did – he ultimately realized it wasn't nearly as bad as he imagined it would be. He stripped the power – and his fear – from that imagined scenario with the knowledge that if he lost his fine robes and had to dress as a peasant, it would not be the end of the world or his self-worth.

Put yourself in the position you fear! Take that solo in the band! Go shirtless even though you don't have six-pack abs! Let those tears flow from time to time! Do this, watch the reaction from those around you, and ask yourself, "is this what I so feared?" In my experience, the reality is never as bad as your imagination leads you to believe it will be.

I realize this is harder to get away with in high school because there is much more social pressure on you, but that's the point of this book. You're in a unique chapter of your life right now. Everyone is trying to figure out where they fit in the social order. Once you get through this mess, however, you'll find that very little of it matters for the rest of your life. In fact, for the past few years I've been *telling* people that I cry at Disney movies! Surprisingly, I've never had anyone make fun of me for it and I've even had a few men pull me aside to tell me that they do too. Seriously! I went through most of my life ashamed, thinking I was alone in this, and it turns out that I wasn't alone – there were other men right there with me, trying to hide our tears at the movies with our friends. There is great power in taking control of your fears and learning to love yourself in spite of your perceived flaws.

I want you to start thinking about these things now, because you'll get a head start developing as a good human being. The bottom line is that it's OK to cry at movies, or still have your favorite stuffed animal or blanket from when you were a baby, or wish that some physical feature looked different ... but you *must* learn to embrace all of these things about yourself and love yourself for who you are.

Life is too short, and you have more important things to do than worry about inconsequential features, characteristics, and quirks that don't change the way you interact with the world. It will take some work, but it's work worth doing. Rise above the noise in your own head and the voices of your loudest critics (real or imagined) and learn to love yourself. Once you do that, the world will reveal itself to be a place with a lot more love in it and you will have the opportunity to love others in ways that will remain hidden from you until then.

Yes, love has many layers and levels. In my opinion, it's the most powerful force in the world. However, I do want to make sure you understand that there are also things that love is *not*.

Love is *not* a Hail-Mary play that you call when you're trying to hook up. That's not how it works. Telling someone that you love them is a big step and it carries a lot of responsibility. Think about all the things that love *is,* above. Are you ready to embody all those characteristics? Even if your intent is purely based in *eros*, saying *I love you* does not give you any right to sex – even if the other person says it back. If you go into a relationship fishing for sex and use the L-word as your lure, you're a predator. That's it.

If you tell someone you love them – even if you've been dating for a few months – and they tell you they aren't ready for sex, you'd better listen. If you pressure them and send them on a guilt trip with "but we've been dating for a while and I really want to – everyone else is doing it," or "but I love you, and if you really loved me back you'd do it," you're not being romantic. You're being a bully.

Sex and love are related, but they're not exclusive. This also goes for sexting. "If we can't have sex, at least send me a pic!" Get the fuck out of here! She doesn't want to see a pic of your wiener and pressuring her to send you naked pics of herself is still bullying. In most places, it's also illegal. I don't care how beautiful she is or how horny you are. It's not worth the risk of being labeled as a sex offender for the rest of your life. Don't do it. Don't be that asshole.

Later in life – in college and beyond – you may find that there are situations where two people are just interested in physical sex, with no expectation of love or even companionship afterward. In high school however, that is almost never the case. You are trying to figure out who you are, and girls are doing the same thing. They are figuring out their bodies, emotions, and core beliefs just as you are. You don't have the right to impose your desires on them at the expense of those things. Moreover, you will see them again! You have to go to school together until you graduate! You don't want to build a reputation as a bully with women – that news will get around too, and could really sabotage future relationships that may have a chance to go somewhere.

She may eventually get to the point that she is also interested in sex, but when she is, she will tell you "yes" in no uncertain terms. It's your responsibility as a good man to make sure that that "yes" is a choice that she makes comfortably – because she wants to – and not because you've become a petulant child who is constantly whining about it and she feels compelled to give in to shut you up. She also shouldn't feel threatened. In other words, if you give her the ultimatum that you'll break up with her unless she agrees to sleep with you so you can find someone who will, you're holding the relationship hostage in exchange for sex. Now that's a weak man's play, and it makes you a complete asshole.

I tried something along these lines my freshman year of high school. I'd been dating a girl for several months and I wanted desperately to sleep with her. Honestly, I probably would have been satisfied with just about any girl who would sleep with me. She just happened to be the girl I was dating at the time. I wrote her a note telling her how much I loved her and how I saw our future together and all that sappy, lure-her-in type of bullshit. I did my best to plead my case as to why we should have sex.

I felt completely disgusted just handing it to her. I *knew* what I was doing, and I felt guilty about it right then and there. This is what I'm talking about – I let my animal instincts lead me down a path that my conscience knew wasn't the right one. I knowingly went against my own code of morality and ethics because my raging hormones and desire for sex had made me desperate. The two wolves were battling within me, and I fed the one that craved shame and self-loathing in an attempt to lose my virginity.

Of course, it didn't work out the way I wanted it to. She still said no, and she also shared that note with her friends. I will always remember the smirk on her best friend's face when she walked past me in the hall and said, "Ooooh, you want to marry her, huh?" Talk about embarrassing! My ears got red hot and I wanted to disappear. I was frustrated, angry, and humiliated. I wished I'd never written that stupid note. She ultimately wound up breaking up with me not too long after that.

Imagine doing something like that yourself, only instead of a hand-written note – where there's only one copy – you sent an email or a text or a DM through one of the social media platforms. It could be forwarded to any number of people! The magnitude of the consequences for something like this is much higher for you than it ever was for me.

I understand that all of these thoughts and possibilities go through your head as a young man with one thing on your mind. It happens to all young men at some point, and it is natural. It's the hard-wiring in our DNA – the animal side of who we are – that drives this. What makes us *human*, however, separating us from the rest of the animals, is our conscience and the ability to discern what is right and what is wrong. It is our ability to *love*. No action that includes pressuring, bullying, or holding a relationship hostage is rooted in love. If you do any of these things and use love as a reason, you're lying to yourself and to her.

But what if she's *asking* for it without actually asking for it? You and your friends may look at how a girl dresses and believe that it's an indicator of her sexual desire. "Damn, she's wearing a low-cut tank top and booty shorts – she's really showing it off today – you know she wants it!" Have you thought about the possibility that she's simply responding to what's popular by today's fashion standards? Sure, she may be trying to catch your eye and appear as attractive as possible, but that doesn't mean that she's looking for sex.

Think about it this way: if you're walking around the house on a Saturday in some gym shorts, a worn-out tee shirt and some old tennis shoes, are you looking to do some yard work? I mean, you're perfectly dressed for it – you're basically *begging* to pull that lawn mower out of the shed! You clearly can't wait to get your hands dirty pulling weeds, right? Of course not! The clothes you wear are not always a beacon of intent.

The bottom line is this: a girl saying "I love you" does not equal sex. A girl saying "I want to have sex" *sometimes* equals sex. Don't ever get the two confused, and make sure that the second one is not a result of you bullying her into anything.

There's one more thought I want to leave you with: just because a girl wants to have sex with you doesn't mean you *should* have sex with her. That girl I wrote the note to was a girlfriend of convenience. She was fun to hang out with, and it was nice to be able to say I had a girlfriend, but we never really had much in common. Today, I'm *really* glad I *didn't* have sex with her. The only thing worse than going through life thinking you'll never have sex, is going through life *regretting* the decision to have sex with someone – because you can't take that one back.

Having sex is not the greatest thing ever. Having sex with the *right person* can be. Don't get those two things confused either. If you don't like jelly donuts, you don't have to eat them just because they're there. You can be upset that there are jelly donuts instead of chocolate cake, but if you wait a little longer, eventually you'll find that piece of cake and you won't have that jelly donut in your stomach making you feel nauseous. Choose wisely. There is plenty of time and there are plenty of people out there. Don't just settle for the first one to come along – even if your hormones are raging, you'll be better off listening to your conscience in the long run.

Good luck, and feel free to give me a shout if you ever want to talk this through in more detail.

> Love,
> Tom

P.S.
The part of this letter about what love is *not,* focused on sex because that's the primary area of my life where

this applied. However, there are other areas that may be in your life that also represent what love is not.

I specifically want to direct this at anyone who feels unloved or unappreciated for who you are. I'll say it again: until you are truly able to love yourself for who you are, regardless of your faults and flaws (*philautia*), you may struggle with the belief that you are unlovable. Your teenage years can be a dangerous time for you because you are naturally more vulnerable to people who will seek to prey on your weakness to their advantage.

These people have learned to identify young men whose desire for friendship, family, and belonging are stronger than their sense of self-worth and morality. This is how young men can be recruited into gangs. The promise of camaraderie and the shared struggle are enticing to someone who has no sense of self-love. They may try to lure you by sharing your pain – expressing empathy for your situation and telling you that they are the same as you. They may promise a "family," or a group of people with the same problems – outcasts of society – sticking together and fighting for one another against a common enemy. What they are really doing is using love as bait – manipulating your mind to see them as a solution to a problem. In reality, they are ensnaring you in a problem that will become larger than any you would have experienced on your own. I have seen this firsthand.

I worked with an organization in Colorado that mentored high schoolers who were on the wrong path. The program was completely voluntary, meaning that each of the students who participated had self-selected into the program. I was paired with a 16-year old sophomore named Jake.

At the time he joined the program, Jake was an active gang member. Over time, he confided in me that he wanted to get out. He had been with his crew since he was eight years old. He started as a runner, carrying drugs from one location to another. He moved up the ranks to enforcer, where he intimidated other individuals and occasionally got into fights over turf, money, or simply because somebody allegedly said something about one of his "family" members. By the time I met him, he was considered an "OG," (old-school, or original gangster) at only 16-years old. He got to this point simply by surviving. Many of the older members of his "family" were either in jail or dead, leaving him as one of the longest-tenured members in the area. He had been to juvenile corrections facilities and changed high schools several times to try and escape the influence of his gang. No matter what he tried or how he tried to correct his course, he kept falling back into the same routine.

On the outside, Jake showed all the signs of confidence. He walked tall, carried an arrogance about him, postured aggressively toward other students in the program, and talked loudly about how tough he was. Inside, however, was a completely different story. Jake's suit of armor was a facade – a mask he wore in public to hide his personal shame and inner feelings of worthlessness.

Jake was the result of an unplanned pregnancy between his mom and dad, who were never married. He lived with his mom, who had two other kids. In the four or five meetings I had with her, I could tell that she genuinely loved her son and cared a great deal about the trouble he was in. Unfortunately, she was rarely home because she had to work to support the four of them. She also had a live-in girlfriend – a lifestyle Jake didn't understand or accept. As a result, he tried to stay out of the house as much as possible.

Occasionally, he would get to see his dad, who wanted nothing to do with him. Every time they were together, usually at family picnics or gatherings, his dad would remind him that he was a "mistake" and tell him that he wasn't a man, constantly belittling him in front of his cousins and uncles. Despite this, Jake still gravitated toward his father, longing for his approval and acceptance, and determined to prove him wrong.

Jake's involvement in the gang was a direct result of a lack of self-love. The belief that he was a mistake, that he wasn't a man, and that his father didn't love him is what drove him to seek those feelings of acceptance elsewhere. Now, having realized that the path he was on was destined to lead him to prison, or worse, Jake was struggling to find something to hold on to. He needed something or someone stable in his life that would help him find his sense of self-worth.

I wish I could tell you that the story ended well, and that Jake was able to find those things. Ultimately, he stopped talking to me. He stopped returning my calls and texts and just disappeared. The last I heard from his mother, she believed he had made his way to California, where they had some family, but where his gang's presence was even more influential. She's not sure which of the two had drawn him in, but based on him ending all contact with me, I imagine it was the latter.

The point of the story is this: in the times that you feel the most down, lonely, worthless, or unlovable, you are also the most vulnerable. I'm not telling you what to do, I'm just telling you that this pitfall exists and that there are plenty of people out there who are not afraid to exploit your emotional turmoil to bend you to do things for them that go against your better judgement. While it may *feel* like you've found a home – a family of sorts – you have ultimately found a prison. It's one without bars, for now, but getting out can be harder than you imagine once you get yourself in.

Being in a gang is basically prostitution for young men. Your "pimp" tells you what to do – often something you'd rather not do if you had a choice – and basically rules your life. If you don't provide enough, try to get out of the gang, or skip a day's work, you may catch a beating or worse. What kind of a family is that? Does that sound like love to you? Even if this is the kind of thing you experience in your biological family, it's unacceptable.

Jake wanted out. That's why he opted into the mentorship program. The gang life pulled him back in because, in all his searching, he was never able to achieve the one thing that would have been instrumental in helping him stay out: self-love and self-respect.

Trust your instincts. Find a mentor – an adult whom you trust or a program at your school that offers a mentorship opportunity. The path is yours to choose. All I'm offering is a suggestion: learn to love yourself. Appreciate your unique qualities and accept the flaws and faults you see – we all have them. Even if you feel unloved by your own family, don't let that stop you from choosing to love yourself. Your self-worth is dictated by you alone. Nobody else has the power to affect that unless you let them. Again, once you have learned to love yourself in spite of what anyone else has to say about you, you will be able to love others and find love in so many more places than you ever thought to look in the past.

You are not alone, although I know it feels that way at times. There are others out there going through the same thing as you and, believe it or not, some going through much worse. I have met plenty of people in my life who have come from some really harsh backgrounds – beaten by their parents, emotionally, psychologically, and sexually abused by family members or other influential people in their lives, and even completely abandoned. The strong ones, the ones who learn to love themselves, ultimately come to understand that the abusers in their lives were full of fear and self-loathing themselves – they just chose to take it out on someone else. When these people refused to let their abusers pin them down, they were able to move on and lead loving, prosperous lives. The choice is yours and there are resources available to you if you would like to use them.

> "Your task is not to seek for love, but merely to seek and find all the barriers within yourself that you have built against it."
> — Rumi

Chapter 14

The truth about bullying

Dear Ivan,

On one of the darkest days of my life, I found myself huddled against a bay of lockers on the floor of a classroom workshop with a sandy-haired, blue-eyed classmate standing over me. His feet were about six inches from where I cowered. His fists were clenched. His chin jutted forward in a forced underbite as adrenaline and malice coursed through him. He stared straight ahead, stony-eyed, as if he didn't see me on the ground. He stared as if I didn't exist, even though he was the one who put me there.

I didn't know what to do. I couldn't speak. I could hardly breathe. I had a lump in my throat so big it was hard to swallow, like I'd had the wind knocked out of me.

I was doing everything I could to hold back a flood of tears that had so much pressure behind them it felt like my head might explode. I was frozen, and I didn't know if I would ever be able to move. Everything had happened so fast, it felt like I was being smothered under an avalanche of shame, fear, and self-doubt. I just wanted to disappear.

Have you ever noticed that certain days or events remain in your mind as crystal clear as if they happened yesterday, while the majority of your days blend together into a blob of time that has no real distinguishing characteristics? These crystalline memories tend to be at the extreme ends of the spectrum: the most joyous and most traumatizing events in your life. I believe your subconscious records these events with hyper-awareness, capturing every second in minute detail and earmarking them for future reflection and analysis. Later, you're able to re-live those experiences, frame by frame, like a referee in the replay booth trying to determine if a runner's knee was down before the ball crossed the goal line.

It's been more than 20 years since that day, but I still remember it in great detail.

It's not easy for me to look back on this time because it still makes me mad, but it turned out to be one of the most critical points in my personal development. I was in 7th grade. I was being bullied at school and trying hard not to let anyone else in my life know about it. I was successful in hiding this secret. In fact, I recently shared this with one of my brothers and he looked at me like I was crazy when I told him I had been bullied. He simply couldn't believe it. I put on a good show around my family. I'm sure my mom and dad didn't know either.

As the oldest of four boys, I was used to being the top dog. Inside my family, I felt confident of my place in the pecking order. I often asserted dominance over my brothers, sometimes even physically, but I also felt the responsibility to set a good example for them to follow and I put a lot of effort into creating the image of what I considered an ideal role model. As a result, my family saw the full, shiny suit of armor that I wanted them to see, projecting strength, confidence, and happiness. The other side of me, however, the side facing my peers in school and other social settings, felt completely naked and vulnerable. I was lonely, timid, unsure of myself, and scared much of the time.

I constantly worked to maintain these two completely separate and contradictory identities – one that I was proud of, and another that I was completely ashamed of. I worked even harder to ensure my two worlds never met. I didn't want my family to see how much I was struggling outside our home, and I didn't want anyone from the outside to accidentally reveal my secret to them either. It was mentally exhausting. In effect, I created a personal prison. It was one of the loneliest places I have ever been. I felt completely helpless – stuck with no way out.

Seventh grade was the worst year that I ever endured as a student. The deck was stacked against me a little bit. I had just moved from Arizona, where 6th grade was still considered elementary school, to Virginia, where 6th grade was the first year of middle school, and I was thrust into the midst of it. It was my first time changing classes, having different teachers for each subject, and having a locker. I was the new kid again, and unlike previous moves, when I was younger and making friends wasn't too hard, this one proved to be a lot more difficult. In many ways, 7th grade really marked the beginning of "growing up" for me. I was stepping out of childhood and into young adulthood, and it turned my life upside down.

I felt inferior to almost every other guy I met. I still don't know why this was my default setting. I'm sure part of it was due to constantly being the "new kid" every time we moved. I had to learn what was considered "cool" in my new environment, and I was never very good at putting myself out there to make new friends.

By 7th grade, most kids have an established group of friends they've grown up with. As an outsider, especially an introverted one, it can be difficult to break into one of these groups. Even groups of seemingly like-minded guys were intimidating to me. I already knew the reasons – my perceived weaknesses and insecurities – why they would never accept me, so I rarely even tried.

I had also never learned how to hold my own in a confrontational setting or assert myself in status-determining interactions with my peers. I never had anyone in my life to model this for me. My dad wasn't timid or weak by any means, but I also never saw him in conflict with anyone. In my eyes, he was the boss at work and at home, and nobody ever questioned or challenged that. He was respectful of everyone he met, and they returned that respect. I modeled myself after him in every way I could, but I didn't know how to ask him about *earning* the respect of my classmates and managing confrontation if necessary. I didn't want him to think I was in trouble, looking to *cause* trouble, or that I was too weak to figure it out myself. I just stayed silent.

Honestly, I wasn't exactly most-popular-kid-in-school material. I moved to a street where the kids my age were into role-playing games like Dungeons and Dragons, card games like Magic: The Gathering, and spending their time outside running around the woods pretending to be wizards and elves rather than building tree forts and trying to shoot one another with paintball or airsoft guns. These were the kids I hung out with, which didn't help my social status at school.

To be fair, this is exactly where I belonged. Even though I preferred sports to mystical card games and fantasy RPGs, a vivid imagination has always been one of my defining characteristics. As recently as the previous year, as a 6th grader in Arizona, my room had been full of stuffed animals with names and imaginary personalities. I even had a baby doll that my grandma had given me when my youngest brother was born. Each of my brothers got one, and I named mine Bill. I was six-years old when I got it, but I held onto it for many years after that because it was a gift from my grandma, and I didn't want to hurt her feelings if I threw it away. Bill sat in my room for much of my childhood.

Now, having traded stuffed animals for baseball memorabilia and age-appropriate posters, I tried my best to fit in. I wore jeans and an unbuttoned flannel over my tee shirt, trying to imitate the iconic look of the grunge movement and the "skater" kids, which was popular at the time. But my jeans were the wrong style, purchased at a discount store, and I didn't have skater shoes, like Vans or Airwalks. Instead, I wore cheap, off-brand high-tops, lacing them all the way up and then tucking my jeans behind the tongue. I had never used a skateboard for anything other than cruising down a long hill in the seated position or being pulled behind a bike. I was a full-blown "poser," which probably made me more of a target.

As if I weren't in a deep enough hole already, my mom insisted that I join the school band. I liked music, but I felt that being a "band nerd" would certainly seal my fate at the bottom of the social ladder.

Could it get more awkward? Oh yes. Yes, it could. Paired with the sagging jeans look, I noticed that you could see the boxer shorts other guys were wearing underneath. I had never seen boxer shorts. My mom had always bought me tighty-whities, so that was all I'd ever known. In my attempt to fit in, I asked her to buy me some boxers. However, I didn't understand that boxers were a form of underwear themselves, rather than an accessory, so I wore my tighty-whities under my boxers. I couldn't figure out how to get my tighty-whitey waistband to stay hidden under my boxers. How did the other kids do it? I didn't learn that boxers could be worn *instead* of tighty-whities until my freshman year of high school, so I wore two pairs of underwear every day for almost two years.

To top it all off, 7th grade was the first time I tried using a styling product in my hair. I have thick, fluffy hair that seems to expand as it grows, poofing up like a dandelion if I let it get too long. In Arizona, some of the kids called me "floppy," because my hair would fluff up like a parachute every time I jumped and then flop back down when I landed. To combat this, I began using styling mousse, but I overdid it to the point that my hair looked like it was plastered to my head, almost as if I was wearing a helmet. One kid even signed my yearbook, "I hope you have a good summer. PS – why doesn't your hair ever move?"

If you can't figure it out from these last few paragraphs, I was trying a little bit of everything to fit in. I was trying to re-invent myself by taking little pieces from every different clique I saw in school and creating a mash-up of what I thought it took to be "cool." In truth, I was completely lost. I felt helpless and alone.

I didn't feel like I had anyone in my life at the time who could help me make sense of all the conflicting observations. I couldn't ask my dad. How would he know anything about current teenage fashion? My brothers are all younger than me and were in elementary school at the time, where it was still ok to wear short shorts and tube socks that came up just below their knees. I couldn't ask my friends from the neighborhood – they'd have me wearing a cape and carrying a plastic sword to school! I truly felt like I was in this on my own.

I quickly realized that I was uncool. I tried to rationalize this by comparing myself to some of the other unpopular kids in school. One kid, Winston, was a terrible saxophone player and overall poor student. One time he literally stuck a paperclip in an electrical socket during biology lab, shocked the hell out of himself, and started a small fire in class. I wasn't *that* bad, I told myself. I also wasn't as bad as Kenny, who never combed his hair, always carried *all* of his books in his backpack (probably so he didn't get picked on at his locker), and still wore Velcro shoes – *Velcro shoes*. Surely, I was cooler than him.

Then I learned that those kids felt the same way about me and considered me to be just like them, if not lower in the pecking order.

I remember walking into the gym at my first school dance and the first person to greet me was none other than *Winston*. He seemed excited to see me. He smiled and jumped up to the pull-up bar on the wall next to us, grabbing it and hanging by one arm like he'd just dunked a basketball, then he dropped down and tried to high-five me. That was the moment I realized I was in *that* group.

Now that we've established that I was, in fact, not very cool at this point in my life, let me tell you how ugly it really got.

The Bullied

Justin and Carlos were buddies. They weren't super popular either. Carlos was in the band too, and not very good. Looking back on it now, I realize they were probably just trying to ensure that they didn't fall to the bottom rung of the social ladder themselves, and picking on me was the best way to guarantee they had superiority over someone else.

I really only had to deal with them a couple times each week in wood shop class, but that made me hate those days even more than the rest. Everyone taking shop had a little locker under one of the tables in the classroom to keep our projects and supplies in. It just so happened that my locker was right under Justin's seat.

They started out by calling me names under their breath and telling me how shitty my projects were every time I went to my locker at the start of class. This went on for the first few weeks of school, and it affected me more than I let on. I remember getting nauseous every day I had shop. The last class I had before shop was pre-algebra, followed by lunch. I would get so sick thinking about shop class that there were several times when I went to the nurse's office and had my mom come pick me up so I wouldn't have to go.

This only made things worse because I *knew* I wasn't sick, and it made me feel like such a little bitch that I was unable to deal with two shit-heads in my class. Here I was, trying to be a role model for my three younger brothers, while my only friends were nerds, I had no idea how to navigate the social norms of my new school, and I just wanted to disappear. It seemed like there was no tangible way out of the situation and I was doomed to suffer through the next five and a half years of middle and high school.

Then it got worse.

Justin and Carlos hadn't gotten the response they were looking for just by calling me names. One day, toward the end of the semester, I went to my locker to get the project I was working on, and Justin bumped into me with his shoulder. At first, I thought it was just an accident, but when I crouched down to enter my locker combination, he used his foot to push me face first into the lockers, knocking me over. I looked up and saw him staring straight ahead – not looking at me – chin stuck out and hands clenched into fists. He was looking for a fight. Carlos was standing behind him, looking at me with wildness in his eyes, ready to watch his friend kick my ass.

Now, I still believe I could have absolutely beat the shit out of him, and if it had been one of my brothers – even my brother Mike, who was stronger than me – I would have done just that. I didn't. I just froze. I was paralyzed by a million thoughts going through my mind at that moment. Some of them included:

1. If I fight, I might be suspended, and I hate getting in trouble.
2. If I try to get up, Justin will be on me, punching me, before I can get to my feet.
3. Carlos will obviously jump in, and I'll be beaten to a pulp before I can take my first swing.
4. I'm absolutely terrified right now because these guys have been bullying me all year and have finally broken me. I am deathly afraid of them for no real reason.

I'm pretty sure the fourth one was the real issue. I mean, Justin and Carlos were both scrawny little guys like me. It's not like it would have been David vs. Goliath or anything – not physically at least – but it sure felt that way in my mind. That's the thing about bullies – in a lot of cases, their power is primarily psychological. At the same time, their actions are inspired by the underlying fears and feelings of inadequacy that they have about themselves. They beat you down mentally and emotionally first, as these guys did to me with their words, then they impose themselves physically to convince themselves and their victims that they do indeed have power over you.

I probably could have won in a fight if I had just been introduced to Justin for the first time that day and someone dropped a microphone into the middle of the class and said, "Let's get it on!," but by the time this incident occurred, I was already mentally beaten to the point of rolling over and playing dead. That's exactly what I did. I crawled out from under that table, away from Justin's reach, and walked back to my table fighting back tears. Thankfully, one of my friends went over and got my stuff out of my locker for me.

I never did fight Justin or Carlos, but I spent the rest of that semester in fear that they would seek me out and finish the beat down they'd planned.

It was the lowest I've ever felt in my life – like I didn't matter. My life was hell and there was literally *nothing* I could do about it. Knowing this, it's even more shameful to admit that later in life, I *became* the bully.

The Bully

If I could go back in time, I'd go back to my senior year of high school and slap the shit out of myself. What was I doing? Knowing what I went through in 7th grade, how could I turn around and do the same thing to another person? I can honestly say I regret it to this day.

Let's set the stage: I got lucky. The district was building a new high school and it opened just in time for my freshman year. They redrew the school zones so half of the kids from my middle school would go to this new high school and half of the kids from another local middle school would also go. To add a cherry on top, they decided to let all of the kids who were rising seniors stay at their current high schools, so there was no senior class my first year - no big bad seniors to pick on me!

I was still terrified of high school and absolutely did not want to go. Every TV show and movie I'd watched about high school taught me that freshmen always get picked on relentlessly. I was fully anticipating getting locked in my locker, hung by my underwear from the towel rack in the locker room, and getting cold-cocked for no apparent reason while walking down the hall. I reiterate: I was terrified.

Ironically, my mom's insistence on me remaining in the band turned out to be my saving grace. Part of high school band included the marching band, which performed the halftime show at football games. Band camp – where we learned that year's show – started three weeks before school did, which meant that I got to meet a bunch of new people before showing up on day one for classes.

I didn't want to forfeit the last few weeks of my summer, so of course I rebelled. Despite some heated exchanges and vehement "you're not the boss of me" tirades, I reluctantly went. Then a funny thing happened. Forced into a common setting with a bunch of other kids – many of whom were also not very excited about band camp – I began to make new friends. Many of these kids were from the other school and had never met me or heard anything about me. I had another opportunity to make a new first impression – a brand new start – with people who had no preconceived expectations of me.

I flourished in this setting. Once I became comfortable around this new group of people and realized that the upperclassmen weren't out to get me, I emerged from my social cave and began to let my personality and sense of humor show. I started school with a large group of new friends, a new haircut with much less styling product, and a much lower anxiety level about being bullied. Even though Justin and Carlos were both at my school, it was big enough that I almost never saw them.

By the time I reached my senior year, my confidence and ego had grown as I became more popular. I was a starting outfielder for the varsity baseball team, had a starring role in the school musical, and was dating one of the prettiest girls in school. I was seen as a leader and a person of high integrity. I got way too full of myself, and it got the best of me.

I was appointed as a section leader in marching band that year. That meant I was supposed to mentor the younger saxophone players and help them learn the ropes during band camp. It did *not* make me their boss or direct supervisor in any way, but my ego told me otherwise.

I honestly cannot remember what it was about this kid that put him in my crosshairs. I don't remember if he was a sophomore or a junior, but he was younger than me. He didn't follow directions well – from the band director or from me. He wasn't the best marcher and didn't know all of the music, and maybe that was part of it. I didn't like his looks – he was a bit overweight, but really just an average guy – or his general "I don't give a fuck" attitude, so I began to pick on him.

Just as Justin and Carlos had started with me, I began with name-calling. I tried a few options until I found one that really bothered him: Porky. I called him that to his face and sometimes in front of other people. I began the process of wearing him down mentally and emotionally. I would physically move him when he wasn't standing in the right position for a given set. Finally, I broke him, and one day he told me to fuck off or he'd kick my ass. Challenge accepted! I told him where and when to meet me and we'd have it out.

The fight never happened. I don't think either of us ever fully intended to fight, and once the school year started, the whole thing fell by the wayside, more or less. I still saw him at band practice and continued to pick on him through the fall marching season. It was limited to band activities, just as Justin and Carlos had limited their bullying to shop class. I never picked on him at school or made a point to seek him out. I'm really thankful for that.

It still amazes me that after everything I went through in 7th grade, knowing how sick and angry and helpless I felt every time I went to shop class, my newly-found ego wasn't going to allow someone whom I saw as less worthy than me to be happy.

What underlying, self-perceived inadequacy did I see in myself that I was trying to overcome by picking on him? Maybe I just wanted to show the rest of my peers that I was *the man*. Maybe it was the fact that I'd failed math the previous year, knew I had to re-take the class this coming year, and was afraid that my identity as a "good student" was in jeopardy so I decided to take the tough guy route to validate that? Maybe it was the fact that I still secretly cried at movies, which made me feel weak, and picking on someone else proved that I was tough and helped me cope with that thing I hated about myself?

It was most likely a combination of all these insecurities and more. People now thought I was "cool," but I didn't feel any different inside. I felt like an impostor and a fraud. I still saw myself as the soft-hearted kid who played with stuffed animals, not the varsity baseball player who gets the hot girlfriend. I was afraid everyone else would figure it out – figure out who I *really* was – and I'd lose all my social capital. My inner turmoil – trying to figure out who I was, where I fit, and what I was going to do with my life – manifested in an outward projection of animosity toward a target I perceived as weaker than myself.

Regardless of the reason, it *doesn't matter*. I was a bully and I behaved like a complete ass. There is no way to rationalize, justify, or make it acceptable. It seemed so important to me at the time, and it *felt so good* to have that kind of power over someone. It is a great high, but it is toxic and cannot be sustained. My desire to feel it came from a dark place – my own sense of inadequacy and self-loathing.

Bullying others, whether mentally or physically, will never fill that void inside you. You have to face your own fears and address the lies you believe about yourself. Most of them are unfounded and downright untrue. The longer you put off looking in the mirror and acknowledging your fears, the longer you will be stuck in this dark place of self-doubt. You will miss out on many great opportunities in your life because you are stuck believing some lie you told yourself about how you're unworthy of the experience.

Start working on yourself now, because in the long run, you will understand that what other people think of you matters very little compared to what you think of yourself. The secret to happiness is not having others like you or look up to you – that can actually be a very lonely place.

Whether you find yourself being bullied or you realize that you *are* the bully, the secret to happiness is in accepting yourself for who you are, for better and for worse, loving yourself as you are, and taking proactive steps to change the parts of you that you can improve.

Bullying is a terrible thing. It's important to know that whichever side of this equation you currently find yourself on, there is another page in the story, and you are not destined to remain in either camp. Maybe you are reading this and thinking that you've never been in either situation. If that's the case, I challenge you to look closer at the relationships in your life and the way you interact with the people around you.

When I was bullying the kid in band, I didn't see myself as a bully at the time. I never picked a fight with him, slammed him into a locker, or wrote him a threatening or demeaning note. I never stole his lunch money, wrote something negative about him in the bathroom stall or on social media, egged his house, or any of the other "classic" bully moves. On the contrary, I was nice to just about everyone else at school. If you asked any of my teachers, coaches, administrators, or other adults I associated with, they'd probably tell you I was a model student!

It wasn't until later in my life, when I began to understand a lot more about the nature of bullying, the catalysts for it, and the many forms that bullying can take, that I realized, "holy shit! I was a bully!"

What did I get out of that experience? In the long run, nothing but a feeling of deep remorse. Every time I've gone back home to visit, I keep an eye out for that kid, hoping that I'll see him somewhere. I have searched social media and come up empty. I want nothing more than to apologize for the way I treated him and ask his forgiveness. I want him to know that I've regretted the way I treated him every day since I realized how terrible I must have made him feel.

I know I'm not the only former bully to feel this way. I know it because Justin revealed that he felt the same way about the way he had treated me.

It happened when I was a junior in high school – nearly four years after he'd slammed me into the lockers and tried to pick a fight with me in shop class. I was at the vending machine after school, about to buy a Snickers bar before heading out to baseball practice. There was almost nobody else around.

I had seen Justin in passing – in the hallways between classes and stuff like that – but I hadn't spoken to him or interacted with him since 7th grade, so it was strange when he approached me that afternoon. I'd grown taller than him by that point and I remember looking down at him as he sheepishly walked toward me and stopped about four feet away. "Hey Tom," he said, "how are you doing?"

I looked at him with a confused look on my face. He'd never said a nice word to me before, but I could tell that there was no malice in his eyes. He was legitimately asking how I was doing – from a safe enough distance that I couldn't punch him if the thought crossed my mind. I just said, "Hey Justin, I'm good."

I said it in that slightly confused tone that you might use when your buddy comes up to you all excited and says, "Hey, guess what! You're never gonna guess!" and you respond with a furrowed brow and "Uh, ok, so then just tell me."

Justin moved his head from side to side a little bit and then said, "Ok, cool. Well, I just wanted to see how you were doing." And that was it. He turned around and walked off.

I didn't think too much about it at the time, but now I realize that that was his attempt at an apology. He didn't directly say it, but why else would he have sought me out to ask how I was doing after not having talked to me in four years? I don't think we ever spoke again after that either.

It must have taken some guts for him to do that. Even though he didn't apologize directly, he had clearly confronted himself about what he'd done and felt bad about it. He risked getting his ass kicked by a kid he bullied, who was now bigger and more popular than him, to clear his conscience of the wrong he'd done.

I still get mad when I think about the way he treated me in 7th grade, and I occasionally have to stop myself from fantasizing about what would have happened if I'd gotten up and fought back. I'm still working on that, but at the same time, I appreciate the effort it took on his part to recognize the wrong he'd done and take a step to make amends. I also forgive him. Letting go of that anger feels good and holding onto it would only fester and create more toxins in my life.

So again, I challenge you to look closely at the way that you treat *everyone* around you. If there is someone in your life who currently makes you feel good when you put them down or belittle them in *any* way. Stop it. Take a long look in the mirror, dig deep, and find the underlying issue that's causing you to act this way. It's really hard to do – especially if you currently feel invincible and that you have a handle on everything that's going on in your life. Find the courage to apologize and accept whatever consequences come your way as a result. You will be better for it in the long run.

I was far too immature in middle and high school to see what was happening, as both the victim and the bully. It's my hope that in sharing these stories with you I can help you realize your own mistakes and encourage you to make amends before you move on, carrying this baggage that will stay with you for years, and possibly the rest of your life.

If you have been the kid being bullied – maybe it's going on right now – it's not your fault. I hope you can begin to understand through reading this that bullies choose to take action based on fears and doubts about *themselves* and choose to take it out on you. It sucks. I *know* how much it sucks. It is truly one of the worst feelings in the world to think that there is something wrong with you that would cause a person or a group of people to attack you for no real reason at all.

I was very lucky to go through school just before social media platforms became as popular as they are now. During my formative years, bullies had to do their work in person. Today, they can hide behind their keyboards and cell phones, sending messages in private and forcing themselves into your life even when you're in your own sacred space physically. I can't imagine how devastating that must be. My situation will never be as hard as yours because of this technology, *but* – and it's a BIG but – the underlying motives for those bullies are the same.

As hard as it is to imagine right now, this too shall pass. There is some truth to the saying, "what doesn't kill you makes you stronger," but I also believe that in this case, "what doesn't kill you can make you *softer*." Your experience is making you keenly aware of the hate that exists in the world, and whether that hate is outwardly directed at you (the *bullied*) or inwardly directed at themselves, whether they realize it or not (the *bully*), you will ultimately go forth in your life with a more compassionate heart and the ability to help others who will find themselves where you are now.

It's not right, it's not fair, and it's not fun, but you *will* weather this storm and it has the power to make you a better person on the other side if you can see it from the right perspective. You will not see it immediately. It may take years for this perspective to come into focus for you, but when it does, you will begin to recognize other injustices in the world, and you will find that you are better equipped to deal with them than many others.

You also need to realize that *you are not alone*. I know how lonely it feels to be bullied. I didn't tell my family or friends about it because I was ashamed. Even though it wasn't my fault that this was happening to me, I was *ashamed* that I couldn't handle it myself and I was *ashamed* of how weak and powerless I felt against it. There are countless others out there right now who are going through the same experiences you are. Shame is a powerful feeling and can drive you to the worst possible thoughts for fixing or escaping a situation. There is so much more to life than middle and high school. No amount of bullying, bad grades, "letting down" your parents, etc. can validate the choice to take your own life.

When I was a freshman in high school, my friend Tianna's younger sister died by suicide. She was in 7th grade. The toll it took on Tianna and her family was devastating. I know that she would do anything to have her sister back. She felt like her best friend had been taken from her.

Many people who choose suicide believe that they are doing the world a favor by listening to the voices – both internal and external – that say everything would be better without them, but that's a lie. For one thing, those external voices don't matter. They're not your friends and they don't care about you. The insecurity and self-hatred they have for themselves is so strong and so deep that they may be struggling to justify their own existence.

In taking her own life, Tianna's sister robbed her family of a lifetime of amazing experiences. Tianna has to live the rest of her life without her best friend. She didn't get to tell her sister about the boys she liked or cry on her shoulder when those relationships fell apart. Her sister wasn't there to be the Maid of Honor at her wedding and give a toast, recalling funny stories from their childhood. She wasn't there to meet her nieces and nephews and help teach them how to overcome the bullies in their own lives.

It can be really hard to look past the despair of your current situation and imagine the happiness, joy, and opportunity that is yet to come. This time will pass, and you will have many opportunities to re-write your life story to be whatever you want it to be, but the decision to take your own life is final, and the people you hurt the most will be the people you truly love and care about. If you have had thoughts about harming yourself in the past, or are having them now, please talk to someone. You can always reach a friendly ear by calling the National Suicide Prevention Hotline at 800-273-8255.

While I did not have to deal with the immense challenges posed by the abundance of social media platforms, I also grew up at a time when bullying wasn't taken as seriously as it is today. There are groups all across the country and the world dedicated to fighting bullying and providing support to people who need help. There is no weakness or shame in seeking an ally to help you out of your current situation. It takes a lot of strength and courage to admit that you need help. Be strong. Be courageous. You don't have to tolerate a bully and you don't have to fight this alone.

If you take one thing from this book, let it be this: **the world is a better place with you in it.**

High school feels like the pinnacle of your life right now – like who you are today and how other people see you in this moment will follow you forever. The reality is that high school, like a broken bone or a bad case of food poisoning, fades into the past sooner than you think. You will recover from the suffering you are feeling right now. You will always remember certain parts of it, but it will be in the past and you will be able to move forward and make a positive impact on the world through your unique gifts and experiences.

You may think you have nothing special to offer, but as I talked about in an earlier letter, that's not true. You just may not be able to see it yet. The opportunities in this world are so vast that you cannot even imagine how many paths there are to be explored and how each of those paths will have an impact on others around you. Your gift – and how to use it – will be revealed to you in time, but there's only one way to get there: stay the course, ride out the storm, and lean on your friends, family, and others who are going through the same experience as you are for support.

Love,
Tom

National Suicide Prevention Hotline: 800-273-8255

Chapter 15

The truth about drugs and alcohol

Dear Ivan,

In the second semester of my freshman year of college, I stood and helplessly watched my roommate's body convulsing on the floor of our dorm room. He was foaming at the mouth and laying in a pool of his own vomit. He was suffering from acute alcohol poisoning, and at just 18-years old, he was about to die.

Writing about my experience with drugs and alcohol is a very difficult task. It's a sensitive topic for many reasons. I know you have personally seen the damage that drugs and alcohol can create in the lives of those around you. Hopefully that is enough to at least make you stop and think carefully before deciding to partake, but I remember what I was like at your age and the pressure that came with it.

I think it's a very important subject to discuss with young men your age because it *will* come up and you *will* be put in a position to make a very difficult decision at some point. It's not something that's talked about often enough, and certainly not openly enough between parents and their children in many cases. If you're anything like I was, you don't like to be told what you should or shouldn't do by any authority figure in your life, *especially* your parents, which means the conversation doesn't land with nearly as much impact as it should, and you don't give it the careful consideration it deserves.

My mom used to try to talk to me about drugs, alcohol, and sex. It would usually happen after she heard about an incident involving some other kid at school. Either somebody got pregnant, or somebody got busted for smoking pot in the parking lot before school – something like that. In nearly every case, I would know about the incident before she did, and I'd already be on high alert for the imminent conversation. She'd try to tiptoe into the topic as gently as possible, like an animal control worker trying to calm a stray dog in an effort to make it feel comfortable enough to trust them. She would approach me as if she had no agenda, and then casually ask something like, "What do you think about drinking?" or "Do you and your friends know anybody who uses marijuana?"

As soon as the words left her lips, I turned into the dog who sees the dog-catcher's pole. I immediately panicked and tried to find an escape route. I remember feeling instantly uncomfortable in those situations. My ears would get hot, and I'd get butterflies in my stomach, like when you get caught red-handed doing something you know you're not supposed to be doing. Of course, I was doing absolutely nothing wrong at the time, but it felt like an accusation of wrongdoing, or some unsolicited advice was right around the corner, and both made me extremely anxious and uncomfortable.

I trusted my mom. In hindsight, I realize she was trying to protect me, but at the time it felt like she was trying to pry a bit too far into my life. In my mind, she was trying to live vicariously through me – to experience all my deviance through the stories I would tell because she never did any of that stuff in her life and felt like she missed out. I thought I knew the direction the conversation would ultimately go, and I did not want my parents telling me what to do. The only escape I had was to turn inward. I would either offer a vague response in as few words as possible or clam up entirely and ignore her until she moved on.

It's hard to comprehend, but our parents were once our age too. They went through similar experiences and did a lot of shit they don't tell us about. They made mistakes and learned hard lessons through their experiences. Your parents, like mine, were probably a lot cooler in their day than you think they were.

Even if you can believe and accept that, having these difficult conversations with your parents or other adults can be excruciating! This is your life after all, and they should trust you to make your own decisions!

I'm in a unique position because I don't have kids of my own. More importantly, *you're* not my kid. I completely understand why most parents and adults are afraid to talk about these topics with the young people in their lives. For one thing, they don't want to believe that you're old enough to be considering these decisions. For another, they fear they will just wind up saying something along the lines of, "just say no," which is the easy way out because there's no risk when it's said without context around *why* they think this is the best option, or any reference to their own personal experiences. For a third, they may still be using drugs, alcohol, or both and feel conflicted about doing the very thing they're telling you not to do. It's not an enviable predicament!

There is internal conflict and resistance for both you and them in these conversations. I, on the other hand, don't have a dog in this fight. I want the best for you, and I believe you will make the right decision for yourself at the time you feel it's appropriate. However, I also know that I could have benefitted from a real heart-to-heart on these topics, so I'm going to give you my unfiltered opinion. You can do with it what you want, but this is what I wish I'd known about these issues when I was your age.

There will come a point in your life – and perhaps it's already happened – where a friend of yours will offer you the opportunity to drink or use drugs. Maybe their parents are out for the night, and they invite you over to their house to raid the liquor cabinet. Maybe an older sibling bought them a case of beer and they ask you to meet them somewhere to share the illicit goods. Maybe you are home alone and find a stash of booze or pills and decide to try it. Whatever the case might be, you will be propositioned or tempted, and you need to be prepared for how you intend to respond.

As promised, here is my unfiltered opinion: don't do it. Not yet anyway. It's complicated, so bear with me and let's talk this thing through.

First, let's start with some facts that you already know, but are worth repeating: drugs and alcohol contain substances that alter your mindset and create physiological changes in your body. They are toxins that your body will do its best to clear from your system. Think about that for a second – your body knows what's best for it, and it sees these substances as dangerous to your wellbeing and tries to eliminate them from your system as fast as possible. That should be your first clue that they are not a *healthy* choice.

Regardless, at your age, you're not always thinking about your health as a top priority. I know I wasn't! You're young! You feel like you've got your whole life ahead of you and there's a feeling of invincibility that comes with that. Part of the reason for that feeling, however, is due to the fact that your body and your brain have not yet reached maturity. You're on your way to becoming an adult, but you're not there yet, and that's an important distinction. I'm not saying you're not *old enough* to make these choices. I'm saying that, from a physiological perspective, your body and mind have not reached the point of physical maturity.

As I shared in a previous letter, your brain won't be fully developed until you're about 25-years old. You may not want to accept this, but believe me when I tell you that a lot of the shit you think is cool now is going to leave you shaking your head when you're older and wondering how you ever survived being that stupid.

There are a lot of things I did that I thought were cool at the time, but I look back now and I want to kick my own ass for being that naïve. I realize now that I was very lucky to escape several situations without harming myself or others. That's actually a huge part of why I wanted to write these letters. If I could, I would go back in time and slap some sense into 16-year old Tom and tell him exactly what I'm telling you.

Adding toxins to your body during the development of your brain is a bad idea. Essentially, you're adding poison to a young, growing organism. If you really simplify it, it's not much different from starting a garden and then mixing just a little bit of gasoline into the can you use to water your plants, or adding just a tiny piece of rat poison to the food you give your puppy. I think we can agree that both of those are dumb ideas, right? I'm not sure about you, but I feel like the person who purposefully feeds their puppy rat poison – even in a small dose – deserves to get strung up, spread eagle, on a busy street and have everyone walking by kick him straight in the balls.

I was very fortunate when I was in high school that my closest friends were not into drugs or alcohol. We got in plenty of trouble without it.

One night, I had borrowed my dad's truck to go over to my girlfriend's house. I had only planned on staying a few minutes, so I left the keys in the driver's seat when I parked it in her driveway. It was a nice neighborhood, so I wasn't worried. I wound up staying about an hour, but when I walked outside to leave, the truck wasn't in the driveway.

Of course, I freaked out. My dad had let me borrow his truck – the one he needed to get to work – and I had carelessly left the keys on the front seat and it had been stolen! My girlfriend and I were in full-blown panic mode as we talked through our options. The last thing I wanted to do was call my dad, because I was pretty sure that if I did that, my life would be over, so literally *anything* seemed like a better idea at the time. After several minutes of pacing the driveway, and shaking with anxiety, my girlfriend's dad came outside holding the phone and said it was for me.

What the fuck was this? Was someone about to ransom me for my dad's truck? I didn't care – I would have paid up to save my skin. I took the phone with shaking hands, took a deep breath, and put it to my ear. I summoned all the courage I could muster, trying to remain calm, and said, "hello?"

On the other end of the line, I recognized the voice of one of my best friends, John, who causally asked, "missing something?"

Chills of relief went through my entire body as I realized they'd caught me. I heard two voices howling and I swung around to see John and my best friend, Chuckie, parked just up the street watching me. They opened the doors of John's car and started laughing their asses off. My dad's truck was parked right behind John's car. They had swung by my house a little earlier, looking for me, and my parents had told them where I was. They had obviously found the keys sitting in the driver's seat and decided to mess with me.

That's just how it was with my group of friends. We spent our time pranking one another by stealing one another's cars when they were left unlocked, filling them with leaves when a sunroof was left open, coating the door handles with peanut butter, or putting them up on cinder blocks and removing the tires. When it wasn't cars, it was going out in public and doing dumb stunts like faking massive diarrhea in the bathroom of local restaurants or climbing street signs or local landmarks in our town. Dumb shit like that. We had a ton of fun and got into trouble without any need for drugs or alcohol.

That doesn't mean I wasn't tempted. I felt a lot of pressure from the guys on the baseball team to drink. It wasn't overt – they didn't make fun of me or anything like that – but I was invited to parties, hosted by one of my teammate's parents, where alcohol was available. His parents' line of thinking was that if we were going to drink, we should at least do it responsibly. They took everyone's keys when they arrived, and attendees were required to spend the night there. My parents never let me go to these parties. I honestly can't remember if I told them that there would be alcohol or if they discovered it on their own, but I wasn't allowed to go. I would hear my teammates talking about it at practice and wishing I could be a part of it.

If I had to guess, I'd bet that I told my parents that there would be alcohol at those parties because I was afraid of whether or not I'd be able to go through with actually drinking when I got there. I wanted to be able to tell the guys that my parents wouldn't let me go and that's why I couldn't ever join them. I wanted that safety net of being able to *talk* about drinking with them without ever actually having to back it up.

It's kind of like when you imagine going to war and how cool it would be to run around carrying a gun and taking out bad guys, but at the same time, if you're really honest with yourself, part of you knows you'd be scared shitless the first time someone started shooting back at you and the possibility of your own death became a reality. It's that same feeling of invincibility. You don't always honestly evaluate the consequences of your actions until they're literally staring you in the face. No rational person I know has ever wanted to go to war *just because*. That's why we have things like paintball and airsoft – it affords the opportunity to get as close to war as possible without any real risk.

With all that being said, the first time I got drunk was the summer right after I graduated high school. There is a tradition where I'm from in southeastern Virginia called Beach Week, where the graduating seniors rent houses in North Carolina's Outer Banks and spend a week after graduation hanging out on the beach during the day and getting drunk and partying after dark. I wanted to go to Beach Week more than anything. All of my friends, including my girlfriend, were going. I saw it as my last chance to hang out with the people I'd spent the last four years with before we all headed off on different paths – colleges across the country, trade schools, or jobs.

My parents were well aware of Beach Week. I didn't have to tell them about it, and this time I genuinely wanted to go. They were having no part of it, so while all my friends were down in North Carolina having a great time, I was stuck at home with my family.

I was feeling especially resentful one night after talking to my girlfriend on the phone. She told me how much fun she was having and that she'd had a couple drinks the night before and was planning to do the same that evening. Fuck that. I wasn't going to be left out! If my parents wouldn't let me go to Beach Week, then I was going to have my own Beach Week right there at home.

My parents weren't big drinkers. My dad drank a couple beers around the holidays, and my mom occasionally had a glass of wine when they had friends over, but that was about it. Consequently, there was very little alcohol in the house. When my parents went to bed that night, my brother, Mike, and I stayed up playing video games. After I was sure my parents were asleep, I went to the refrigerator in the garage and grabbed one of the beers my mom used for making stew. It was cheap, but it was cold. It tasted disgusting. I'd tasted beer before, but only a sip or two. I'd never tried to consume it in volume. Over the course of about two hours, I drank my way through an entire six pack. I offered one to Mike, because if I was going to go down for this, I wanted to bring someone with me – just like the incident with the photography magazine! He declined, but I'm sure he enjoyed watching the shit show that ensued.

I don't remember much from that night. I know we were playing Mario Kart and I was making bad drunk-driving jokes. At one point, we let the dog outside to use the bathroom. He came back in and tracked mud all over the white carpet in the den, which really set me off. "We're going to get in so much trouble!" I said to Mike in alarm. "Mom is going to kill us when she sees this mess." I'm sure there is more to the story, but I don't remember it. By the time the night was over, I had consumed every beer in the house.

Another thing I didn't remember was that I had a doctor's appointment the following morning. My mom woke me up in a rush, telling me we had to leave in 30 minutes. My head hurt. Every heartbeat felt like someone was smashing my temples with a hammer. I felt nauseous, like I had been in a small boat on the ocean for several hours.

I made my way downstairs, where I realized that being drunk had not affected my love for the environment. The recycle bin was full of empty beer bottles, so my parents knew exactly what I'd done the night before.

Surprisingly, my mom wasn't as mad as I thought she'd be. She knew what a hangover was, and she knew she didn't have to punish me because I would be punishing myself all day. For starters, I couldn't eat breakfast. The mere thought of food almost made me throw up. She drove me to my doctor's appointment hungry, nauseous, and with a headache that wouldn't quit. The glare of the sun through the windshield made the headache even worse and the 20-minute drive felt like it took five hours. I didn't start feeling somewhat back to normal until late afternoon, shortly before dinner.

All told, the fun and rebellion of the previous night had basically cost me the entirety of the next day. Instead of doing what I *wanted* to do, I languished between my bed and the couch, unable to do anything other than lay there. It was a terrible trade off: a couple hours of "fun" in exchange for an entire day of suffering. It would be like me loaning you four dollars tonight, but you'd have to pay me back 20 dollars tomorrow. Would you make that deal?

You would think an experience like that would have been enough to convince me to never drink again, but I was young and determined.

When I went away to college, I drank a lot. Every weekend was a drunken affair, and occasionally my friends and I would even drink during the week. My buddy, Bryce, and I had German together freshman year, and once we were still drunk when we went to class the following day. We had an oral exam, where we had to have a conversation in German in front of the class. He and I were partners and we both fumbled our way through the exam. We actually passed, but it was an experience neither of us wanted to repeat. We thought it would be really funny when we were drinking the night before, but we underestimated how foggy our brains would be at 8 AM after partying until 2 that same morning. It was a harmless incident, but even then we realized it had been a stupid decision and could have been detrimental to our grades. Not only that, but if we'd been reported by our professor, we could have been in some serious trouble with the administration as well. I didn't want to get kicked out of school.

There were also times when alcohol affected my decision making and I put myself in very real danger. That same year, my roommate Adam was pledging a fraternity, so I would often go with him to the parties he was invited to. One Saturday I was back in my dorm room, opting for a low-key night after partying the night before, when the phone rang. It was Adam. He told me how much fun he was having at this party and that I should come out. I could hear the loud music in the background, and he had to yell into the phone to make sure I could hear him. His speech was already slightly slurred, and I knew he was drunk.

The party was at a house off campus, and I didn't have a car. Adam assured me he was good to drive, and we decided that he would come pick me up. In my mind, I knew this was a bad idea. As you know from a previous letter, I had attended the funeral of a friend who was killed in a drunk driving accident in high school, but I was at a point in my life where I felt like nothing bad could happen to me.

Twenty minutes later, I pushed those thoughts aside and hopped into the car with Adam. We peeled out of the parking lot, going way too fast. Adam ran a red light and blew through a couple stop signs in his rush to get back to the party. By some miracle, we arrived safely.

Once we got inside, some of the frat brothers found Adam and made him bong two beers simultaneously. He consumed 24 ounces of beer in a matter of seconds. Almost immediately afterward, he ran outside and puked in the bushes in front of the house. After he'd finished, he looked up at me and yelled, "puke and rally!" We headed back into the party.

We stayed for another hour or so, playing drinking games, bonging beers, taking shots of liquor, and dancing with the sorority girls who were there. When it came time to leave, I was pretty drunk, but not nearly as drunk as Adam, who could barely stand. In our only smart move of the night, we decided to leave his car at the house and walk home. I probably dragged him half of the way back to our dorm, where he passed out on my bed – the bottom bunk – while I went to brush my teeth and wash up.

When I came back to the room, I tried to get Adam to move so I could go to bed. I poked and slapped him, but his only response was a low moan. I was getting fed up, so I grabbed him by the feet and dragged him off the bed. He hit the ground with a dull thud. As far as I was concerned, Adam could spend the night on the floor.

Just as I was about to turn off the light, Adam started to move. It started as a slight twitching, but quickly escalated into a full-blown seizure. His body was spasming violently and he started foaming at the mouth. I freaked out. It was 3 AM, I was underage, and I was drunk. I didn't know who to call and I was afraid of getting in trouble.

I ran through the small closet that connected our room to our suitemate's room in a panic. Luckily, our suitemate Matt was in his room, sober and still awake. He ran back through the narrow passageway with me and quickly assessed the situation. He immediately rolled Adam onto his side. Almost on cue, Adam projectile vomited all over the stack of textbooks next to my desk. My initial reaction was anger – those books cost a LOT of money! Matt kept his cool, however, and told me to call 911.

The epic spasm of vomit brought Adam back to consciousness, and he tried to push Matt away from him while telling me not to call 911. I was paralyzed for a moment, unsure of whose direction to follow. I was thinking again about the trouble I figured Adam and I would both be in if we got caught in the dorm while drunk. I was about to put the phone down when Adam threw up again and then passed out. His breaths were coming in short gasps now and I began to understand that he might really be in trouble. I dialed the phone and told the dispatcher where we were and what was going on.

An ambulance arrived shortly afterward and the EMTs put Adam on a stretcher and rolled him out of our room and down the hallway. Every guy who lived on that floor was in the hall watching it go down. Adam was barely conscious as he was being wheeled out, but he managed to give us all a slight wave. It was almost his last.

We learned the next day that Adam's heart had stopped in the ambulance on the way to the hospital. Thankfully, the EMTs had been able to resuscitate him and bring him back, but for a few moments, my roommate was dead. When he came back to campus the next day, he told me he was never going to drink again.

I'm not sure if dying and being resuscitated had reinforced his feeling of invincibility or if he was just giving in to the pressure of the fraternity he was pledging, but that change of heart only lasted a couple weeks. Adam went right back to partying after that.

The incident affected me differently. I couldn't stop thinking about what would have happened if the timing hadn't worked out exactly the way it did. What if I'd turned off the light, gotten into bed and passed out before Adam's seizure started? What if Matt hadn't been in his room and come to help me? What if we'd delayed calling the ambulance for even a few more minutes? I would have woken up the next day and found Adam dead on the floor of our room, laying on his back, having drowned in his own vomit. It was a wake-up call for me, and I was much more cautious about my own drinking after that. I still drank, but I was much more aware of my surroundings, aware of the amount I was consuming, and I had a plan to get home or an alternative place to sleep if I needed it.

I didn't really try drugs in college. During my freshman year, Bryce and I were hanging out with some upper classmen – kids that Bryce had gone to high school with and their friends. One of the guys asked us if we'd ever tried ecstasy, which neither of us had. He offered to supply us if we ever wanted to give it a go.

Being the nerds that we were, Bryce and I went back to his dorm later that night and researched the drug. Based on what we read – including an article that told us that it caused your brain to bleed and the drips of blood down into your spinal column is what makes you feel the euphoria – we decided not to take the guy up on his offer. We also learned that your body could overheat, and if you didn't drink enough water you could die from a heat stroke. Bryce and I had flashbacks of Adam's alcohol-induced seizure and we didn't want to have anything remotely similar happen to us. That little bit of research was enough to convince us that we didn't want to risk our lives or compromise our brains.

It turns out the first article wasn't entirely accurate, though an estimated eight percent of the population does have abnormalities in the blood vessels in their brains, which can rupture and cause a stroke as a result of using ecstasy. The second one is definitely true. People who take ecstasy and then go to a rave to dance for hours can get dehydrated with all the sweating. If they don't drink enough water, they can absolutely overheat, and some have died.

I did smoke marijuana once in college, and I've done it several times since then. For most people, it has the opposite effect on your mood than alcohol does. For example, I've never met anyone that was high on pot – *only* pot – and looking for a fight. It tends to mellow people out. On the other hand, I've met plenty of raging drunks who wanted to throw fists. Regardless, marijuana does affect your senses.

You may believe you're functioning at a level that makes it safe to drive, or do other tasks that require fine motor skills, when you're actually not. It's also still undetermined what effect it has on the still-developing brain of younger users. Like alcohol, my recommendation is that you stay away from it at least until your brain and body have matured. You'll be in a better head space to make a rational decision about whether or not it's something you're interested in, rather than just doing it "because everyone else is."

Another thing you should consider is that you never know how any particular substance will affect you until you use it, which can turn a fun experience into a scary or dangerous one very quickly. I have one friend who has a metabolic condition that allows him to process alcohol so quickly that he physically cannot get drunk. His doctor told him if he ever wanted to feel what it's like to be drunk, he should make sure he does it in the ER parking lot because he would have to drink so much so fast that he would feel drunk for a couple minutes before he experienced acute alcohol poisoning and require immediate medical attention! Another friend of mine is allergic to alcohol. She swells up with hives all over her body after just one sip.

The same goes for marijuana. Most of the people I know who use it recreationally do so as a means to relax and relieve stress, but I also have friends who say that getting high makes them anxious and paranoid, which is the opposite of a good time, especially if you're in an unfamiliar place around unfamiliar people!

There's also a big difference between smoking and taking an edible. You feel the effects from smoking much faster, so you're better able to regulate how much you consume and how high you get. It can take an hour or longer to start feeling the effects of an edible. Many people get impatient, think it's not working, and take more. By the time the first dose kicks in, it's too late. You can easily wind up so high that you don't know where you are. It can be difficult to move or even differentiate between if you're in a dream or reality. Edibles can last four to six hours or more. It can be scary, and it's not fun.

There is also the question of what you're truly putting into your body. Unless you know the source of the product you're using for sure, you can't know if anything else is in it. People can drop a pill into your drink or lace a marijuana cigarette with other substances like PCP or methamphetamine that you are unaware of. If you're going to try these things, make sure you do it in a safe environment with people you trust. Even then, you may trust the friend who is offering it to you, but do you trust the person who sold it to him? A random party, where egos are running hot, and people are trying to out-drink or out-smoke one another to determine who's the manlier man is not a good setting for a new experiment.

As I said, I did not drink or use any drugs in high school. I smoked marijuana once in my senior year of college, but that was it. I have plenty of friends who didn't drink at all and still *loved* their college experience. I don't feel like I missed out on anything in high school by not using drugs and alcohol. There is not a single experience that I look back on and think, "dang, that would have been a lot more fun if I was drunk or high!" On the other hand, there are *plenty* of times that I look back on an event and think, "dang, that would have been a lot more fun if I was sober."

One time, in my early 20s, I went to a concert with a bunch of friends at an outdoor amphitheater in the middle of the summer. We had lawn seats, which meant we could sit anywhere on the big lawn at the top of the amphitheater, behind the sections with actual seats. We got there early so we could party in the parking lot before the gates opened. I wasn't driving, so I partied pretty hard. I was completely wasted before we even went in.

I remember bits and pieces of the opening act, but that's pretty much it. I was blacked out for the majority of the show. The next day, one of my friends showed me pictures from the concert. Apparently, at some point, I had decided to take off my clothes and throw them into the crowd. I was running around in my underwear and taking pictures with random people. My friends had to find my clothes and hold onto them until we got home. I could have been arrested for that little stunt, and I didn't even remember doing it! I certainly wouldn't have done it if I had been sober.

Not only did I make a total ass of myself in that situation, but I completely missed the concert that I had been so excited to see. I basically paid for a ticket to a show I didn't even attend. I definitely would have enjoyed that experience a whole lot more if I'd been sober, and I regret my decision that day.

I'm not going to lie to you. Drugs and alcohol can be fun and contribute to a good time when used in moderation, around the right people, and in the right setting.

There is a reason some people use them, after all. In my opinion, however, high school is not that time or setting.

You can have a great high school experience without drugs or alcohol if you're with the right crowd. If you haven't found that crowd yet, seek them out! As I told you earlier, you will discover that your true friends are the ones who share your values. You'll have plenty of opportunities in your life, once you're in a more mature place mentally, to decide if you want to experiment with these substances. You'll also be in a better place to evaluate the potential risks.

I've tried a lot of things in the years since college, including multiple varieties, concentrations, and methods of consuming marijuana. I've experienced opiates like Percocet, Vicodin, and Dilaudid. They were prescribed to me after surgery when I had my elbow reconstruction, and again after I broke my ankle snowboarding. After my elbow surgery, I held onto some of them for "recreation" after I no longer needed them for pain management. I've also tried cocaine and magic mushrooms. I've had some great times and some absolutely terrible experiences. There is no such thing as a guaranteed good time when drinking or using drugs. Every substance and every experience is a roll of the dice.

I don't use any of these drugs often, and I plan to never use prescription opiates or cocaine ever again. I tried them and I didn't like them. I certainly didn't like them enough to trade my life for them. There are other substances, like crystal meth and heroin for example, that I will never try because the risk is just too great to even make one experimental use worth it. I don't care how good it might feel – a few minutes or even a few hours of artificially-induced euphoria cannot compare to a lifetime of joy and happiness that I would be putting in jeopardy.

I'm not telling you about my own drug use to brag or sound cool. I just want you to understand that I am speaking from experience and not just telling you to "just say no" because I did. I understand the danger that comes with using opiates in particular. With the omnipresent news stories about the "opioid crisis" and the climbing death toll in this country, you should too. The risk of addiction is very high. Choosing to use them recreationally, or even at all, is a game of Russian Roulette – eventually, you will lose. When that happens, everything else I am sharing with you in these letters will be irrelevant. Once addiction takes hold, it consumes you and becomes the focal point of your day-to-day life. Think how much time you will waste if you are trading two or three hours of pleasure a day for *every other waking moment of your life.* Say goodbye to any dreams and goals you have for your future. Stay away from that shit!

After my second surgery, I threw out the remainder of the prescribed pain killers as soon as I could manage the pain on non-prescription options alone. Keep in mind, when I broke my ankle it was the most intense and excruciating pain of my life. I was in so much pain that I couldn't sleep. My sheets were soaked with sweat because my muscles were in a constant state of contraction. It felt like I was in a never-ending workout, and I could not make my body stop! After the surgery, in which my foot was literally reattached to my leg with metal plates screwed into my bones and my skin was stapled shut, I was so tense from the throbbing pain that I couldn't even relax enough to pee.

Imagine waking up in the morning with a full bladder and not being physically able to pee! My wife had to help me to the bathroom, and I had to *sit* on the toilet, propping my surgically-repaired ankle up so the blood would flow back down toward my torso and the pain would abate just enough that I could relax my bladder and pee. Despite this, I still tried to get off the opiates as soon as I could. I chose to live with a little more pain for a few days rather than risk forming a dependence on those pills and wasting my life chasing a temporary feeling. That's how seriously I took the risk of opioid addiction.

At the end of the day, you will have to make your own choices. I can't tell you what to do any more than your parents can. I just hope that this letter makes you think a little bit more about the potential consequences of your choices. Maybe it will even make you more curious about your parents' choices.

If you're feeling up to it, try asking *them* about their experiences with drugs and alcohol earlier in their lives. You may be surprised by what they have to say. They may be more open to sharing their story with you if you start the conversation. It might even allow you to see them in a new light and bring you closer together as a result.

Again, when your body and brain have matured and you have the capacity to make an informed decision regarding drugs and alcohol, you can do whatever you want. If you want to try it all, go for it! Until that time, take care of yourself and respect your body and your gut instincts. If that little voice in your head is telling you something is a bad idea – like when I decided to get into the car with Adam – it probably is. Don't ignore it.

Peer pressure can be really hard to resist, but as your self-confidence grows and you really take the time to discover who you are and what's important to you in life – as I hope you have been doing as you read these letters – you will be able to weigh those long-term aspirations against any temporary labels that others may throw at you.

Remember, in a few short years, high school will just be a memory, and you will have the benefit of being able to make rational decisions on *your* terms with the right precautions in place. A rash and impulsive choice now could leave you carrying around the weight of guilt and shame well into your future – if you even make it that far.

If you ever want to talk more about this subject, or anything in any of these letters, let me know. I'll be here for you, without judgment.

    Love,
    Tom

Chapter 16

The truth about strength and fitness

Ivan –

I spent nearly 10 years as a strength and nutrition coach, so these next two letters are very important to me. I want to tell you right up front that *this* letter focuses on the value of weight training and some broad guidance on how to get started. However, I want to emphasize that while lifting weights is my preferred method of training, it's not the only way to improve your fitness. If you prefer running, swimming, biking, or any other form of physical activity, that's great! Do something that you enjoy and that you'll stick with. Regardless of how you choose to stay active, including some form of weight or resistance training *will* make you better at whatever else you decide to do, so I encourage you not to ignore the weights entirely.

With that said, I will make this very simple for you: lift weights. Get strong. This isn't just for athletics or to look good for the ladies. This is for your mental, emotional, and physical health and longevity – things that will mean a lot more to you in the years to come. It's something I wish I had taken more seriously and started earlier in my life.

I'm not suggesting you need to spend several hours a day in the gym or put up huge numbers in the squat rack. Strength is relative. If you want to *compete* in a strength sport like weightlifting, powerlifting, or even football, you may need to spend more time in the gym and put up some bigger numbers, but you can get strong and improve your health in 30-40 minutes, four or five days a week.

Right now, you are – there's no other way to say it – you're pretty weak. There's nothing wrong with that. You're young and you've never physically trained your body in any real capacity. With that said, however, *now* is the time to get started on it. As I've gotten older, I've noticed that a lot of the strongest people I know have one thing in common – they started young. At your age, your body is primed to learn the movement patterns and build the base strength you need to carry through the rest of your life. The longer you wait to get started, the harder it will be to achieve.

Here's the thing about strength – it never really goes away once you've got it. I'm not saying that you can get strong, then stop working out completely, spend your days playing video games, and still be able to lift like a boss, but if you take the time to get strong while you're young, you'll teach your body, specifically your central nervous system, that you are capable of moving big loads. Then, even if you take some time off, you will be able to get back to that peak physical strength much faster than someone who has never trained and is starting from scratch.

Here's another reason to take strength and fitness seriously: strong people are harder to kill. I'm not talking specifically about going to war or even getting in a fist fight – although being strong helps in both of those scenarios too. I'm talking about your body's ability to handle more stress. That can be an acute stress, like breaking a bone, or a stress that accumulates more slowly, like a virus or infection. The healthier you are, the better your immune response will be, increasing your resistance to injury and disease.

You will become more resilient and increase and your ability to tolerate pain and suffering because you'll have made your body accustomed to being in stressful, physically uncomfortable situations. Lifting weights will increase your bone density, making them harder to break, which will help significantly in your older years. Your coordination will also improve because your brain will have developed the neural pathways to help your muscles work together to move heavy loads with precision.

On top of all that, working out is an awesome way to safely let out anger, aggression, and frustration that has built up in other areas of your life. I have never finished a training session with more stress than I started with. It's a great way to clear your head while also benefiting your body. The benefits of strength training are incalculable and there is almost no risk – if you do it correctly.

While I do believe there is a genetic component to this – some people are more naturally inclined to be stronger and run faster than others – the genes you're born with are only a small part of this equation. Neither of my parents are particularly athletic. My uncle was a very good baseball player by all accounts, but with that exception, I don't know if anyone else in my family, other than my brothers, even played sports growing up. I certainly didn't have anyone encouraging me to go to the gym! Going outside to play was just about the only exercise I got, and while I got a lot of it running around the neighborhood and building forts in the woods near my house, it didn't help me get strong. If you're spending hours a day playing video games and watching TV, you're not even getting that basic exercise!

The two biggest things that held me back when I was younger were that I didn't have anyone encouraging me to lift, and I had no idea what I *should* be doing, let alone how to do it correctly. If you don't grow up in a household or community where health and fitness are taken seriously, where do you even begin?

With all the dreaming I did about becoming a professional baseball player, you'd think I would have put a lot more thought into how to get stronger to improve my game. Without any guidance however, I didn't even consider that taking an active role in getting stronger would make me better. I thought my skills were good enough for my age, and that they'd magically get better as I matured and my body filled out. I never had a coach who understood the value and *necessity* of weight training in achieving that goal. I also never received an education on how it all worked. I didn't understand the biomechanics of how muscles are built and that strengthening my legs and back would help me throw harder than if I just focused on strengthening my arms and shoulders.

In fact, I had the opposite thought: if I started lifting weights, my muscles would get so big that I would become inflexible and injury prone. In my mind, I was sure that if I even *looked* at a barbell for too long, I'd get muscles like Mr. Olympia and I'd be too bulky to play the game I loved. I equated any form of strength and performance training to bodybuilding because I didn't know the difference. I didn't understand exactly what steroids were and how they worked, I just thought that anyone who lifted weights would naturally start to look that way.

By the time I reached high school, I still made the excuse that I was afraid of getting too bulky to play, but in reality, I was just lazy. The thought of getting bulky and inflexible was a convenient lie I allowed myself to believe to justify my laziness. Lifting weights seemed like a lot of work. Our off-season baseball workouts were disorganized and most of them were optional, so I opted out at every chance I got. However, high school is also when the majority of young people begin to blossom physically.

I was a thin, wiry 165 pounds as a sophomore, and I wanted to impress the ladies! I got a set of weights for Christmas that year. It was a very small set. The bar was probably only 25 pounds, and the biggest plates in the set were 25 pounds each. I'm having a hard time remembering the specifics because I hardly used it!

Again, with no instruction or coaching, and doubling down on my unfounded theory that even looking at the bar would morph me into a raging hulk, I figured I could take some creatine, crush a few sets, and be jacked in no time.

I bought some creatine, which I thought was essentially legal steroids, and started with the "pre-loading" phase that was recommended on the package. I choked down two servings a day for two weeks, doing some biceps curls with a set of five-pound dumbbells my mom had. I figured some light pre-training reps would get the blood moving and let my muscles know that bigger weights were right around the corner. At the end of that two-week loading phase, I put as much weight on the bar as I could handle and spent an hour in the garage doing bench press and curls and mixing in sit-ups between sets. I rotated through those exercises until I physically couldn't do another rep.

I went to bed that night expecting to wake up looking like a Greek statue. The next morning, I was a statue alright – I could hardly move my upper body at all. My arms were on fire. Once I got one moving, I had to keep it moving or it would lock up on me and the pain would start all over again.

I went to the movies with my girlfriend that afternoon. When I put my arm around her and left it there for five minutes, I had to physically use my other arm to remove it. It was horrible. I started to regain normal movement after a couple days, but I was sore for about a week.

Looking back, I'm sure I had severe inflammation in both shoulders and elbows. I had tried to do too much weight and too many reps before my body was adequately prepared for the workload, and my ligaments were damaged from the effort. I was lucky I didn't get Rhabdomyolysis, which can occur when the acute breakdown of muscle tissue releases a damaging protein into the blood. This can cause severe kidney damage and require hospitalization.

Like I said, there's very little risk to weight training if you do it *correctly*, but I had no idea what I was doing. Rather than take personal responsibility for doing it wrong and invest the time and effort to learn to do it right, I decided that I was not destined to be strong after all and I swore off weights for two years, skipping every off-season strength-training session and telling myself that, as a pitcher, I had to stay nimble and flexible.

The next time I set foot in a weight room was my freshman year of college. I went with my suitemate, who had played football in high school and had a physique that I admired. I tried to do everything that he was doing. Obviously, he could lift far more weight than I could, so I did the same rep scheme using a lighter load. I lasted all of 20 minutes before I ran outside and puked in the bushes. I went back into the gym and watched him finish his workout before once again deciding that I would never be strong.

Finally, in my junior year of college, I got my first "coach," but it's not the coach you'd expect. A friend of mine introduced me to a book on strength training, written by Pavel Tsatsouline. Pavel is a Russian strength coach who is widely recognized as the man who introduced the kettlebell to the United States.

This book recalibrated my mind and gave me a fresh perspective on fitness. Pavel's training method focuses on practical strength and mobility. He emphasizes that bigger does not always mean stronger. Through his writing, I began to understand strength training in a new way. I began following the programming in his book, including his philosophy of using the minimum effective dose. To paraphrase Pavel, you should leave the gym feeling like you're *ready* for a fight, not like you just lost one. These critical lessons changed the trajectory of my path to fitness. For the first time, I truly felt like the results I wanted were achievable – they would just take more time to develop than I initially thought. This new knowledge changed my life.

I learned that the body responds best when it is trained in balance. This means that you cannot spend all your time doing bench press, biceps curls, and sit-ups. Those are what I like to call *mirror muscles* – the ones that are fun to look at in the mirror. If you really want to develop them fully, however, you need to focus on the muscles you cannot easily see, specifically your back, glutes, and hamstrings.

Think of your body from an architectural standpoint. If you are building a tower and stack twice as many bricks on one side, what will happen? The tower will start to lean to the heavier side. The same thing happens to your body if you only work the front half. If you've ever seen a strong-looking guy walking around with his shoulders rolled forward and his arms swinging in front of him rather than at his sides, he is probably suffering from this phenomenon. He's not necessarily doing that on purpose. His pecs and shoulders are overdeveloped and out of balance with his back, so the stronger muscles on his front side are pulling his shoulders forward, creating that look.

He might look like a superhero cartoon, but he's probably pretty inflexible, which can lead to injury if his arms and legs are forced into a position they're not used to being in – if he slipped and fell awkwardly, for example – and he probably could not lift a heavy object off the ground without hurting his back. How practical is that? Think about how you use those muscles in day-to-day life. How many times do you find yourself laying on the ground and needing to push a large object off of you? Hopefully not often! On the other hand, how frequently do you need to stand up from a seated position or lift something off the ground and carry it somewhere? Literally every day! This is why building your body in balance is the key to true, functional strength.

To build your body in balance, you have to work on the biggest muscle group in your body: your posterior chain. This includes those muscles I mentioned earlier, your back, glutes, and hamstrings. As these muscles get stronger, they will allow your mirror muscles to get stronger because the balance has been restored and they can continue to grow, even if you don't train them directly.

Here's a true story to illustrate that point. Toward the end of college and in the years right afterward, when I was focused solely on my looks, I slipped back into my old method of working out. I spent most of my time in the gym working my pecs, biceps, and abs. I was benching three days a week. After about 18 months of this routine, I could still barely bench 200 pounds.

A few years after that, I found CrossFit, which changed my mindset again. Some aspects of the training methodology reminded me of what I had read in Pavel's book. I took an interest in learning more about different training philosophies, like progressive overload, where you slowly increase the amount of resistance (weight) over time, and I started focusing on building my entire body in balance. I transitioned away from the bench and spent more time on the deadlift and the squat.

CrossFit also introduced me to Olympic Weightlifting. I was mesmerized by the speed and technical precision these lifts demanded. I was amazed to learn that some of the smallest weightlifters in the world could easily outlift the biggest dudes in a CrossFit gym – any gym for that matter – and I was immediately hooked.

Just like that, I went from being "allergic to the barbell" to falling in love with it. I tailored my training program to get better at the two competitive lifts, the snatch and clean & jerk, which meant a lot more deadlifts and squats! I cut the bench press out of my training program almost completely. I probably benched a total of five times over the next few years.

One day, after I'd finished my training, I saw a friend of mine doing some bench press. Just for fun, I decided to join him and see how heavy I could go – maybe I could still bench 200! I wound up maxing out at 305 pounds.

I had increased my bench by more than 100 pounds without specifically training that lift at all for more than three years! I was able to do this because all the snatches, cleans, squats and deadlifts had made my body much stronger as a whole. Each of those exercises is a compound lift, meaning it requires multiple muscle groups to work together to execute them. Compound lifts strengthen the neural pathways that teach your muscles to work together and allow them to grow in balance to perform the necessary task. The overall strength I accumulated had increased my bench without me even having to think about it, let alone train it.

You can do this too, even if you're not interested in the sport of Weightlifting. You just have to think about building a strong body as a *whole* rather than as individual muscle groups. To maximize your strength, you should stick to free weights, like barbells, dumbbells, and kettlebells. Stay away from the machines.

Machines are convenient for targeting specific muscles, which can be helpful if you're a body builder or trying to rehab an injury, but they are a very poor method for turning your body into a cohesive unit. This is because machines limit the range of motion you can achieve. They are locked in a specific path of motion, and you can only move within that pre-defined path. As a result, the muscles used to move weight on that specific path get stronger, but the small stabilizer muscles around the primary movers are hardly doing anything at all, so they remain comparatively weak.

When you use free weights, all of those smaller stabilizing muscles have to work just as hard as the major muscle groups to keep you balanced and in a good mechanical position to move the load. It's also more practical for everyday use.

When was the last time you had to move an object that was locked into a specific path of motion? When you pick up your backpack, or get up from a chair, or even reach into the car to help carry the groceries into the house – are those objects and movements limited to one direction or movement pathway? No! They can move in three dimensions: up and down, front to back, and side to side. Free weights allow your body to sense these different dimensions of movement, training all of your muscles to work together to prevent that external object from pushing you into an awkward position while under a heavy load. You can strengthen your entire body at the same time and build everything in balance by using compound movements.

I've seen guys who post pictures of themselves on social media using the leg press machine with 800+ pounds on it, but I have also trained with them and know they can't squat half that weight using a barbell. That leg press isn't going to help them if they are trying to lift a fallen tree off a fence because their back and core stabilizers won't be strong enough to support the load. If you're going to spend time in the gym getting strong, get the most bang for your buck and stick to the free weights. Teach your body how to manipulate objects in space and prepare yourself for real world applications rather than just an ego boost and a social media post.

The single best exercise to train your entire body at the same time is the deadlift. If you could only do one exercise for the rest of your life – or if you want to spend as little time in the gym as possible and still get strong – the deadlift will be your best friend.

The deadlift is a simple lift. It's just a loaded barbell that you pick up off the floor and set back down again. When it is done correctly, it uses just about every muscle in your body, from your fingers and forearms, to your biceps and shoulders, to your lats and back, to your core, to your glutes, hamstrings and even your calves and quads. One lift to rule them all.

To execute the deadlift safely, start with the bar on the ground. Don't load it on a rack and then put it on the ground. Remember, use small plates – maybe 25 pounds on each side – to start. You want to keep the bar as close to the center of your body as you can, so when you set up for your lift, set your feet about shoulder-width apart and step up to the bar so it's covering the knots in your shoelaces when you look down. Bend at the waist and grab the bar with both hands, making sure your hands are outside your knees. From there, bend your knees to bring your shins in contact with the bar. Every person's position is going to look a little different based on the length of their limbs, but following these steps will put you in the best position for *your* body type.

Once you have your grip set, lock in your back and torso. Take a breath and force the air into your core like you're bracing for a punch to the stomach. Flatten your back – you should not have a curve of any kind in your spine when pulling your deadlift. Pull your shoulder blades back and lock them in. Imagine trying to hold a pencil between them. With your back and shoulders set, squeeze every muscle in your body and slowly push the floor away from you. By focusing on pushing the floor down rather than pulling the bar up, you will have a better chance of resisting the urge to use your arms to move the bar. Your arms should remain straight throughout the entire lift. Keep your back straight the entire time. Once the bar passes your knees, use your hips to straighten out and stand up.

To put the bar down, keep everything tight. You can take a breath at the top of the lift and re-set your core if you need to. Start by hinging at the hip. Push your butt slightly backward like you're going to sit down. Once the bar passes your knees again, lower your entire body back down to the starting position, all the while keeping your back and shoulders set.

If things start to fall apart and you feel your back start to round or your body start to shake uncontrollably, you can always just drop the bar. It will make some noise, and you may startle some of the people around you, but it's always better to be safe than sorry! Don't go too heavy with the deadlift – or any lift for that matter – until you have mastered the technique. Never compromise your form. If your legs feel strong enough to move the weight but your back starts to round, take some weight off the bar and continue training with lighter weight that allows you to keep your back straight. As your back gets stronger, bigger weights will come, but give it time to catch up to the rest of your muscles! Remember the mantra of *minimum effective dose*.

The second most important lift is the squat. You do this movement every day without even thinking about it. Every time you sit down to eat or take a dump and then stand back up again, you've done a squat. Every time you sit down in class and then get back up when the bell rings, you've done a squat. You can get more efficient at this by adding weight to a barbell, taking it on your shoulders, and doing a similar motion. In addition, the weight helps train the stabilizing muscles in your core, which protect your back. By strengthening these stabilizing muscles, you will greatly reduce the risk of hurting your back if you twist the wrong way while standing up or doing some other mundane task – even with little or no weight involved.

The keys to a good squat are achieving a full range of motion and maintaining a strong core throughout the lift. When you take the bar out of the rack, take a breath, push the air into your abdomen and brace your core the same way you do when you deadlift. Keep that tenson throughout the lift. Once your core is set, bend your knees and let your butt travel slightly backward as you sit down into a full squat. Your chest should stay upright the entire time, facing the wall in front of you. If someone was standing in front of you, they should be able to read what's on your tee shirt through the whole lift. If you start to round your back or your chest starts pointing toward the floor, your core and stabilizer muscles are not strong enough to manage the load and you've gone too heavy. If you are truly achieving full range of motion, your glutes and hamstrings will make contact with your calves at the bottom. Once you feel that contact, stand back up.

You can do a simple test to know if you're truly reaching your full range of motion. When you're at the bottom of the squat, you should be able to sit there with your glutes and hamstrings resting on your calves without your quads getting tired. Make sure you're keeping your back straight, your chest upright, and your core engaged the whole time. You can do this exercise without any weight at all, just extend your arms out in front of you to help maintain your balance. Don't forget to breathe at the top between reps.

The third tool I'll recommend to you is the kettlebell, essentially a cannon ball with a handle on it. While the deadlift is the best single exercise for a full-body strength workout, the kettlebell is the most versatile tool. One kettlebell will allow you to do tons of exercises that build explosive strength, mobility, and balance. If you can only invest in one piece of equipment to work out at home, the kettlebell should be your choice. It's such a simple piece of equipment that even if you can't buy one, you can make one yourself. There are plenty of do-it-yourself kettlebell options out there!

Kettlebells allow you to do swings, snatches, cleans, presses, get-ups, windmills, deadlifts, squats, and pretty much any movement you can think of. They are especially effective at developing shoulder strength and stability because you are controlling an external object through a full range of motion that can include going overhead. Developing strong shoulders is critical for *every* sport, as well as everyday life, and can help protect you from injury whether you're playing on a varsity team or in the driveway with your friends.

These movements alone will help you jump higher, run faster, throw harder, react faster, and apply more force and power to any athletic feat you attempt. They can also get you shredded if you're still primarily interested in looks. I will say, however, that most of the aesthetics are achieved through eating a healthy diet, which I'll talk about in my next letter.

When you decide to start some kind of strength training regimen, please make sure you read some books and watch some videos on proper form and technique. My descriptions of the movements are very general and there are more details you need to be aware of before you try adding weight or working out on your own. If you can, find a qualified strength coach in your community to help you. You can learn the basics and make sure you're using proper mechanics with just a couple hours of knowledgeable coaching. Once you have that, you will feel more confident in working out on your own and increasing the load as you are able. You will also reduce the risk of doing it incorrectly and injuring yourself. Don't do what I did and just assume you know what you're doing. It hurts and it's not worth it!

Remember that strength gains are progressive, so you'll need to be patient. If you do it correctly, you can expect to see very significant gains in a few months. Start with light weight. Make sure your technique is dialed in and your movement patterns are nearly perfect. Give your smaller muscles time to catch up to the big ones. You cannot make any serious progress until your form is excellent and your muscles are ready to share the load as a team. Lifting with poor form and bad technique will put you in a weak position, which means that you won't be able to lift as much weight as you are physically capable of, and you will substantially increase your risk of injury.

Give your body time to recover. Muscles aren't built in the gym. They're built while you're resting. To realize your full physical potential and get the best return on your investment for the time you spend working out, you need to make sure you're getting enough sleep and giving your body the opportunity to rebuild stronger muscles that will allow you to increase your work capacity.

Remember the principle of minimum effective dose. Don't work out to the point of exhaustion or failure. Always walk away from the bar or kettlebell feeling like you might have had at least one more rep in you. Imagine your body as a battery. When you begin your workout, you're at a full charge. Use 80 percent of it in your workout and leave the gym feeling like you've got that other 20 percent in reserve. You will see much greater progress over time using this approach than if you drain that battery entirely and beat yourself down every time you train.

If you don't have access to a gym, you can still work on building strength and agility using your bodyweight alone! You can run sprints, do squats, pushups, pullups, sit-ups, and plenty more exercises without any equipment at all. If you want to add weight, try doing squats, pushups and pullups while wearing your fully loaded backpack. You can do sit-ups while holding the bag over your head. Starting this type of training now will give you a tremendous head start for when you are eventually able to access a gym with some free weights.

If you're feeling inspired and want to get started on your strength journey immediately, here's something to get you started: try to do 100 push-ups, 100 squats and 100 sit-ups every day. If you have a kettlebell, add 100 swings to the mix. Now, if you try to do this all at once, it's going to take you a LONG time. However, if you do 10 reps of each movement once every hour or so, you can get through the whole thing in about 15 minutes of total time over the course of your day. Do a couple sets before school. Mix them in between homework assignments and during the ads that pop up between videos. It's easy to find a spare minute here and there. If you do this for a few months, even if you just start with 50 reps of each movement a day, I promise you'll get stronger and have some new muscle to show for it!

There is literally no excuse for you not to get stronger if you want to. I have seen people in wheelchairs lifting big weights, pulling themselves and their chairs up a rope with just their arms, and getting absolutely jacked.

I personally know a guy whose legs end just below his knees. He was born that way and has two prosthetic legs that he wears to walk. He competes in strongman events and the Highland Games. I follow an athlete on social media who was born with only one arm and still competes in Olympic Weightlifting. If you *want* to get strong, you can do it. Any excuse you come up with is merely in your head. Overcoming that mental hurdle is often the most difficult part of the whole process.

As I mentioned up front, I focused primarily on lifting weights in this letter because that's what I like to do. However, fitness is far more than just lifting weights. If you want to exercise and get into better shape but aren't as concerned about moving a bunch of weight, do yoga, take up dance, or swim some laps! Do whatever makes you happy! Participating in some form of physical activity will provide incredible value to your physical and emotional health, both now and into the future. The best exercise program is the one that you enjoy and will stick with!

>Love,
>Tom

Chapter 17

The truth about nutrition

Dear Ivan,

Hopefully you read my letter on the importance of fitness and you're inspired to get moving. Now we need to talk about what you're eating. There's a truism that says, "you can't out-work a bad diet." Basically, there's no amount of working out that you can do to completely offset the effects of eating a bunch of crap.

Before I get into the details, I want to start off by acknowledging that there's a good chance your body doesn't look the way you want it to right now. You may think you're too skinny or too fat. Some of this can be attributed to what you eat, but at this point in your life, it's more likely a product of the hormonal changes your body is going through. Everyone's body is a little bit different. Two guys could eat the exact same thing and have completely different physiques, so changing your diet and working out won't necessarily guarantee a dramatic change to your body's appearance at this point in your physical development. There is nothing wrong with the way you look right now. You just have to ride it out and let nature take its course.

There are people I went to high school and college with who were skinny as a rail. They could eat whatever they wanted and not gain a pound. Years later, once their bodies reached maturity, they got fat because they continued to eat the same way they always had, despite the fact that their metabolism had changed. Even though they went to the gym regularly, they couldn't get back to that slim frame they had in school because they refused to change their eating habits. On the other hand, when I was a personal trainer, I worked with plenty of people who were grossly overweight when they started but were able to shed a ton of fat and regain their muscle tone by changing what they ate in addition to exercising.

In both cases, exercise is about 20 percent of the equation. The biggest factor in determining your body composition is making good food choices. If you start making healthy choices now, you will be in a much better position to create your ideal body in the years ahead.

When I was in high school, I hardly thought about nutrition at all. I picked up little bits and pieces about what it meant to "eat healthy" over the years, but it was always anecdotal. The source of the information was often questionable, like an advertisement from a food or supplement company, and the sources often contradicted one another. For example, there was an ad campaign for milk that used to run in some of the biggest sports magazines I read. The full-page ads featured elite athletes with milk moustaches claiming that drinking milk helped them in competition and suggested it could help me too. At the same time, there was another ad campaign running on TV telling me that drinking milk would make me bloated and gassy, so I should drink *almond* milk instead, which isn't really milk at all. How do you make sense of these mixed messages? How do you know who or what to believe?

My first memory of anything nutrition-related happened in kindergarten. I don't remember anything about the in-class lesson, but the homework assignment was to eat a healthy breakfast the next day and then tell the class about it. The reward was a gold star sticker I would get to wear! At that age, I was highly motivated by positive recognition from my teacher, and I was determined to get that star.

The next morning in class, we all sat in a circle around the teacher, who called us up one by one to tell her what we'd had for breakfast. When my name was called, I proudly marched to the center of the circle and took a knee, as if I were about to be knighted.

"Good morning, Tommy," she said. "What did you have for breakfast today?"

I recited my breakfast menu in a very matter-of-fact tone: a fried egg and toast with a glass of orange juice. My teacher commended me for my excellent choices and the rest of the class applauded. I was struck by a dizzying sensation as a flood of dopamine hit my brain and she bestowed the coveted gold star sticker on my shirt.

My classmate, Michael, was next. The teacher called him into the circle and asked him to share what he'd had for breakfast. Michael took a knee, just as I had, and proudly told the class that he'd had not one, but *two* bowls of Lucky Charms.

I was immediately struck with envy. Lucky Charms! That son of a gun! My mom *never* let me eat those delicious, kid-friendly cereals!

While Michael waited expectantly for his gold star sticker, I stared off into space, daydreaming about what a bowl of Lucky Charms must taste like. I began scheming up ways to convince my mom that I needed to get a piece of that action.

"I'm sorry, Michael," the teacher lamented. "That is not a very healthy breakfast."

My head snapped to attention and my daydream evaporated in a puff of powdered sugar. I looked to the center of the circle. The confident smile had left Michael's face. With slumped shoulders, his expressionless eyes stared at the floor in disbelief, as if he'd just missed a wide open jumper at the buzzer and lost a championship game.

As he grappled with the realization that he would not be getting a gold star sticker, I found myself just as confused as Michael. How could Lucky Charms, heavily advertised as "part of this nutritious breakfast," *not* be healthy?

We never got an explanation that I can recall. The teacher had said it wasn't a very healthy breakfast. That was it. Period. End of story.

I don't remember any other formal education on nutrition or what constituted a "healthy" meal until I started doing the research for myself much later in life, well after high school and college. I have a feeling this experience is not unique to me, so my goal with this letter is to help you with some of the basic fundamentals of nutrition and get you started in the right direction.

Nutrition and fitness have some similarities. For one thing, they're both easier to maintain and improve over time if you start early and build good habits. For another, there's more than one right answer. Just as one person may prefer to lift weights while another prefers long-distance running, one person may prefer to eat a meat-heavy diet while another prefers to go vegan. Just like with fitness, the best option is the one that you enjoy, will stick with, and keeps you healthy. As long as you're smart about it and understand the fundamentals, it's hard to screw it up.

It's important to get your information from a good source. Learning to lift from a crappy coach who doesn't understand the technique, or a social media influencer who has no idea what they're actually talking about, can lead to injury. In the same way, taking your nutritional cues from an advertising campaign with ulterior motives, or an influencer with a poor understanding of the science of nutrition, can leave you confused about what to eat, how much to eat, and when to eat it.

The best advice I've heard regarding eating comes from Michael Pollan, one of the top writers about food and food science of our time. It's very brief and straightforward:

"Eat food. Not too much. Mostly plants."

Keep this simple mantra in mind when you decide to start making changes to the way you eat. You can branch out into all different types of food, but this general rule will hold true for all of them. It's crucial to remember there is no single diet that is right for everyone, and no single diet that will be right for you for the rest of your life. Things will change. Your hormones, metabolism, and overall energy needs will fluctuate over the course of your life, so don't waste time trying to find the *perfect* solution – it doesn't exist. I don't have the answer for myself, let alone the ability to offer it to you. All I can do is offer some general guidelines to help you get started on your own personal journey.

Just a heads-up, this letter gets a little *sciency* from this point on. I will try to keep it pretty light, so hopefully you will find the value in it!

First, let's talk about the word *diet* itself. In our society, this word is often associated with a desire to lose weight, so we tend to think of it as a restrictive word. "I can't eat *that*. I'm on a diet!" This negative connotation of the word is partly responsible for my early disregard for nutrition. I wasn't fat, so why should I care about a diet?

In reality, a diet is just a general encapsulation of the things you eat. It's easier to comprehend when you think about it from a non-human perspective. A monkey's diet consists primarily of fruit, nuts, and seeds. A lion's diet consists primarily of zebra, wildebeest, and other animals they're able to hunt in their native habitat. *Your* diet simply consists of the things you eat and drink, whatever they are.

Following a *specific* diet can help you achieve certain goals. Sure, you can go on a diet to lose weight, but did you know you can also go on a diet to *gain* weight? The word diet itself isn't important. The key is making smart choices about what you include or exclude from your diet to ultimately achieve the outcome you want. The point I really want to drive home before I go any further is that when I use the word diet, it doesn't necessarily mean restriction or weight loss.

Ok, so now that you understand I'm not saying you have to lose weight, let's talk about your diet and how to evaluate your food and drink choices to achieve your personal goals. I'm going to cover some general terms to help you understand the basic science of the food choices you make. I'll try to keep this as simple as possible, but I do tend to geek out on this stuff from time to time, so just bear with me!

What is a calorie? Simply put, a calorie is a measure of energy. All the food you put into your body is converted into energy to power everything from your muscles during a workout, to your brain during a test, to maintaining your body temperature while you sleep. Your body is constantly burning calories, even when you don't feel like you're actually *doing* anything.

Everyone has different caloric needs depending on where they are in life and what they do on a daily basis. A young man like yourself may need more calories than someone my size because you're still growing, even though your body is smaller than mine. Your body demands that extra energy to build more cells and increase your overall size, while still covering the needs of your muscles during that workout, your brain during that test, and your body temperature while you sleep – among many other things!

Many people – and adults in particular – make a big deal out of the number of calories in the food they eat. That's why you see estimated calorie counts next to every item on many restaurant menus these days. It's important to remember that your caloric needs are different from everyone else, so when you see general recommendations that suggest a man needs to eat 2,500 calories a day, remember that number is an *average*. That average includes you, your dad, your grandpa, and every other man in this country. It's not a number that's carved in stone. It's not the *law*. Your specific calorie needs will change over time depending on your rate of energy expenditure.

For perspective, back in 2008, American swimmer Michael Phelps won eight gold medals at the Olympic Games in Beijing. During that time, he was eating 12,000 calories a day! That's nearly the general recommended daily amount for FIVE men, and he was absolutely shredded! His body needed that amount of energy input to maintain his activity level. If he had been sitting on the couch at home *watching* the Olympics and consuming 12,000 calories a day, he would probably *be* the size of five men. It's all relative, so don't focus too much on a specific number of calories, but more on matching the number of calories you're consuming to the amount of work that you're asking your body to do.

The number of calories in a particular food does not directly correlate to the size of the meal, its nutritional value, or how long that food will keep you feeling full. For example, one large, hard-boiled egg has about 78 calories in it, while one medium sized avocado has about 250 calories, and one Double Stuf Oreo has 70 calories. You could eat three large, hard-boiled eggs, plus a bite of a fourth; or one medium sized avocado; or three and a half Double Stuf Oreos and wind up consuming about the same number of calories. Which of these options do you think would keep you full the longest?

I've tried them all at some point in my life. I can tell you that for me, three hard-boiled eggs is about my limit.

After I finish that third one, I'm full, and the thought of starting a fourth is almost enough to make me gag. The eggs alone are enough to keep me satisfied until lunch. The avocado is also filling. I don't feel sick after I finish it and it can also get me to lunch on most days. The Oreos, on the other hand, well, I don't think I've ever sat down and had just three cookies! There have been plenty of times I've crushed an entire row of 10 or more without even thinking about it! That's 700 calories without even counting the milk that goes with it! On top of all the extra calories, I'm usually pretty hungry again within an hour or two, so I have to eat something else between breakfast and lunch, which adds to the calorie count. Why is this the case?

I've talked a lot about hormones in these letters – usually as they relate to the changes you're seeing in your body as you go through puberty. Those hormones can contribute to issues like acne and are also responsible for sending your sex drive through the roof. Hormones are not limited to puberty, however, and you'll be dealing with them for the rest of your life. Hormones also play a significant role in how your body processes food.

Hormones are the chemical messengers of your body. When your body needs fuel, your stomach produces a hormone called ghrelin, which signals your brain to create that feeling of hunger. When you've eaten enough, ghrelin's counterpart, leptin, signals the brain to send the feeling of fullness so you stop eating. It seems like a very simple system, so why do people get fat?

Here's where things get a little more complicated. Throughout much of human history, food has not been plentiful. It was dependent on hunting and gathering. When food was scarce in the winter, people had to survive on what little they could find, in addition to tapping into any body fat they'd accumulated over the summer months.

Finding a large quantity of calorie-dense food, like a beehive full of honey for example, was rare. When a high-calorie meal presented itself, people had to take advantage of it! If the hormonal signals of ghrelin and leptin worked as normal, people would stop eating when they were full, but our bodies are smart. The body knows additional calories will be needed in the winter when hunting and gathering becomes much harder, so it has a built-in mechanism to override the leptin signal of fullness when it's presented with a calorie-dense opportunity. This override switch allowed our ancestors to consume far more of these calorie-dense foods than they needed to be full. Their bodies converted the extra calories to fat, storing the energy for later when there wouldn't be enough to eat on a day-to-day basis.

Today, we live in a world of plenty. If you're hungry, you can go to any number of stores and buy almost any type of food you want. Despite this, the survival instincts of our ancestors are still hard-wired into us. The calorie-dense foods that trigger our override switch are simple carbohydrates like sugar – or the honey that our ancestors would have found. This is why you can feel completely full after a meal but still find room for dessert.

Carbohydrates, or carbs for short, are one of the three major macronutrient groups. The other two are fats and proteins. Most of the foods you eat are made up of some combination of the three. Rather than dealing with fractions, we tend to classify foods based on the macronutrient that makes up the majority of that food.

Some foods can even be manipulated to shift between categories. Take milk for example. Raw milk, straight from the cow, contains all three macronutrients. If you let the milk sit for a while, the cream, which is primarily fat, rises to the top. We use that cream to make other products like whipping cream, half-and-half, and butter. Those foods would fall into the "fat" macronutrient category. On the other end of the spectrum, if you skim off the cream, you're left with *skim* milk, which is much higher in carbohydrates. Sure, skim milk also has protein in it, but it's got more carbs than protein, so it would be classified as a carbohydrate.

Without getting too deep into the science of each of these groups and how your body processes them, the key thing to realize is that simple carbohydrates are the easiest for your body to metabolize, or break down to use as energy. This is why you get jacked up and hyper when you eat a candy bar or drink a bottle of soda. The "sugar high" you experience is due to an almost immediate increase in the amount of energy coursing through your bloodstream, topping off your cells like millions of tiny gas tanks.

Most of the things we classify as junk food, including chips, cookies, candy, soda, and products made from refined white flour are primarily composed of these simple carbohydrates, which are all quickly broken down in your body into sugar.

If you've ever experienced a sugar high, you've probably also experienced the crash that follows, where you begin to feel tired and need a nap shortly after eating a bunch of it. This is the result of another hormone, insulin. Insulin's job is to remove excess sugar from your blood. If too much sugar stays in your blood stream, it is toxic to your body and it can damage your organs. This is why people with Type I diabetes need supplemental insulin. Their bodies don't make enough insulin naturally, so they have to compensate by adding it to their body to help remove excess sugar and prevent this kind of damage. As insulin pulls the sugar out of your bloodstream, your energy level falls, which results in that lazy feeling. The insulin stores the excess in your fat cells.

Not all cells in your body are the same. Muscle cells, for example, have a limited storage capacity for energy. This is why many athletes, especially endurance athletes like marathoners, eat during training and even during competition. They need to constantly replenish the energy they're burning. Once the fuel tanks in those muscle cells are full, however, there's no room to store any extra. Any unused energy remaining in the bloodstream after the muscle cells have been topped off will be stored as fat, and unlike muscle cells, your body has no limit to the amount of fat it can store.

This is a big reason why many people get fat. Our lives have become so easy! Think about how much physical activity an average person does in a day relative to the amount of work our ancestors had to do – constantly moving to hunt and gather food. Combine that with the easy access to calorie-dense foods that our brains are hard-wired to consume in excess and you wind up with the perfect recipe for obesity.

Over time, obesity can create many other problems in your body. This is collectively referred to as "metabolic syndrome," which includes Type II diabetes and heart disease, among other maladies. Metabolic syndrome can throw your hormone ratios out of whack and damage your insulin receptors, inhibiting the normal function of storing excess sugar as fat. When this happens, your blood sugar will continue to rise because the insulin can't effectively unload the sugar into the fat cell and return to grab more of it. Your body responds by producing more insulin. Now you've got high levels of insulin, as well as high levels of circulating blood sugar. If this imbalance isn't corrected through changing your diet, it can lead to Type II diabetes.

I'm not saying carbohydrates are bad or trying to scare you into eating better by threatening you with diabetes. What I *am* saying is that consuming too many simple carbs without burning an equal amount of energy is a bad long-term health strategy. As long as you are aware of the potential problems, you can make your own choices and live however you want! If you want to eat candy, do it. If you want to drink a soda with your pizza, do it. Maybe just not every day.

There are also complex carbohydrates, which are the carbs you get from fibrous foods like vegetables, beans, and oatmeal for example. These carbs are also broken down into sugar in your body, but the process of extracting it takes longer, which in turn slows the rate of sugar hitting your blood stream. This not only gives your muscles time to use their energy stores and be ready to take on more, but it also prevents insulin spikes, which cause that feeling of a sugar crash. It's the difference between throwing gasoline on a fire and just adding another log.

Protein is broken down in your body using the same chemical pathways as carbohydrates. Like complex carbs, however, it takes longer to process the protein, so the sugars that are metabolized from that steak you're eating don't hit with the same impact as the cake you're about to have for dessert.

Proteins are the building blocks for muscle, but with that said, if you eat a ton of protein or drink protein shakes with the intention of getting jacked, you have to make sure you're also lifting weights! If you're consuming a lot of protein but not spending any time in the gym, all that extra protein will be eventually broken down into sugars and stored as fat.

With all this talk about excess carbs and proteins being stored as fat, why would you ever need to actually *eat* any fat? It's a good question! When I was in high school, I thought eating fat would not only make me fat, but also give me a heart attack. I avoided eating fat whenever I could. I cut the extra fat off my steak, only ate the crispy parts of the bacon strips, and used margarine instead of butter because I thought it was the healthier choice. Years later, after reading a lot of books and doing a lot of independent research, I completely changed my opinion of this misunderstood macronutrient.

Contrary to how it sounds, eating fat won't *make* you fat. Fats are broken down in your body using a different metabolic pathway than proteins and carbs. Fat does not trigger a hormonal response from your body in the same way proteins and carbs do. There is no insulin response when you eat a chunk of lard or a spoonful of olive oil.

Fat is actually the *most* important macronutrient. You literally cannot live without it. Some of your most vital organs, including your brain and heart, prefer fat as a fuel source and need it to function properly.

Have you ever heard about the phenomenon of "rabbit starvation?" Here it is: if you were stranded on an island that had abundant, edible plant life, a good water source, and a huge population of rabbits, you would starve to death. Even if you were able to make a leafy green salad every night and design some traps and snares that constantly caught rabbits without you having to expend much energy, you would starve to death because rabbits are so lean that you wouldn't be able to consume enough fat to survive. Look it up if you don't believe me.

In fact, there are some native populations living in the arctic region whose diets consist almost entirely of saturated fat, and yet they have almost no instance of heart disease. The variety of nutrients available in fat, combined with its energy density – nearly twice the calories per gram of proteins and carbs – make it the ideal fuel for your body.

If you think about it, it makes perfect sense. Your body's preferred method of energy storage is saturated fat – that's what your fat cells are made of. If there is no food to put in your mouth, your body will begin breaking down your fat cells and using that energy to keep your body working in prime condition until the fat stores run out.

This was put to the test back in the 1960s, before many of the current restrictions around using human test subjects in experiments were put into place. An extremely obese man named Angus Barbieri, under his doctor's supervision, fasted for 382 days – more than a *year*! During that time, he drank nothing but water, unsweetened tea, and black coffee. He ate nothing but some salt and mineral supplements that had no caloric value and he lost 276 pounds! He remained completely healthy and went on to live a normal life.

Barbieri weighed 456 pounds when he started his fast, so he had a lot of fuel to work with. An average person can only live about 40 days before their body fat stores run out. It's not an experiment I would recommend, but it is definitely something to keep in mind the next time you're feeling so hungry you think you might die!

There are three major types of fats: saturated fat, mono-unsaturated fat, and poly-unsaturated fat.

Saturated fats include your body fat, and foods like butter and coconut oil. They are solid at room temperature because their chemical structure is more stable. It does not mean that they solidify in your arteries. In fact, much of the new research on fat and its relation to heart disease indicates that saturated fats can be *better* for you than the mono- and poly-unsaturated varieties. The reason for this is again due to their structure.

Imagine you are living in the time of Genghis Khan and given the responsibility of building a wall around your city to protect against invasion. The safest fortress would be one with no doors. Granted, it would be difficult to get in and out of – you'd have to carry everything over the top using ladders lowered from the inside – but there would be no weak point for the enemy to attack, providing a very formidable defense against the pillaging hoards. Alternatively, you could build your wall with only one door. All commerce would be limited to this one entry point to your city, which might get a bit congested at times, but it would be easier to defend since you could concentrate your defenses around that single weak link in the wall. Finally, you could build *several* doors in your wall, opening the city for trade and encouraging a free flow of people and goods. This option, however, would allow your adversary to evaluate multiple weak spots in your design and exploit the weakest point. They could also attack multiple doors at once, splitting your defenses and increasing your odds of defeat. Ultimately, fewer doors are better in this scenario because your primary objective is to keep unwanted people out and protect the integrity of your city and its citizens!

You can think of the three types of fats in the same way. The chemical chain of saturated fat is closed, there are no spaces for other compounds, called free radicals, to bind to them and create inflammatory particles through the process of oxidation. They are the most stable fats. Over time, of course, all organic matter will break down and the chain will weaken, creating an opportunity for oxidation to occur. However, the durability of saturated fat is much more robust than mono-unsaturated fats, like olive oil, which have one opening in their chemical structure, and poly-unsaturated fats, like canola, corn, sunflower, and other oils derived from nuts and seeds, which have multiple openings.

Each opening in the chemical chain is an opportunity for oxidation – a weak point in the wall around your city. The oxidized particles are what ultimately get stuck in the arteries and lead to heart disease. The more saturated a fatty acid chain is, the more stable and less susceptible to oxidation it is. That's why butter and coconut oil maintain their shape at room temperature, while olive oil has a consistency that's closer to maple syrup and vegetable oils have an almost water-like consistency. If your heart is the city you're trying to protect, high-quality saturated fats are the safest option.

When you hear recommendations to stay away from fatty foods, it's usually in relation to the junk foods I talked about earlier. Most chips are fried in vegetable oil and most pastries and snack cakes that you can find in your traditional grocery stores are made with vegetable oil because it's much cheaper than other fats. When you combine these simple carbohydrates with a fat that is highly susceptible to oxidation, you are consuming the worst of both macronutrient groups! The good fats generally get lumped in with the bad ones, which leads people to think that eating fat is bad for you in general.

Hopefully I didn't bore you with the science lecture and you're still reading this. Believe me, it's a lot more complicated and nuanced than the overview I just gave you. I'm not a doctor or a food scientist, so I strongly recommend doing your own research if you find this subject interesting. My goal is to give you some basic information you can use as a jumping off point for making your own decisions about what you put in your body.

To wrap it up, I'm going to come back around to Michael Pollan's advice: "Eat food. Not too much. Mostly plants."

You can create any number of meals based on this principle. If you're going to eat meat, try to choose high quality meats. The way an animal is raised greatly impacts the quality and nutritional value of its fat. If you're going to go vegetarian or vegan, make sure you do the necessary research to ensure you're getting all the essential proteins you need to be healthy, as well as enough fat from good sources. Stay away from vegetable oil!

If you're going to eat dairy products, stick to the full-fat version rather than the low- or no-fat options. These "healthy" alternatives often have added sugars to make up for the flavor that's lost when the fat is taken out. Limit the amount of simple carbohydrates you eat and try to match the amount of fuel you're putting in your body to the amount of energy you're burning on an average day. These basic steps will help keep you on a healthy path at a healthy body weight well into the future, even if you change things up from time to time.

Remember that you don't have to be perfect. You could definitely eat nothing but cake, candy, and chips, while drinking nothing but soda for a month and not die or become obese. It's just not a good long-term strategy, especially if you're trying to look good and perform in the gym or on the sports field. The good news is you can always choose to go back to eating healthy, once you know what that means.

Consider this letter as a general guideline to start making healthier food choices where you can. Save it and re-read it in the future to remind yourself of how to get back on track if you find yourself in a place you don't want to be.

Most importantly, do your own research! Find something that works for you and that you enjoy. Try lots of foods and pay attention to how they make you feel. This is *your* journey and the only way to truly realize what is best for you when it comes to nutrition is to try it out and make small adjustments as you go.

Love,
Tom

Chapter 18

The truth about school

Dear Ivan,

It may seem a bit strange that in a series of letters about all the shit I wish I knew in high school, the letter about school is at the end.

Honestly, for most of my time in high school, academics were an afterthought, which might explain why the academic side of high school was an afterthought in this book. It seems pretty straightforward. You take classes. You do your best. You get graded accordingly. It's the one part of high school that doesn't need much explanation and doesn't present questions that don't have a ready answer. Most of the stuff I wish I'd known in high school had nothing to do with academics.

The more I think about it, however, the more I realize there are some valuable insights that I only started to become aware of at the end of high school, and others that didn't crystalize until many years later, after I'd already started my professional career. I would be doing you a disservice if I didn't share this with you now, even though it may not feel as urgent or valuable as the content in the previous pages. It may help you get your priorities in line a little bit.

The big take-away, from my perspective, is do what you're good at. Put most of your thought and effort into the subjects you enjoy and understand the best.

I was not a bad high school student, but I didn't graduate with honors either. Perhaps part of the problem is that I have recently been diagnosed with ADHD and I'm learning what that means and how to deal with it as an adult. I'm sure I suffered from it in high school as well. I had a really hard time focusing on anything for very long, especially subjects that didn't come naturally to me.

When it came to subjects that demanded black-and-white answers, I struggled mightily. The sciences were not easy for me. I did alright in biology – I enjoyed learning how cells work and about the life cycles of plants, animals, fungi, etc. However, the formulas, equations and calculations required for chemistry and physics were torture. I could understand the general concepts of those courses, but writing them down on paper and proving how and why they work caused the gears in my brain to lock up and I'd drift off into a daydream about something I enjoyed and was easier for me to comprehend. Having said that, it should come as no surprise that I was also terrible at mathematics.

I remember struggling with math as early as 2nd grade. One night, my dad was helping me with my homework on counting and using multiples. One of the questions was, "What is your favorite way to count to ten?" I didn't know the word *fuck* when I was in 2nd grade, but in my head I was screaming the childhood equivalent of *what the actual fuck?!?* I flipped out and threw a small tantrum because I didn't have the language to articulate my feelings.

The easy answer, of course, is by twos, by fives, or by tens. I couldn't grasp the concept, so instead I started singing. I watched a lot of Sesame Street back in the day, and I sang a song I'd learned to help kids learn to count. That seemed like a very logical answer to me, but I couldn't figure out how to *write* it on my homework assignment.

My fear and insecurity with mathematics continued all the way through school. As soon as I ran into a concept that I couldn't immediately understand, the gears in my head would lock up again.

Sometimes I would *really* try to learn the material. I'd read the chapter in the textbook several times. Occasionally, I was even confident that I'd figured it out. However, it seemed like the moment I looked away from the book, the information would be extracted from my head, locked in an encrypted file, and rendered inaccessible by the time I got my eyes back on my homework. It was maddening, and I didn't know what to do about it.

On the other hand, I had a natural gift for "soft" skills, like interpreting language and the arts, where there can be more than one right answer as long as you can defend your position. I was very good at English. I couldn't tell you the rules of sentence structure or what the different parts of speech were, but I could intuit what an author was trying to say in a novel or poem and articulate my own thoughts very clearly. I was adept at defining and defending my conclusions. I don't know how else to explain this ability other than that it just felt natural and effortless. I assumed that everyone found it as easy as I did.

Aside from English, I excelled in other classes that required these intuitive skills. My natural proclivity for language made learning German an easy task. I also excelled in public speaking, history, government, drama, and band.

I started playing the saxophone in 6th grade, and by the time I reached high school I was pretty good. I found music to be strangely similar to English, almost a language itself. As I mentioned, I struggled with the technical aspects of language – I couldn't identify parts of speech or explain why a certain sentence structure made sense grammatically – I was just naturally able to read and write. In band, I was not very good at music theory, and I never memorized my scales, much to the band director's dismay. However, I could sight read music and *feel* the direction the composition was supposed to flow and how the music was supposed to move. I experienced the emotive changes of tempo and volume in a musical composition in much the same way that I experienced the words of a well-written novel or poem. Despite the similarities, I never considered playing saxophone – or any kind of music – as a possible career opportunity. I didn't see it as anything other than an easy A.

My freshman year was the first year my high school was open. It was a brand-new school. The band director was brand new too – it was his first job out of college. During band camp, which was held during the last few weeks of summer before school actually started, he recognized my intuition for music and placed me at the top of the saxophone section, above my friend Chuckie, who also played sax. This really bothered Chuckie. Unlike me, Chuckie had to work hard to be good at music. He had a much stronger work ethic than I did, and he made it his job to improve in all academic pursuits.

Chuckie was very good from a technical aspect, but he had no finesse – no *feel* for the music. Everything he played was robotic: technically correct, nearly perfect really, but there was no feeling in it. The tone wasn't quite right, and the dynamics – the rise and fall of the volume and intensity – were forced. It was like listening to someone perform "The Star-Spangled Banner" as a chant, articulating each syllable and timing the space between words perfectly, but not actually creating the emotion that accompanies the best renditions of that anthem.

Once we were actually in school, we were seated – essentially ranked – based on our ability to memorize musical scales and play assigned pieces of music with technical accuracy. Like I said, I never memorized my scales. For me, it was not an important part of the process. I just played what sounded right in my head. Because of this, I wound up seated behind Chuckie. I was still a better musician than he was, but the rank was based on technicality, not artistry. This continued all through high school. I was bothered by the ranking system more than I let on, so in my senior year I decided to rebel in my own way.

The whole point of band camp is to learn the halftime show for football season. It has to be held during the summer because football season starts almost as soon as school does and there's a lot to learn. Each year there is a new theme, new music that must be memorized, and new positions to learn to create the designs on the field that coincide with the music.

The marching band show my senior year featured a trumpet solo, which I learned to play on the saxophone. At the last football game of the year, the soloist, who was an underclassman, agreed to let me play the solo. When the moment came, I broke ranks, made my way to the center of the field, and let it rip. It was the pinnacle of my marching band experience and would also serve me well later in the year.

My high school had a very strong band program, so every person in the band was required to audition for the All-District Band, which was comprised of the best musicians from every high school in the district. The audition consisted – again – of memorized scales and a prepared piece of music that was handed out in advance. Everyone who auditioned on a particular instrument would be graded on three scales, selected at random, and the same piece of prepared music.

I didn't care about All-District Band at all. I was far more interested in baseball and hanging out with my girlfriend, so I did not make any effort to learn my scales, which had already relegated me to the second tier of saxophones in my own high school. I certainly wasn't going to put in the time to learn a piece of music that was technically challenging but completely unappealing to my ear. Instead, I decided to "stick it to the Man." If the band director was going to force me to burn a Saturday to go audition for this nonsense, I would show him just how little I cared.

The auditions took place at another local high school. After getting ready in a general warm-up room, musicians were called individually into private rooms with the judges sitting behind a curtain to prevent playing favorites with kids they might know. When my number was called, I walked into the audition room and sat down with a smug look on my face. I don't remember the scales I was asked to play or if I played them correctly or not. My mind was on the prepared piece of music.

The judge thanked me after I completed my scales and invited me to begin my prepared piece when I was ready. I briefly closed my eyes to revel in the moment. I shook out my fingers and slowly brought the mouthpiece to my lips. I drew a deep breath and absolutely *blasted* the trumpet solo from the marching band show as loud as I could, putting as much passion and effort into it as I had when I'd played in on the field and wanted to make sure the people at the top of the stands could hear me.

When I was finished, I quickly picked up my things and turned to leave while the judge was still trying to figure out what had just happened. He or she had no frame of reference for what I had played, so they may have thought I'd been given the wrong piece of music to prepare. The only one who knew what I had done was Chuckie, because I'd told him my plan ahead of time. At least that's what I thought.

I was feeling pretty good about myself as I gently closed the door to the audition room behind me and prepared to enjoy what was left of my Saturday. As I turned to walk back to the warm-up room, I almost ran into my band director, who had been standing outside my audition room listening. I froze, and my smile disappeared as I looked into the face of the man who had recognized my intuitive gift for music early on and had failed to help me care enough to learn the technical side of it. I thought he would be furious with me, that he might pin me to the wall and berate me for embarrassing him, but I read something else in his expression. He gently shook his head, and without speaking a word, his soft, sorrowful eyes said, "I can't believe you're throwing this away."

For the first time, I realized I had misinterpreted his intentions over the past three and a half years. He saw a gift in me, but it was a gift I had no interest in. His desire was for me to recognize this gift – that not everyone can play intuitively and make music sound the way it's supposed to. He hadn't been trying to knock me down by forcing me to learn scales and audition for the All-District Band. He was trying to show me that I could have a future in music if I wanted it. He wanted me to recognize that if I was willing to put in just a little more effort to learn the parts of it that *could* be taught, the gift I had that *couldn't* be taught would put me on a trajectory for great success.

I didn't fully understand it then, but I do now. Choosing not to use the gifts you are given is worse than not receiving a gift at all.

At that time, I did not understand that my natural talent for language and the arts is not given to everyone. I took it for granted – an automatic A – and I did the bare minimum to get that A. Sadly, this blind spot followed me through most of college as well. If I had recognized my gifts for what they were when I was your age, I would have put a lot more effort and focus into improving those skills.

Even the most naturally gifted people must work hard to sharpen their skills and learn how to wield that gift before they are able to maximize their individual potential. We tend to look at people like Michael Jordan, for example, and think they are just *naturally* better than everyone else. In reality, guys like Michael Jordan and Travis Mash – the world champion powerlifter I told you about – put in an *insane* amount of work to maximize their natural abilities and achieve their utmost potential. If either of these men had rested solely on their natural gift without putting in the extra time and effort to hone it, we may never have known their names.

What is your gift? It might be something you're passionate about, or it might be something you take for granted. I was extremely passionate about baseball, and I put in the practice to get better at it, but just like Chuckie on the saxophone, I could have been technically perfect (which I wasn't) and still not had the natural gift to make it a viable career option.

I had a gift for music, but it was nowhere near as good as my brother's gift for music. I could have practiced every day of my life for hours at a time and I still wouldn't be anywhere close to the musician he is. I didn't want to be the second best in my own family, so I didn't put in the effort to develop that gift.

I also had a gift for writing and language. At first, I didn't see it as a gift. Everyone can speak and write, can't they? How special could it be? Once I got to college, however, I learned that most people are terrified of public speaking. Once I began reading other students' work, I also realized that not everyone can clearly transcribe their thoughts into writing. I began working for the school newspaper and then got a part-time job at the local newspaper in my college town covering high school sports. I learned to appreciate being able to tell stories and convey the full range of emotions to people who didn't attend the game in person.

After I graduated college, I briefly considered going to law school. I enjoyed writing and arguing, which is basically a lawyer's job, and the money sounded pretty good. However, I was burned out on school and I didn't want to take on the huge debt that law school would demand. I decided to head off into the workforce and see what happened.

I worked at several unfulfilling jobs over the next five years before my experience as a journalist helped me land a position as the editor for a non-profit association's monthly journal. I edited and re-wrote articles that were submitted by members of the association, for whom writing was not a strong suit. I also wrote several articles myself that were published for the world to read. I leveraged that experience to transition to a different non-profit association, where I not only managed the annual magazine, but also the marketing and membership responsibilities.

I found that I enjoyed the marketing side of things. To me, marketing is simply making an argument for why someone should join your organization or buy your product. To be good at it, one must be able to make a clear, compelling case – an argument in writing!

Without any formal education or experience in marketing, and without ever considering it as a potential career when I was in high school or college, my meandering path had led me to a job where I could exercise my natural talents and begin to really explore my gift. Through this position, I connected with marketing managers, creative designers, and public relations professionals at numerous companies that were members of the association I worked for. I learned a lot from each of them and used that knowledge to sharpen my own talent.

I still work in marketing today, but as you know if you're reading this, I have also started working on side projects like this book. My true passion – and the gift that I have chosen to really work hard on – is writing.

As I shared in a previous letter, you don't have to have it all figured out right now. You don't have to know what you want to do or be "when you grow up," but if you play to your strengths and work to improve the natural gifts you have been given, you will eventually figure it out.

Everyone has something that they are naturally inclined toward. Once you recognize your unique gift, you need to start looking for opportunities that will allow you to improve and sharpen it. This will look different for everyone – there is no single path to any outcome.

Your gift doesn't necessarily have to be a school subject either. Maybe you have a knack for putting together unique clothing combinations or making delicious sandwiches out of random ingredients. There are people out there who are willing to pay for that kind of expertise, among innumerable other things! If you're particularly good at something and you enjoy it, there's a good chance there's a market for it out there somewhere.

My own path was not a straight line by any stretch of the imagination. It has zigged and zagged, completely broken off from the original line, jumped backward, and then started moving forward again. Every experience and opportunity has been a steppingstone on the path that ultimately got me to where I am today. I took the positive lessons from every failure and used them to improve my next attempt.

Don't anticipate an easy, clear-cut path. Sometimes you have to take a side road that you don't want to take because the main road is blocked. Other times, you'll have to make your own road. Look at each of these detours as an opportunity to learn. Every job I've ever had has taught me something that I've carried with me ever since – even the ones that had literally nothing to do with speaking, writing, or marketing.

For me, a college degree was a requirement. It would have been very difficult to reach my current position without the journalism and creative writing experience I had in college. In addition, the jobs I was able to get that ultimately led me to discover marketing all required a college degree to even apply. This is not the case for everyone!

What if your gift is working with your hands? Do you need a college degree to become a carpenter, plumber, gunsmith, mechanic, or electrician? Not necessarily.

With a high school diploma, you can attend a trade school, or perhaps find a local tradesman who needs an apprentice. There are literally thousands of jobs that do not require a four-year college degree – and you can make a lot of money in any of them if you are truly gifted in your craft.

Skilled tradesmen are hard to find. The ones who recognize their gifts and work to improve them can start their own businesses, work for themselves instead of someone else, and charge premium prices for their products and services because there are so few people who can do what they do. The market rewards scarcity. The harder it is to find something – especially something that other people want and need – the more money it's worth.

I'm not saying you *shouldn't* go to college or that academics aren't important. I'm also not saying you definitely *should* go to college. You need to take some time to evaluate what path is best for your situation. What are you good at and what do you enjoy doing? Is college really going to help you master your gift and achieve your maximum potential?

You *do* need to graduate high school. Whether you love school or hate it, having that diploma will open a lot of doors for you that will remain closed without it. Even if you are incredibly gifted with a skill that doesn't require a college degree, it's a lot harder to find an opportunity to take the next step on your path to improvement without a high school diploma. A higher GPA definitely helps, but as long as you graduate it shows that you are persistent and determined – that you are willing to stay the course, put in the work, and overcome adversity to achieve a challenging goal. That's an important quality that any future school or employer will be looking for.

I was terrible at math in school. I hated it. I thought I would never need it and it was pointless to learn. For the most part, that's proven to be true for me. I haven't used anything higher than basic math since I graduated high school. I mean, if you really analyzed every decision I've made and every action I've taken, you could probably find some very, very basic algebra that I've used at some point, but I've never faced a decision in my personal or professional life that required trigonometry, that's for sure!

As much as I hated math and insisted that I would never need it in "real life," I fought and clawed my way through every math class I ever took. I did whatever I had to do to pass the class and reach that next steppingstone. None of what I've accomplished in my life would have been possible if I'd simply given up and dropped out.

You, on the other hand, may love math. You may be *great* at math. It may come as naturally to you as writing does to me, but there's probably something that frustrates the heck out of you. Whatever it is, do what you need to do to get by. Focus on your strong suit. Keep your eyes on the goal – a high school diploma – and then dedicate yourself to your gift and the things you enjoy doing once you've got that in your back pocket.

I can honestly say I learned more overall in high school than I did in college. While college can provide a lot greater depth and specificity in a particular field of study, high school does a much better job of presenting a broad platform of knowledge. Don't take that for granted. After all, specificity is only helpful if you're sure you know what you want to do.

I mentioned this in an earlier letter, but it's worth repeating here in the context of this conversation: about 80 percent of college graduates will change their major at least once during their college career. After graduation, more than 50 percent will ultimately find a job in a field outside of their major.

What this should tell you is that the specificity college can offer in a particular field of study still doesn't guarantee you a job in that field – or that you'll even be interested in it after you get started. College alone isn't the key to success. Before you make your decision one way or the other, focus on graduating high school and figuring out what you are *good at*. Of the things you're good at, choose the ones that you like the best and let them be your guide as you decide what your next step should be.

For most people, a career path is long and winding. It all starts here. Take your classwork seriously – even the stuff that you think is unnecessary and a waste of time. That diploma really is the springboard into the world of opportunities on the other side.

    Love,
    Tom

Chapter 19

The last word

Dear Ivan,

The world is full of conflict and assholes. The two go hand-in-hand, like peanut butter and jelly. They can make life difficult and uncomfortable at times, but I'd argue they're necessary. If everything was always easy and everyone was always nice, how boring would it be? We need conflict and assholes in our lives for contrast – a barometer to measure the good times and nice people against.

Let's be honest, at one point or another we've *all* been assholes and we probably will be again. Every person in history – even those who are generally agreed to have done wonderful things – has been an asshole at some point. There's no way around it.

Imagine traveling back in time and finding yourself in a busy market. You're enjoying the sun on your face and casually perusing the wares of the street vendors when you hear a commotion up ahead. As you turn to see what's going on, a flustered old man in ornate garments rushes through the crowd, heading away from the ruckus, and approaches another man in similar apparel at the cart next to you.

"Yo, Jebbediah! What's poppin' man?" asks the man at the cart, turning to meet his friend. "You close that deal with the goatherd yet?"

"No, dude," says the first man, trying to catch his breath. "I was waiting for him to show up and watching Azaria change some money for a wheat farmer when some *asshole* started shouting that we were offending God. He started throwing shit and turning over our tables ... the whole temple's a mess, bro!"

"Son of a..." mutters the man at the cart, throwing a half-eaten fig to the ground in contempt. "Caesar needs to hear about this. Go find Pontious and let him deal with it!"

Ok, I may have taken a *little* bit of creative liberty with the dialogue there, but the story may sound familiar. They're talking about Jesus – yes, *that* Jesus. The extraordinary man, whom many around the world believe to be divine, was an asshole ... from *their perspective.*

Life is all a matter of perspective. One man's truth is another man's lie. One man's savior is another man's asshole. The difference in perspective is what creates conflict, and life as we know it cannot exist without it. Therefore, do not strive to live a "perfect" life or make everyone happy, but rather to limit your time spent as an asshole and the amount of conflict you create.

The beauty of perspective is that we ultimately get to *choose* how much these conflicts affect us. I hope these letters have helped you put some things in perspective and given you some new tools to deal with the inevitable conflicts and assholes in your life.

As you prepare to take the next step in your journey, I challenge you to think critically. Almost nothing in life can be taken at face value. There's always another side to every story. The ability to think *around* an issue or situation and evaluate it from multiple angles – different perspectives – is the key to freeing your mind and discovering your own truth.

One thing most successful people have in common is a love for books and a general hunger for knowledge. Read books. Read as much as you can. Read content that interests you and can advance your understanding of a subject. Read content that offers a perspective that differs from yours and will help you understand another point of view.

As you read, think critically about the content. Just because something is written in a book doesn't make it true, whether you agree with it or not. That goes for this book as well! The stories I tell are told from my perspective. The advice I offer and lessons I learned are, to a certain extent, a matter of opinion shaped by my perspective. Give yourself the freedom to challenge your beliefs. There is no risk involved! You may read something you strongly disagree with and think, "this guy is a real asshole!" If that's the case, and you can make a clear counter-argument, all you've done is strengthen your own position.

On the other hand, you may discover a perspective you hadn't considered before – like I did when my suitemate and I nearly came to blows over whether or not Paul O'Neill was a crybaby. You may still disagree with the author's argument, but now the author is just a *person* with a different *perspective*, rather than an asshole. The animosity you feel toward that person, and others who agree with their point of view, will temper. You'll reduce the amount of energy you expend in anger and stress. You will waste less time stewing in those negative emotions and your life will get better and more productive as a result.

Everything is a matter of perspective, and not everyone will share yours. All you can do is follow your own moral compass and do the best you can. Learn to accept that not everyone will like or agree with you, and some will even think you're an asshole. The more thoughts and ideas you expose yourself to through reading, and the more critically you evaluate them by weighing them against your currently-held beliefs and calibrating them against your moral compass, the fewer assholes you'll find.

When you can see things from another person's perspective, even if you disagree with the premise, it adds a layer of humanity to that individual: a better understanding of where they're coming from, what experiences have formed their opinion, and why they may be acting the way they are. Try to find the common threads of humanity in your conflicts and use them to work toward a resolution.

At the end of the day, all people have value. When you strip away the "accessories," like money, social status, and the rest of the *stuff* we accumulate in our lives, we're all equal. Striving for status, however we define it, and striving to be part of the "in-group," is an innate part of being human, but in the end, we can't take any of it with us. When we die, we will be remembered for the impact we had on *others*.

Imagine standing on a rocky bank beside a mountain lake. The water is clear, and the surface is smooth as glass. Look around you and choose a rock. You can pick any size or shape you want. Now cast it into the lake. The sound of the rock splashing into the water momentarily fills the air and drops of water shoot skyward. The rock is swallowed by the lake and silence returns. The only remaining evidence of the rock are the ripples that emanate in ever-widening circles from its point of entry.

That last paragraph encapsulates your life.

The moment the rock touches the water is when you're born and the instant it's swallowed by the lake is when you die. In the big scheme of things, we're all here for the briefest of moments. We make a splash and then we're gone. However, the impact we have on the world – the size of our splash and the ripples we create – has the potential to carry on long after we've slipped beneath the surface. At that point, nobody cares if your rock was a nugget of pure gold or a chunk of old concrete from a demolished building. What matters is how much water you displaced and how many ripples you created.

As long as your ripples remain, you will not be forgotten, and your legacy will live on. Think about that for a moment. Think about all the names you've learned in history class over the years. Why do we know them? Why do we still care about someone who died 50, 100, 1000 years ago? Their ripples are still rolling across the lake. Their splashes were so significant – for better or for worse – that their impact still resonates today. The impact you have on the people in your life will be passed to other people in *their* lives, possibly for generations to come, with the potential to carry on forever!

Everyone, regardless of their current station in life, will take a turn standing beside that lake. What kind of rock will you choose? How strong and far-reaching will your ripples be?

Your rock has just barely broken the surface of the water. The majority of your life is still ahead of you – well beyond your high school years – and there is plenty of time to shape your rock as you go. How you choose to shape it is up to you. My advice is to start with love and lead with *agape* – the selfless form of love that is extended to all of humanity purely out of the fact that you are also a part of humanity. Even the smallest ripple can have a significant and lasting impact on those it touches.

Ultimately, the last word is yours. You get to choose your own path and live the way you want.

In the vast wilderness of life, there is nowhere to go but forward into the unknown. Just like the pioneers in their covered wagons, none of us really know exactly where we're headed, what we'll find along the way, or how long the journey will be. We follow in the footsteps of those who have gone before us and use whatever guidance they can offer to our advantage.

Think of this book as *my* rudimentary map, drawn to the best of my ability, based on my own expedition into the wilderness and the maps handed down from those who preceded me. I'm handing it down to you with the hope that you can use it to your advantage. Each of these letters is an icon in the legend, intended to provide some general guidance and point out key landmarks to help you along the way.

You must plot your own course and map your journey as you go, relying on your own ingenuity, survival instincts, and moral compass. You will inevitably get lost somewhere along the way. We all do. When that happens, you can refer back to this map and reorient yourself before moving on.

Wherever your journey leads you, I hope that in the end you can look back with a smile and think, "Wow. What a great trip!"

Love,
Tom

Gratitude

I would like to thank all of the men who saw the value in this project and took the time to read my early drafts with a critical eye and provide constructive feedback. I couldn't have done it without you.

Thank you to Mike Borak, Gerry Borak, Justin Pascale, Alexander Moore, PhD, James Willis, PhD, Kevin Pei, Will Marble, Chris Bentley, and Connor Hannigan.

Special thanks as well to my friend and colleague, Jim Woods, for his cover design.

Thank you to my wife, Annah, for her unwavering support and encouragement, in this and all of my endeavors. (Team T&A!)

Thank you to my brothers, Mike, Andy, and Mark, who tolerated me as an older brother and colored my life experience in a way nobody else could.

Most of all, thank you to my parents, Holly and Gerry Borak. I would not be who I am today without the unconditional love they have always shown one another and modeled for me and my brothers. The values and morals they instilled in me laid the foundation for this work, and the ripples that eminate from these pages are theirs as much as mine.

www.ingramcontent.com/pod-product-compliance
Lightning Source LLC
LaVergne TN
LVHW012053070526
838201LV00083B/4182